BLUE GUIDE

ITALY
FOOD
COMPANION

Glossary & Miscellany

T0021611

Somerset Books • London

Blue Guide Italy Food Companion:
Phrasebook & Miscellany
Third edition 2023

Published by Blue Guides Limited, a Somerset Books Company
Unit 2, Old Brewery Road, Wiveliscombe, Somerset TA4 2PW
www.blueguides.com
'Blue Guide' is a registered trade mark.

Compiled by Ellen Grady, Robin Saikia, Annabel Barber, Tom Brompton.
With thanks from Ellen Grady to the following for their invaluable
expertise: Eleonora Consoli, Damiano Ferraro, Nadia Foiadelli, Amelia
Fragola, Fiorella Giubbi, Maria Grammatico, Tania Lo Cicero, Silvia
Maccari, Nigel McGilchrist, Daniele Nannetti, Aldo Tomarchio, and
Simonetta Agnello Hornby, for her *Un filo d'olio* (Sellerio editore, Palermo).

ISBN 978-1-905131-96-9

A CIP catalogue record of this book is available
from the British Library.

Distributed in the United States of America by WW Norton & Company,
Inc. of 500 Fifth Avenue, New York, NY 10110.

Drawings by Jim Urquhart. Photo p. 119 by Ellen Grady.
Cover photo: iStock © TheArtist
Wine label by Anikó Kuzmich
Map by Dimap Bt.
Design, typesetting and image pre-press by Anikó Kuzmich, Blue Guides.

Printed and bound in Hungary by Pauker Nyomdaipari Kft.

CONTENTS

INTRODUCTION

Pasta, pizza and ice cream, washed down with Chianti and followed by an espresso standing up at the bar. Does that sum up the kind of food you can expect in Italy? Not quite; it is that and much, much more. When you look at where Italy is on the map, it immediately becomes clear that a superb and varied cuisine is only to be expected. The serendipity of her position in the mildest, sunniest part of Europe, stretching her foot and her islands far into the Mediterranean, almost as far as Africa, makes for a perfect climate, infinite soil types, and coasts and lakes rich with fish. Taking advantage of its strategic value, people of various ethnic origins have settled here through the ages, and have used their ancestral methods of farming, fishing and food preparation to exploit the culinary opportunities offered by this bountiful land. Arabs and Angevins, Byzantines and Bourbons, Celts and Castilians, Greeks and Goths, Elymians and Etruscans, Latins and Lombards, Phoenicians and Picenes, Sicans and Sicels—and that list is by no means complete.

Many of these settlers introduced new varieties of plants and new domestic animals. It is reasonable to suppose that rice, oranges, sugar cane, dates, aubergines, artichokes, pistachios, tea, cotton, mulberries, mangoes, peaches and apricots were cultivated here for the first time in Europe. Over 7,000 edible vegetables can be found in Italy, more than in all the rest of Europe put together. Over 1,000 native grape-vines (France, the land of wine, only has 200); 533 different cultivars of olive (Spain, the closest runner-up, has 70); 140 varieties of durum wheat (in the USA, the world's most important producer, only six types are grown); and 51 types of honey, a world record. Even in the preparation of food, there are many differences between the 20 regions that make up the country, and even within the same region there can be subtle variations in the recipes. Sicily's famous *caponata* varies from town to town, and even from household to household. Modena and Bologna, only 50km apart, proudly defend their distinct versions of *tortellini*, and the dispute continues to this day: is the filling better when *mortadella* is used, or *prosciutto crudo*?

The fame of Italy's food and wine is spreading rapidly. The healthful advantages of following a Mediterranean diet, with abundant fruit, vegetables, pasta, cheese, olive oil and fish, are now known to all. Italian food today is more popular than it has ever been and each year sees a new selection of books on the subject. More than half a century has passed since the publication in 1954 of Elizabeth David's classic, *Italian Food*, the book which showed English-speaking food lovers that there was more to gastronomy than French cuisine and that much could be gained from an exploration of the diverse culinary heritage of Italy and her islands. In the USA, meanwhile, a thriving Italian immigrant community had transplanted, preserved and developed the traditions of the old country. Over the last 50 years, both in Britain and in North America, there has been a growing awareness of the vast regional diversity of Italy's food, promoted both by food writers and by Italian expatriate chefs. Excellent books have emerged, notably Gillian Riley's *Oxford Companion to Italian Food*, Oretta Zanini De Vita's *Encyclopedia of Pasta* (English translation by Maureen Fant) and Fred Plotkin's *Italy for the Gourmet Traveler*. All three are essential reading for anyone interested in the subject of Italian food, as is *The Silver Spoon*, Phaidon's important English edition of the Italian classic first published in 1950.

This little miscellany in no way attempts to rival these books, either in scope or in scholarship. What it does offer is portability. This slim volume, sufficiently neat to put into a handbag or pocket, is designed to be a convenient tool for ready reference in restaurants, bars and cafés. We hope that readers will find it useful, entertaining and informative. Please do not hesitate to take us to task for any errors or omissions. The compilers are uneasily aware that there are rare, rich and obscure pastas made only on one day of the year in a secluded valley in Alto Adige, that have not yet made it into these pages. Please tell us about these and any other delights you may have experienced in the foothills of Monte Albo or on the shores of the wine-dark sea.

HOW TO USE THIS BOOK

The book is divided into two parts, a glossary and miscellany and a phrasebook. The Italian-English glossary contains short definitions of over 2,000 terms that one might expect to encounter, principally on menus. These range from simple translations of common food items to more obscure examples taken from local dialects and folklore. Some of the entries are longer and more discursive, such as those on pizza and truffles. Others have required little more than a line or a word.

GLOSSARY & MISCELLANY

abbacchio [a-**bac**-ki-o] a milk-fed lamb no more than four weeks old, popular in Rome and elsewhere in Lazio, also known as *agnellino da latte*, 'little lamb of milk'. Abbacchio is cooked in variety of ways, often roasted or casseroled. *Abbacchio scottadito* are cutlets, preferably charcoal-grilled.

abboccato [ab-boc-**ca**-to] semi-dry, very slightly sweet (wine).

abbotta pezziende [ab-**bot**-ta-pet-si-**en**-de] meaning 'feed the beggar', a soft, sweet bread roll from the town of Agnone in Molise, flavoured with sugar and lemon.

abbrustolito/a [ab-brus-to-**li**-to] toasted, e.g. *pane abbrustolito*: toast.

abissini [a-bis-**si**-ni] the smallest type of shell-shaped pasta, suitable for soups. They were named after Italy's former African colony. Nowadays they are more commonly known as *cocciolette*. They resemble small CONCHIGLIE.

Abruzzo [a-**bruts**-zo] mountainous region in the centre of the Italian peninsula known for its durum wheat, used for a wide variety of pastas, which are often flavoured with PEPERONCINO, another local speciality. Other noted Abruzzo products are nougat (*torrone*) and lentils. Montepulciano d'Abruzzo is the best-known wine.

acciuga [at-**chu**-ga] (pl. *acciughe*) anchovy, preserved in salt, which gives it a distinctive silvery-brown colour. Salted whole, their flavour is enhanced by the gradual disintegration of the bones and intestines—perhaps a modern-day survival of the popular ancient Roman fish sauce called garum, which was made from salted and fermented fish guts. Fresh anchovies are known as *alici* (*masculini* in Sicily).

acerbo [a-**cher**-bo] sour, unripe or harsh.

aceto [a-**che**-to] vinegar.

aceto balsamico [a-**che**-to bal-**sa**-mi-co] traditional balsamic vinegar is produced in and around Modena in Emilia-Romagna and is made mainly using the local white grape, Trebbiano di Castelvetro. It is misleadingly named, since it is not a vinegar but a syrup made from grape must, subjected to a lengthy and sophisticated ageing process. The must is boiled down to a sweet syrup which is left to ferment for a year or more in a barrel. After this initial period of fermentation, the must is decanted each year into a series of progressively smaller barrels (as time goes on, moisture evaporates) made from a variety of different woods, each of which, connoisseurs insist, imparts a new note to the aroma. Standard balsamic vinegar (not *Tradizionale*) is made with a mixture of reduced must (*mosto cotto*) and wine vinegar. As with wine, there is a bewildering spectrum of quality and price. There are even *Riserva* vinegars. The age of the finished product—some vinegars have been aged for almost a century—makes a spectacular difference to taste and price.

acetosa [a-che-**to**-za] sorrel, a vegetable whose leaves resemble spinach but which has a lemony, tangy taste, used in soups and sauces.

acetosella [a-che-to-**zel**-la] wood sorrel, a wild plant with a pleasant faintly lemony taste, good in salads and soups.

acido [a-**chi**-do] sour, acidic, sharp-tasting.

acidulo [a-**chi**-du-lo] high in acid (but not necessarily unpleasant), tart.

acini di pepe [a-chi-ni di **pe**-pe] tiny, pellet-shaped pasta mainly used in soups.

acino [a-**chi**-no] grape.

acquacotta [ac-qua **cot**-ta] typical of Matelica and Fabriano (Marche), a thin broth of meat, fish or vegetables poured over slices of toasted stale bread.

acqua [**ac**-qua] water.

acqua minerale [**ac**-qua mi-ne-**ra**-le] mineral water. *Acqua gassata* or *acqua frizzante* is fizzy water. *Acqua liscia, acqua naturale* or *acqua senza gas* is still water. Useful phrases to know when ordering water are *con/*

senza ghiaccio (with/without ice [ghi-**atch**-o]) and *temperatura ambiente* (room temperature). If you want tap water, ask for *acqua del rubinetto* [**ac**-qua del ru-bi-**net**-to]

acqua pazza [**ac**-qua **pat**-za] literally 'mad water', referring to a recipe for poached white fish, which in the Naples area were cooked in seawater seasoned with herbs, tomatoes and wine. The 'mad water' is the broth itself. The phrase is said to originate in Tuscany, where peasants would boil the seeds, stems, grapeskins and pulp left over from wine production and leave the mush to ferment for several days. The resulting 'mad water' was a much less pleasant drink than wine but often just as intoxicating and a great deal cheaper to produce.

acquadella [ac-qua-**del**-la] see LATTERINO.

Acqualagna see TARTUFO.

acquasale [ac-qua-**sa**-le] literally 'salt water', a thin soup from Basilicata made by pouring a broth made with onions, tomatoes and garlic over slices of dried or stale bread.

acquaviti [ac-qua-**vi**-ti] liqueurs made from distilled grapes or fruit, like German *Schnaps*.

affettati [af-fet-**ta**-ti] cold cuts, sliced meats.

affogato/a [af-fo-**ga**-to] poached.

affogato al caffè [af-fo-**ga**-to al caf-**fè**] ice cream doused with hot ESPRESSO.

affumicato/a [af-fu-mi-**ca**-to] smoked.

aframomo [a-fra-**mo**-mo] grains of paradise, a peppery spice from the ginger family, native to West Africa (*Aframomum melegueta*).

agghiotta di pesce spada [ag-ghi-**ot**-ta di **pe**-she **spa**-da] a popular Sicilian recipe for swordfish (*pesce* = fish, *spada* = sword), cooked in tomato sauce enriched with onion, pine nuts, currants, capers, potatoes and green olives; from the Italian *ghiotto*, meaning both 'tasty' and 'greedy'.

Aglianico [al-**ya**-ni-co] hardy red-wine grape from Campania and Basilicata widely celebrated as the 'noblest' grape of the south. It was the grape used in the ancient Falernian wine, praised by Pliny. Today it is the main grape in TAURASI.

agliata [al-**ya**-ta] a kind of garlic mayonnaise made from garlic, egg yolk and olive oil whipped together until creamy (Liguria).

aglio [**al**-yo] garlic; three Italian strains with protected geographical status (DOP) are *Aglio Bianco Polesano* from the Veneto, *Aglio Rosso di Nubia* from Sicily and *Aglio di Voghiera* from Emilia-Romagna.

aglio e olio [**al**-yo e **o**-li-o] also known as *olio e aglio*, 'garlic and olive oil', a quick sauce for pasta, often with chilli, anchovies and parsley.

aglio orsino [**al**-yo or-**si**-no] wild garlic (*Allium* sp.).

agnello [an-**yel**-lo] lamb, a weaned lamb, therefore older than an ABBACCHIO and having a stronger flavour. It is usually roasted or stewed and served *alla pastora* (with potatoes) or *cacio e uova* (stuffed with grated PECORINO cheese and eggs, a method widespread in Abruzzo and Molise, where it is known as *agnill cac'e 'ove*.

agnolini [an-yo-**li**-ni] *see agnolotti*.

agnolotti [an-yo-**lo**-ti] sometimes known as *agnolini*, a Piedmontese PASTA RIPIENA, in effect a type of RAVIOLI. Originally they were a way of using leftover roast meat, which is why the traditional filling is a meat paste. They are sometimes served in broth and can also be covered in melted butter and sage. *Agnolotti del plin* are mini ravioli filled with meat and cabbage.

agone [a-**go**-ne] the lake shad, a fish found in Lake Como (pl. *agoni*).

agresto [a-**gres**-to] a tart-tasting condiment, known as verjuice in English; a concentrate obtained from the juice of unripened grapes and used to impart a sour tang to sauces; appreciated in the central Marche, it is becoming increasingly popular in Australia, thanks to vintner-chef Maggie Beer.

agretti [a-**gret**-ti] also known as *barba di frate* ('friar's beard') or *roscani*; saltwort. The leaves are either used as a salad vegetable, eaten pickled or very lightly braised with garlic and mint. The taste is slightly salty, faintly reminiscent of fresh spinach.

agric. biol. frequently used on menus, the abbreviation for *agricoltura biologica*: organic farming.

agro [**ag**-ro] sour; *all' agro*, with olive oil and lemon juice.

agrodolce [**ag**-ro **dol**-che] sweet and sour. Recipes vary regionally and according to the meat or vegetables for which the *salsa agrodolce* is destined.

agrumi [ag-**ru**-mi] citrus fruits.

aguglia [ag-**ul**-ya] the garfish, a small, needle-shaped seawater fish (pl. *aguglie*).

al, all' alla in the style of, e.g. *alla rustica*: country style; *al forno*: in the oven, baked.

ala [**a**-la] wing, e.g. *ala di pollo*: chicken wing.

alaccia [al-**lat**-cha] shad, a bony fish of the herring family.

alalonga, alalunga [a-la-**lon**-ga, a-la-**lun**-ga] long-fin tuna.

Alba [**al**-ba] town in Piedmont that hosts an annual truffle fair in autumn (see TARTUFO) and which is also known for its BARBERA wine.

Alba madonna [**al**-ba ma-**don**-na] a white truffle (see TARTUFO).

albero di Giuda [**al**-be-ro di **joo**-da] Judas tree, also known as SILIQUASTRO. Its bright pink flowers are used to make a syrup, are added to FRITTATA or scattered as a decorative element in salads.

albicocca [al-bi-**coc**-ca] apricot (pl. *albicocche*).

alborella [al-bo-**rel**-la] bleak-fish; a small freshwater fish found in the Lombardy lakes, also known as *aola* or *alburno*.

alburno [al-**bur**-no] see ALBORELLA.

Alchermes [al-**ker**-mes] a scarlet, slightly bitter-tasting liqueur made from flowers and spices, traditionally used in ZUPPA INGLESE.

Aleatico [a-le-**a**-ti-co] red-wine grape that grows throughout central Italy (Tuscany, Lazio, Umbria, Marche) and also in Puglia, where it is the principal ingredient of the fruity red wines of the Salento peninsula, the heel of Italy. It is also used to make a sweet dessert wine, described by Napoleon as one of the few available consolations during his exile on the island of Elba.

alfabeto [al-fa-**be**-to]

Fiori albero di Giuda (Judas tree blossom) alongside *strigoli*, on sale at a street market in Ravenna.

internationally popular PASTINA representing the letters of the alphabet.

alfredo [al-**fre**-do] a rich cream, butter and cheese sauce, named after Alfredo di Lelio, whose restaurant in Rome, Alfredo alla Scrofa, was patronised by Mary Pickford and Douglas Fairbanks in the 1920s. They were captivated by Di Lelio's FETTUCCINE and presented him with a gold knife and fork in recognition of his services to gastronomy. The restaurant still exists, as does its successor establishment, Il Vero Alfredo, just a few blocks away from the original, on Piazza Augusto Imperatore; but don't expect to find this dish anywhere else outside the USA.

alici [a-**li**-chi] anchovies, served freshly caught or halved and preserved in brine rather than the salted kind (ACCIUGA).

Alionza [a-li-**ont**-za] white grape from EMILIA-ROMAGNA used both as an eating grape and for vinification.

alisanzas [a-li-**sant**-zas] also *sas alisanzas* [**sas** a-li-**sant**-zas], a Sardinian long pasta typically served with a robust meat ragout.

allegroni [al-le-**gro**-ni] *griù* in dialect, sweet RAVIOLI from the Marche, with a chicken and parmesan filling, and dressed with SAPA. Served as dessert.

allevamento, all' [al-le-va-**men**-to] farmed (of fish and game), i.e. not wild. An *allevatore* is a farmer, breeder.

alloro, foglia di [**fol**-ya di al-**lo**-ro] bay leaf.

alosa [a-**lo**-za] shad, a freshwater relative of the herring, also known as *cheppia*.

alpestre SEE ARQUEBUSE.

alta cucina [**al**-ta cu-**chi**-na] *haute cuisine*.

Alto Adige [**al**-to **a**-di-je] the South Tyrol, the semi-autonomous province of Bolzano, home to Italian, German and Ladin cultures, languages and cuisines. Together with TRENTINO, it forms the region of Trentino-Alto Adige. The cuisine is Alpine and some

good wines are made, notably LAGREIN.

alzavola [al-**za**-vo-la] teal (small wild duck).

amabile [a-**ma**-bi-le] of wine, slightly sweet.

amarena [a-ma-**re**-na] the bitter Morello cherry, often preserved in syrup or brandy.

amaretti [a-ma-**ret**-ti] macaroons; those from Saronno (Lombardy) are hard and crunchy, while those from Sassello (Liguria) are soft and delicate. Both kinds are made exclusively with almonds, egg-white, sugar and peach or apricot kernels (*armellini*) to give a bitter note.

Amaretto [a-ma-**ret**-to] almond-based liqueur.

amaro/a [a-**ma**-ro] bitter. Amaro is also the name of a bitter DIGESTIVO flavoured with herbs.

Amaro Averna [a-**ma**-ro a-**ver**-na] a caramelised herbal DIGESTIVO from Sicily, made according to a secret recipe given to the family centuries ago by a friar; very popular throughout Italy.

Amaro Montenegro [a-**ma**-ro

mon-te-**neg**-ro] a bitter herbal aperitif made in Bologna.

Amarone [a-ma-**ro**-ne] full-bodied, highly-regarded (and invariably expensive) DOCG red wine, a style of VALPOLICELLA made from selected bunches of grapes that are dried (raisined) before pressing in order to concentrate flavours and sugars. The wine is fermented to complete dryness and then aged for at least two years. The resulting wine is complex and high in alcohol. Amarone was 'invented' by accident, when the fermentation process for RECIOTO went on too long, resulting in a wine with no residual sugar. The dry style is much more acceptable to modern palates.

amatriciana [a-ma-tri-**cha**-na] a popular pasta sauce of tomatoes, PECORINO, GUANCIALE and sometimes chilli, a recipe originating from Amatrice in northern Lazio. In origin, the sauce does not contain tomatoes; they came to dominate the mixture after their arrival from the New World.

Ambra di Talamello see FORMAGGIO DI FOSSA.

ambrato [am-**bra**-to] white wine that has turned a darker shade, slightly amber, through oxidation.

Americano [a-me-ri-**ca**-no] 1. a cocktail consisting of equal measures of red vermouth and CAMPARI topped up with soda water; 2. *caffè americano* or *caffè all'americana* is filter coffee or percolated coffee, a much longer, more diluted drink than an *espresso*. The effect can also be achieved by adding water to *espresso*.

ammazzacaffè [a-**mat**-za-caf-**fe**] lit. 'coffee-killer', a small shot of liqueur drunk after a coffee. A chaser.

ammogghiu [a-**mog**-ghi-yu] typical of the province of Trapani (Sicily) and especially of the island of Pantelleria, a dressing of ripe tomatoes, basil, chilli, garlic, salt and olive oil, pounded together and served raw on spaghetti or boiled meats.

anacardo [a-na-**car**-do] cashew.

analcolico [an-al-**co**-li-co] non-alcoholic. *Bevande analcoliche* = alcohol-free drinks.

ananas [**a**-na-nas] pineapple.

anatra [a-na-tra] sometimes called *anitra* [a-ni-tra] duck, often stuffed. In Venetian dialect the *anatra ripiena* (stuffed duck) is often referred to as *anara col pien*. The stuffing is made of duck liver, breadcrumbs, raisins, egg, cheese, herbs and crumbled macaroons. The wild duck of the Venetian lagoon is celebrated in Carpaccio's painting of Venetian sportsmen (Getty Museum, Los Angeles) where several ducks can be seen scudding across the sky.

anchellini [an-kel-**li**-ni] 'little anchors', also known as *piombi* (weights), pasta served in soups.

anelli, anelletti, anellini [a-**nel**-li, an-nel-**let**-i, a-nel-**li**-ni] 'little rings', a pasta shape said to be based on the earrings worn by the women of Benghazi, one of Italy's former colonies; *anelli siciliani*, 'Sicilian rings', are the larger type, the pasta of choice in Palermo for *pasta al forno alla palermitana*. They are mixed with a rich ragout of beef and pork, béchamel, peas, bits of cheese and hard-boiled eggs, baked in the oven in a pan lined with slivers of fried aubergine, then turned out onto its serving dish and placed in the middle of the table, a glorious, fragrant centrepiece.

aneto [a-**ne**-to] dill.

angelica [an-je-li-ca] wild parsnip; the seeds and roots are used to flavour GRAPPA; the stems are put to a variety of uses, candied as sweetmeats or thinly sliced and tossed with slices of Parma ham; leaves are eaten raw in salads.

anguilla [an-**gwil**-la] eel, served in a variety of regional styles, usually stewed. Some of the best freshwater eels are said to come from Lake Bolsena in Lazio. Another important source is the Comacchio lagoon in Emilia-Romagna.

anguria [an-**gu**-ri-a] watermelon.

anice [a-ni-che] anise, a small plant of the parsley family with a distinctive liquorice flavour.

animelle [a-ni-**mel**-le] sweetbreads, the thymus glands of a young calf, usually breaded, sautéed, grilled or chopped and used in pastas as a filling; known as *lacetti* in Piedmont. In

Lazio, *animelle* are often taken to refer either to the thymus gland or the pancreas of a calf or sheep.

Anisetta [a-ni-**set**-ta] anise-flavoured liqueur from the Marche.

annegati [an-ne-**ga**-ti] slices of meat marinated in white wine or MARSALA sauce.

annoso [an-**no**-zo] of wine, aged.

anolini [a-no-**li**-ni] a 'must' on the Christmas table, PASTA RIPIENA from Emilia-Romagna, typically filled with beef that has been stewed until it falls apart its own juices.

antipasti [an-ti-**pas**-ti] starters, *hors d'oeuvres*; literally 'before a meal'. These often consist of a selection of cured meat or fish.

antipastino [an-ti-pas-**ti**-no] a little appetiser, something more than a *bonne bouche* (ASSAGGIO) and less than a full-blown *antipasto*.

antiveleno [an-ti-ve-**le**-no] antidote, the 'hair of the dog'.

aola [a-o-la] see ALBORELLA.

aperitivi [a-pe-ri-**ti**-vi] aperitifs.

Aperol Spritz [a-pe-rol **sprits**] a popular Venetian aperitif made with PROSECCO and Aperol orange liqueur, topped up with soda water.

aperto [a-**per**-to] open.

Apulia (see PUGLIA).

arachidi [a-**ra**-ki-di] peanuts.

aragosta [a-ra-**go**-sta] the clawless rock lobster (*see illustration on p. 21*).

arancia [a-**ran**-cha] orange; popular citrus fruit in season from late autumn throughout the winter, mainly grown in the south of the country, in Sicily, Calabria and Campania.

aranciata [a-ran-**cha**-ta] orangeade, orange soda, a fizzy drink, as opposed to *spremuta di arancia* (freshly squeezed orange juice).

arancini [a-ran-**chi**-ni] or, in Palermo, *arancine* [a-ran-**chi**-ne], typical of Sicily, where they are said to have been introduced by the Arabs, they are fist-sized fried or baked rice balls, round or cone-shaped, coated with breadcrumbs. The outer crust turns golden-orange when cooked, hence the name. The standard filling is a ragout of meat, peas and mozzarella, but many other fillings are found.

In Palazzolo Acreide, near Syracuse, a hard-boiled egg is tucked in with the filling, but this is considered heresy everywhere else. In Roman cuisine, *supplì* are similar to *arancini*. In Naples, rice balls are called *palline di riso*.

arancione [a-ran-**cho**-ne] orange, as in VINO ARANCIONE, orange wine.

Arbëreshe [ar-bu-**re**-she] the Albanian community of southern Italy and Sicily, who retain a distinct cuisine, language and customs.

arborio [ar-**bo**-ri-o] a type of glutinous, short-grain rice from the Po valley, typically used in RISOTTO; one of the oldest varieties grown in Italy.

Archestratus of Gela Sicilian author of the oldest known cookery book (*see box overleaf*).

Arance: oranges

Italian oranges are typically in season from November to February, though some varieties do not ripen until the spring. There are many types, and even of these the individual fruits can change flavour and appearance, depending on the rootstock or the position of the grove. The first to ripen are the small blond *Navelina* varieties. The drop in temperature as winter progresses enhances the deep red colouring of the *sanguinello*, (blood orange), and the intensely crimson *Moro*, but this only occurs in the area close to Mt Etna in Sicily (the only place in the world, in fact); they are protected by the IGP seal as *Arancia Rossa di Sicilia*. The seedless *Tarocco*, a variety native to Sicily, ripens in February near Francofonte; its sweet juicy flesh streaked with red is reminiscent of strawberries. In Sicily, the last to ripen in the spring are Ribera's three DOP varieties, the huge blond *Washington*, the *Brasiliana*, and the *Navelina di Ribera*. Sicily is also the only area where the sweet, seedless *Vaniglia* oranges are grown, also ready in February. Finally, around Sortino, the *Ovale Calabrese* and the *Valencia* are harvested until the end of May.

Archestratus of Gela

The earliest surviving cookery book was written in the 4th century BC by the Sicilian Archestratus of Gela: *Hedypatheia* or 'On Good Taste', is a long poem listing various foods and drinks, how they should be prepared, and how they should be enjoyed. He enthuses about the flavour of lobsters from Lipari, gilt-head bream from Syracuse, swordfish from Messina, tuna from Tindari, also bread, wine and hares, advising cooks to keep condiments to a minimum. His book was translated into Latin and even became the object of the satire of Horace; some of the recipes were included in the book written by the Roman gourmet Apicius (*see p. 185*).

ardente [ar-**den**-te] literally 'burning', high in alcohol content (wine).

aringa [a-**rin**-ga] herring, also *renga* (pl. *renghe*).

arista [a-**ri**-sta] a lean cut of pork particularly suitable for braising or roasting.

arlecchino [ar-lec-**ki**-no] a 'harlequin', a colourful selection or mixture, often of vegetables, e.g. *arlecchino di verdure al vapore*: a mixture of steamed vegetables.

armellini [ar-mel-**li**-ni] in northern Italy, the bitter kernels of apricots or peaches, used in confectionery.

armonie [ar-mo-**ni**-e] also known as *stortini*, a pasta served in soups.

Arneis [ar-**ne**-is] a white grape from Piedmont used to produce dry, flowery wines.

arnia [**ar**-ni-a] a beehive.

aromi, aromati [a-**ro**-mi, a-ro-**ma**-ti] a general term for aromatic herbs like rosemary, thyme, basil, oregano.

arquebuse [ar-kwe-**bu**-ze] a herbal DIGESTIVO from Piedmont. Also known as *alpestre*. See TANACETO.

arrabbiata [ar-rab-bi-**a**-ta] popular spicy pasta sauce made of tomato, chilli and garlic. The name literally translates as 'enraged'.

arraganato/a [ar-ra-ga-**na**-to] a dish thus described is covered with herbs and breadcrumbs, and oven-baked.

arrosticini [ar-ros-ti-**chi**-ni] skewered pieces of meat, often lamb, popular in Abruzzo and Molise; kebabs.

arrosto [ar-**ros**-to] as a noun, a roast; as an adjective, roasted. *Pollo arrosto* = roast chicken.

arselle [ar-**sel**-le] tiny clams, also known as TELLINE or *zighe*. They are often served in broth with FREGULA. *Arselle* is sometimes incorrectly used to denote scallops, the correct names for which are either *pettini* or CAPESANTE.

Artusi, Pellegrino cookery writer (*see box*).

arzilla [art-**zil**-la] around Rome, the name for skate or ray, RAZZA.

ascolana, all' [al as-co-**la**-na] Ascoli-style, from Ascoli Piceno in the MARCHE. *Olive all'ascolana* are a snack of olives stuffed with meat, then breaded and fried.

asiago [a-zi-**a**-go] cow's milk cheese from the Veneto and

Artusi, Pellegrino

A silk merchant from Forlì in Emilia-Romagna who wrote a best-selling cookbook, *La scienza in cucina e l'arte di mangiare bene* ('The Science of Cooking and the Art of Eating Well'). Having made a fortune in silk, Artusi devoted himself to his favourite pastimes, eating and collecting recipes and published his collection himself in 1891, at the age of 71. By the time of his death in 1911 it had sold over 200,000 copies and remains in print in several languages to this day. The most extensive edition is edited by the historian Piero Camporesi. The book is important because it was the first major work on Italian food to appear since the unification of Italy in 1861. It was Artusi who identified turpentine as the best means of neutralising the smell of urine after eating asparagus. A few drops in a chamber pot, or these days in the lavatory pan, convert the strange aroma of asparagus into a flowery fragrance.

Trentino, available as *asiago d'allevo* (the artisanal variety) or *asiago pressato* (processed, and much milder in taste).

asino [a-zi-no] donkey, donkey meat, steadily attaining status as a rarity and therefore a delicacy; *stracotto d'asino*, donkey stew, is made with red wine and juniper berries and plenty of butter and lard. It is typically served with POLENTA.

asparagi [as-**pa**-ra-ji] asparagus. Both white and green varieties are available across Italy. *Asparagi selvatici*, *asparagi di bosco* or *asparagi di campo* are wild asparagus. For *asparagi di mare*, see SALICORNIA. The cookery writer Pellegrino Artusi recommends a method for rendering urine odourless after eating asparagus, for those who might be embarrassed by this unwanted effect.

aspretto [as-**pret**-to] pleasantly sharp (wine).

asprigno/a [as-**prin**-yo] pleasantly tart.

aspro/a [**as**-pro] sour, bitter.

assabesi [as-sa-**be**-zi] either shortbread biscuits flavoured with hazelnuts and cocoa powder, or chewy liquorice sweets, both named in honour of Italy's capture of the port of Assab in Eritrea in 1869. There was a fashion at the time for naming food items after Italy's colonies, and when in 1884 some unfortunate inhabitants of Assab were displayed at the General Exhibition of Turin like animals in a circus, pastry-cooks vied to invent memorable 'black' sweetmeats.

assaggio [as-**sad**-jo] a taster, from *assaggiare*, to try, to sample. ASSAGGI [as-**sad**-ji] are a selection of little tasters or small portions.

Associazione Verace Pizza Napoletana the Authentic Neapolitan Pizza Association, a body dedicated to preserving the integrity of local pizza, ensuring that makers who use the best local ingredients, such as DOP San Marzano tomatoes and DOP MOZZARELLA cheese, are granted due recognition. Neapolitan pizza is recognised by UNESCO as a World Heritage Tradition.

assortimento [as-sor-ti-**men**-to] an assortment, a mixture.

Asti Spumante [**as**-ti spu-**man**-ti] a sweet to medium-sweet sparkling wine from Asti in Piedmont. Despite a harsh press from wine snobs, Asti Spumante has a respectable pedigree. It was invented by the Duke of Savoy's jeweller, Giovanni Battista Croce, around the beginning of the 17th century. When Croce retired he embarked on a successful career as a viticulturalist, producing a varied and popular range of wines using the MOSCATO grape.

astice [**as**-ti-che] lobster (*see illustration below*).

attesa [at-**te**-za] waiting time, e.g. *attesa: 15 minuti*, sometimes found on menus beside dishes which require special preparation.

avemarie [**a**-ve-ma-**ri**-e] small pasta shapes that cook quickly, ready in just the time it takes to recite a Hail Mary. See PATERNOSTER.

avena [a-**ve**-na] oat.

Averna see AMARO.

avocado [a-vo-**ca**-do] excellent quality avocados are grown in southern Italy and Sicily.

azarole [at-sa-**ro**-le] an orange-red, bittersweet, vitamin-rich

Below right: *astice*, true lobster, with pincers. Left: *aragosta*, the clawless lobster or rock lobster.

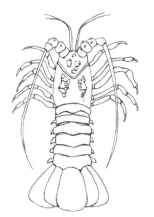
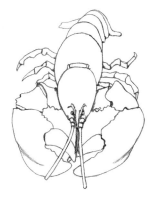

fruit of the hawthorn family.

azzimo [**ads**-zi-mo] unleavened.

azzurro [ads-**zu**-ro] blue, as in the generic description *pesce azzurro*, 'blue fish', stronger tasting, darker-fleshed fish such as *tonno* (tuna), *sgombro* (mackerel), *aringa* (herring), *sarda* (sardine) and *acciuga* (anchovy).

babà [ba-**ba**] a Neapolitan rum-soaked pastry of French origin, shaped like a fat mushroom. It was allegedly invented to console Stanislaw Leszczinsky after his defeat in the War of the Polish Succession in 1735.

babbaluci [bab-ba-**lu**-chi] Sicilian word for small snails, from the Latin *bava lucens*, 'shiny saliva'.

bàcaro [**ba**-ca-ro] a typical Venetian wine shop or wine bar serving drinks, snacks and simple meals. You would typically go to a *bàcaro* in the early evening for an OMBRA and CICCHETI.

bacca [**bac**-ca] berry (pl. *bacche*).

baccalà [bac-ca-**la**] salt cod, served in a variety of ways, usually de-salted by soaking in water, cut into portions and fried, served with regional sauce and pasta. *Baccalà alla vicentina*, a Vicenza dish, uses unsalted cod; *baccalà alla romana* is a speciality of Roman Jewish cuisine. Menus will sometimes offer a more generic *baccalà fritto*, a simple cod-in-batter starter that echoes the best of British fish and chips. *Baccalà mantecato*, in Venetian dialect *bacaeà mantecà*, consists of boiled STOCCAFISSO beaten with olive oil and seasoning into a thick pâté and served spread over bread or POLENTA.

bacio [**ba**-cho] literally, 'a kiss'; in confectionery, *baci* are chocolate and hazelnut sweets, made in Perugia, Umbria.

baggiana [bad-**ja**-na] from Urbania (Marche), a supper dish consisting of dried broad beans simmered until tender, then cooked with chard and a SOFFRITTO of olive oil, garlic and pepper.

bagna cauda [**ban**-ya **ca**-u-da] literally, a 'hot bath', a hot dip made with anchovies, olive oil and garlic, accompanying a selection of raw or cooked vegetables. See also BAGNÈT and BAGNUN.

bagnèt [ban-**yet**] in Piedmont dialect, a 'little bath', a sauce for *bollito misto*, a selection of boiled meats. There are two species of *bagnèt*, red and green. *Bagnèt ross*, or *bagnetto rosso*, is made with tomatoes, carrots, onions and garlic, simmered in wine vinegar with a teaspoonful of sugar. *Bagnèt verd*, or *bagnetto verde*, is made with anchovies, parsley, garlic, vinegar, bread and olive oil.

bagnun [ban-**yoon**] literally a 'big bath' or 'big dip', a Ligurian soup made with fresh anchovies, onion, olive oil, bread and tomatoes. It is easy to make and was therefore popular with fishermen. Today it is something of a cult dish. It is also spelled *bagnon*.

bagòss [ba-**gos**] hard cow's milk cheese, infused with saffron, from the province of Brescia.

balacin [ba-la-**chin**] see FRICO BALACIA.

balilla [ba-**lil**-la] a soft rice with a melting texture, ideal for soups and often used for desserts and ARANCINI.

ballerine [bal-le-**ri**-ne] pasta shapes, literally 'ballerinas', because they resemble a pretty dress; also known as *campanelle*, 'little bells'.

balsamico SEE ACETO BALSAMICO.

banchetto [ban-**ket**-to] banquet.

banco [**ban**-co] bar or counter, the origin of our word 'bank', going right back to the Middle Ages, when money-changers would set up their counters (*banchi*) in town squares. In an Italian café, it is usually cheaper to stand and drink your coffee *al banco*, at the bar, that to sit at a table (*tavola*).

barattolo [ba-**rat**-to-lo] a can, *un barattolo di birra* is a can of beer; *dodici barattoli di birra* is 12 cans of beer.

barbabietola [bar-ba-bi-**e**-to-la] beetroot.

barbaforte [bar-ba-**for**-te] horseradish.

barbagiuai [bar-ba-ju-**a**-i] a type of fried RAVIOLI from Liguria filled with a mixture of pumpkin and cheese. *Barbagiuai* means, in local dialect 'Uncle Giovanni' (*barba* = uncle; lit. 'bearded one'; *giuai* = Giovanni). A certain

Giovanni allegedly invented the dish.

Barbaresco [bar ba-**res**-co] highly-regarded red wine from Piedmont, like BAROLO made from the NEBBIOLO grape (the two wine regions are near neighbours). Typically tannins are softer in a Barbaresco, making the wine quicker to mature than Barolo. Angelo Gaja is one of the most famous producers.

Barbera [bar-**be**-ra] red grape of Piedmont and Lombardy, used to make increasingly fine wine, fruity and dark in colour. A *Barbera Superiore* is an aged Barbera, a *Barbera Barricato* has been aged in a *barrique*, a French-style wooden cask.

barbon [bar-**bon**] Venetian name for TRIGLIA DI FANGO, red mullet.

barbina [bar-**bi**-na] 'little beard', strand-shaped pasta.

barbozzo [bar-**bots**-zo] cured pig's cheek, an Umbrian speciality.

bardele con morai [bar-**de**-le con mo-**ra**-i] a pasta from the Veneto and Lombardy, served with butter, PARMESAN and sage leaves.

Bardolino [bar-do-**li**-no] a popular light red wine from the province of Verona. There is a rosé version, the *Bardolino Chiaretto*, and a *Bardolino Novello*, the new growth released annually in the same manner as Beaujolais Nouveau. The *Bardolino Superiore* has an extra 1 percent strength.

Barolo [ba-**ro**-lo] one of the great Italian red wines, rich, full-flavoured and high in tannin. It is made from the NEBBIOLO grape, grown around the village of Barolo in the low hills of Piedmont.

basilico [ba-**zi**-li-co] basil. Used in tomato sauces, salads, soups and omelettes, it is also the basis for PESTO. Basil has powerful symbolic connotations of fertility and kingship—the name derives from the Greek *basileus* meaning king—and is believed to have flourished on the site in the Holy Land where St Helen discovered the True Cross.

bastardui [bas-tar-**du**-i] pasta from Liguria served in a creamy leek sauce.

bastarduni [bas-tar-**du**-ni]

'big bastards', the finest Sicilian prickly pears, the second crop of the late summer.

batata [ba-**ta**-ta] yam, sweet potato.

batsoà [bat-so-**a**] in Piedmont, meat from a pig's foot, marinated in vinegar, stewed, then dipped in batter and fried.

battolli [bat-**tol**-li] pasta from Liguria, made with chestnut flour and often served with PESTO ALLA GENOVESE.

battuta [bat-**tu**-ta] literally 'pounded', 'beaten'. *Battuta di manzo* is steak tartare. *Battuta di pollo* is a kind of chicken terrine.

battuto [bat-**tu**-to] a mixture of chopped vegetables such as onion, garlic, celery and carrot mixed with herbs and fat (oil, butter or lard) and used to flavour a stew or soup—in other words, a freshly-made stock cube. *Battuta* means beaten or pulverised, in this case with a pestle and mortar. When sautéed, the same ingredients would constitute a SOFFRITTO.

bavarese [ba-va-**re**-ze] a rich custard for desserts, especially trifle, made popular by German visitors to northern Italy.

A bunch of fresh basil (*basilico*), wrapped in paper. Basil is sold this way in markets and supermarkets in Liguria, where it is the main ingredient of the famous pesto sauce.

bavette [ba-**vet**-te] literally, 'strings of drool', a popular if unappetisingly nicknamed pasta, like fine tagliatelle. *Bavette* are served with a variety of regional sauces, notably tuna and capers in the Sicilian archipelago.

bazzotto [bad-**zot**-to] coddled

(of an egg).

beccaccia [bec-**cat**-cha] woodcock.

beccaccino [bec-cat-**chi**-no] snipe.

beccafico [bec-ca-**fi**-co] garden warbler. No longer to be found on menus, the word now indicates a method of cooking, as in the speciality of Palermo *sarde al beccafico*: fresh sardines are filleted, rolled up on a filling of breadcrumbs, pecorino, parsley, pine kernels, garlic and currants, and skewered, separated by bay leaves, before grilling. This was the traditional method of preparing the songbirds.

beciamella, besciamella [be-cha-**mel**-la, be-sha-**mel**-la] Italian transliteration of béchamel, the white sauce made from butter and milk, thickened with flour.

belecot [be le-**cot**] spiced and garlicky pork sausage made with offal, served boiled with mashed potato, typical of Ravenna (Emilia-Romagna).

belga [**bel**-ga] abbreviated form of *indivia belga*, an endive.

Bellini [bel-**li**-ni] a cocktail of fresh peach juice and PROSECCO, invented at Harry's Bar in Venice. As the CARPACCIO is named after one Venetian artist, so is this after another.

Bel Paese [bel pa-**e**-ze] a mild, industrially-produced cheese (made of cow's milk), originating in Melzo in Lombardy, named after a best-selling 19th-century work of popular science by the geologist-priest Father Antonio Stoppani. The book, *Il Bel Paese* (*The Beautiful Country*) consists of 32 fireside 'conversations' extolling the beauties of the Italian landscape and explaining concepts of natural science in straightforward, comprehensible language.

bergamotto [ber-ga-**mot**-to] bergamot; aromatic citrus fruit like a small orange, grown only along the west coast of Calabria, not good for eating, but the essential oil extracted from the rind is excellent as a flavouring for sweets, for the manufacture of medicines, or for 'fixing' perfumes. It provides the fragrance for *eau de cologne*, Napoleon's favourite after-shave, and gives the characteristic aroma to Earl Grey tea.

berlingozzo [ber-lin-**got**-so] a sweet bread (Florence).

bernese [ber-**ne**-ze] béarnaise sauce, made of clarified butter and emulsified egg yolks with herbs and seasoning.

bertù [ber-**tu**] large wholemeal-flour ravioli from Bergamo (Lombardy) filled with COTECHINO, parmesan and egg, traditionally eaten to celebrate the return of Christian troops after their victory at the Battle of Lepanto in 1571; the dish was invented for the occasion.

bevanda [be-**van**-da] a drink, beverage (pl. *bevande*).

bianchetto [bi-an-**ket**-to] whitebait or newborn anchovies or sardines (pl. *bianchetti*).

bianco [bi-**an**-co] 1. white (wine); 2. *in bianco*: cooked without tomatoes; the opposite of *in rosso*. Recipes that require a sauce *in bianco* often predate the arrival of tomatoes from the New World.

bianco carta [bi-**an**-co **car**-ta] a clear, almost colourless white wine.

biancomangiare [bi-**an**-co-man-**ja**-re] a dish dating back to the Middle Ages, often translated as 'blancmange', though the original Italian version could be sweet or savoury. The guiding principal of preparation was the whiteness of the ingredients, which could include cheese, chicken, rice or fish. At its heart, however, a *biancomangiare* was an almond pudding, and it is as a sweet dessert that it mainly survives today, prepared with almond milk or cow's milk and cornflour.

biavetta [bi-a-**vet**-ta] a tiny, rice-shaped egg pasta from Piedmont, the basis of *minestra del bate 'l gran*, 'bash-the-wheat' soup, a hearty chicken broth served to harvest workers at threshing time.

bibarasse [bi-ba-**ras**-se] in the Venice region, small clams similar to VONGOLE.

bibita [**bi**-bi-ta] a soft drink, pl. *bibite* [**bi**-bi-te].

bicchiere [bik-ki-**e**-re] a drinking glass. Wine prices are quoted by the *bicchiere* or by the *bottiglia*.

bicchiere della staffa [bik-ki-**e**-re del-la **sta**-fa] one for the road, literally a *bicchiere* (glass) before I set my foot in the *staffa* (stirrup).

bicchierino [bik-ki-e-**ri**-no] a paper cup for ice cream, or a small glass, usually for wine.

bicerin [bi-che-**rin**] coffee, hot chocolate and whipped cream, a Turin speciality.

bietola [bi-**e**-to-la] Swiss chard.

bietolone [bi-e-to-**lo**-ne] an outsize Swiss chard.

biga [**bi**-ga] a substantial sourdough bread.

bigarade [bi-ga-**ra**-de] meat sauce made with orange juice and citrus zest.

bignè [bin-**yay**] the Italian cream puff, related to the French *beignet*, also known as *bigné di San Giuseppe* because it is traditionally served on St Joseph's day, 19th March.

bigoli [**bi**-go-li] a robust, spaghetti-like pasta (literally 'worms') from Friuli-Venezia Giulia. The strands are thick and hollow, an ideal vehicle for sauces. *Bigoli col'anara* is a substantial Paduan dish in which the pasta is served in a sauce made of duck livers seasoned with sage. *Bigoli co le sardele* is a dish of *bigoli* pasta with a sauce of sardines. *Bigoli col tocio* are served in a minced meat RAGÙ.

bigui [**bi**-gui] = BIGOLI.

biovette [bi-o-**vet**-te] soft, plump bread rolls (Piedmont).

biroldo [bi-**rol**-do] a sausage from western Tuscany made of pork and pig's blood seasoned with garlic, lemon peel and parsley and incorporating raisins and pine nuts.

birra [**bir**-ra] beer; *birra chiara* [ki-**a**-ra] is light beer, lager; *birra rossa* [**ros**-sa] or *scura* [**sku**-ra] is dark beer. In central and northern regions of Italy there may be an emphasis on German beers, but Italians are justifiably proud of native brews such as Nastro Azzurro, brewed by Peroni in Lombardy.

birreria [bi-re-**ri**-a] a beer bar.

bisato [bi-**za**-to] a Venetian word for an eel.

biscotti [bis-**cot**-ti] a generic term for biscuits, in all their regional manifestations (and there are many). The word means cooked (*cotto*) twice (*bis*), descriptive of the preliminary part-baking of a solid lump of dough which is then sliced or cut into shapes before the second and final turn in the oven.

bistecca [bi-**stec**-ca] steak.

bitter [**bit**-ter] alcoholic or non-alcoholic sharp-flavoured aperitif. In Venice and the Veneto, a '*spritz bitter*' is a SPRITZ mixed with CAMPARI.

bitto [**bit**-to] a Lombard country cheese made from a mixture of goat's and cow's milk.

blecs [bleks] literally, 'patches of cloth', pasta from Friuli-Venezia Giulia resembling coarsely-cut patches.

blu [bloo] blue, often on menus denoting blue cheese.

blutnudeln [**bloot**-nu-deln] 'blood noodles', pasta from Trentino made from rye flour and pig's blood, served with sage and local cheese.

boba see BOGA.

boccale [boc-**ca**-le] a jug or pitcher, usually for wine.

boccòn [boc-**con**] pasta from the Veneto traditionally made with RICOTTA cheese and spinach mixed into the dough.

bocconcino/i [boc-con-**chi**-no] a bite-sized morsel(s), a little mouthful, something rather more formal and elaborately

---

Steak (*bistecca*) and how to order it

Bistecca di maiale is a pork chop. If what you want is beef, make sure you are ordering *bistecca di manzo* [**mant**-zo]. The famous *bistecca alla fiorentina* [fi-o-ren-**ti**-na] is a thick T-bone of CHIANINA beef. Purists eat it very rare, grilled over coals, served with nothing but lemon juice and parsley. Other steaks include *b~ alla pizzaiola* [pit-za-i-**o**-la], with tomato and garlic and *b~ di filetto* [fi-**let**-to], rib steak.

When ordering steak, the following terms are important: *quasi cruda* [**kwa**-zi **cru**-da], nearly raw; *al sangue* [al **san**-gway], bloody; *a puntino* [pun-**ti**-no], medium; *ben cotta* [ben **cot**-ta], well done.

Note that prices are often given *per etto* [**et**-to], one *etto* being 100g. Don't order a hearty 900g steak in the mistaken assumption that you will only pay the price quoted *per etto*!

thought-out than an ASSAGGIO, used of delicate portions of stewed veal or fried rolls or balls of veal, ham, and cheese. The word can also be used to imply subtlety and delicacy in more substantial dishes, for example *bocconcini di vitello con funghi porcini e lamelle di tartufo bianco* is a veal stew with PORCINI and finely sliced white TRUFFLES. The veal is served in dainty mouthfuls. In cheese-making, *bocconcini* are the smaller balls of fresh MOZZARELLA: 'mouthfuls' as opposed to the standard size. The word has come to mean all bite-sized cheese rounds or ovals. *Bocconcini* is the diminutive of *bocconi*, which means mouthfuls. *Boccone squadrista*, the 'Airman's Titbit', was a Futurist recipe devised by Filippo MARINETTI consisting of a piece of fish served between two large apple slices, sprinkled with rum and set alight immediately prior to consumption.

boccone del prete [boc-co-ne del **pre**-te] 1. the 'priest's morsel', a choice cut in a stew reserved for the visiting local priest; 2. a kind of pork SALAME.

boga [**bo**-ga] bogue (fish; pl. *boghe*). Also called *boba*.

bogoni [bo-**go**-ni] snails.

boldro [**bol**-dro] frogfish or angler fish (Tuscany), see PESCATRICE.

Bolgheri [**bol**-ghe-ri] wine-growing area of coastal Tuscany, home to some of the SUPERTUSCANS.

bollicine [bol-li-**chi**-ne] bubbles in wine. As a heading on menus, it indicates sparkling wines.

bollito/a [bol-**li**-to] boiled.

bollito misto [bol-**li**-to **mi**-sto] a dish of mixed boiled meats, mainly sausages.

bologna [bo-**lon**-ya] a smooth, mild, often smoked, sausage.

Bolognese sauce the famous meat ragout named after Bologna, its birthplace. It is typically eaten with an egg pasta such as TAGLIATELLE (purists will never eat it with spaghetti) and uses far less tomato in the preparation than commercial Bolognese sauces; some cooks use none at all; this older version is called *ragù bianco*, white ragout. Simmered for several hours (at least two), a glass of milk is added to both versions when it is nearly ready.

bomba di riso [**bom**-ba di **ri**-zo] a rice dish originating in Tuscany as a way of using up leftovers. The cooked rice is formed into a circular receptacle either by hand or by using a mould. The well in the middle is filled with meat and sauce, often pigeon, and then covered with a final layer of rice. The resulting 'bomb' is baked in the oven, turned out onto a dish and served.

bondiola [bon-di-**o**-la] a spiced pork sausage from the province of Ferrara; boiled for a number of hours and served in slices.

bonito [bo-**ni**-to] (or *bonita*), skipjack tuna.

bordatino [bor-da-**ti**-no] a Tuscan soup with cornflour, beans, vegetables, and sometimes fish; excellent versions are made in Pisa and Livorno.

bordolese [bor-do-**le**-ze] beef bone-marrow sauce, bordelaise.

borlengo [bor-**len**-go] a flatbread, often eaten spread with PESTO MODENESE.

borlotti [bor-**lot**-ti] small red and pink speckled beans, often used in soups and stews and mostly bought dried.

borragine, borrana [bor-ra-**ji**-ne, bor-**ra**-na] borage, aromatic plant with edible blue flowers.

boscaiola, alla [bos-ca-i-**o**-la] with aubergine, mushrooms and tomato.

bosco [**bos**-co] the woods, forest; *misto di bosco* is a dish of mixed wild berries.

bosega [bo-**ze**-ga] a type of grey mullet, also known as *muggine*.

botargo, bottarga [bo-**tar**-go, bot-**tar**-ga] the salted and cured roe of grey mullet, popular in north and south. Regional variants are found in Sicily and the Veneto where it is served as an ANTIPASTO, thinly sliced and dressed with olive oil. *Bottarga* can be grated over pasta in the same way as truffles.

botolo [**bo**-to-lo] Venetian name for a type of small mullet.

bottagio [bot-**tad**-jo] a thick stew. The name probably derives from the French *potage*.

botte [**bot**-te] a cask or barrel for wine, as in the proverb *non si può avere la botte piena e la moglie ubriaca*: you can't have your barrel full and your wife drunk (you can't have your cake and eat it).

bottiglia [bot-**til**-ya] bottle.

bovino [bo-**vi**-no] beef.

bovoletto [bo-vo-**let**-to] a little snail.

bovoli [**bo**-vo-li] snails.

Bra [bra] a cheese from Piedmont available in two varieties, *duro* (hard, and used for seasoning and grating in favour of the more expensive PECORINO) and *tenero* (soft and milder in taste).

bracciatelle [brat-cha-**tel**-le] 'bracelets', ring-shaped loaves from Emilia-Romagna; also known as *brazadei* (brat-sa-**de**-i).

brace, alla [**bra**-che] cooked over embers.

Brachetto [bra-**ket**-to] sweet Piedmontese red wine.

braciola [bra-**cho**-la] a cutlet or chop, usually pork but may also describe lamb, beef, game and, sometimes, fish. The word is also used of a minute steak. *Braciola di maiale* is pork loin, served in Naples in a sauce made with tomatoes, garlic, capers and pine nuts. *Braciole*, in the plural, are chops.

bramangiare [bra-man-**ja**-re] see BIANCOMANGIARE.

branzi [**brant**-si] a fragrant alpine cheese from Bergamo, Lombardy.

branzino [brant-**si**-no] sea bass, also known as *spigola*. In Venetian dialect, *branzin* [brant-**zin**].

brasato [bra-**za**-to] a pot roast consisting of braised beef marinated in wine and braised with vegetables, often *al* BAROLO, i.e. with the red wine of that name. There are striking regional differences in flavour depending on the wine used.

brazadei see BRACCIATELLE.

bresaola [bre-**za**-o-la] salted, air-dried beef, dark red in appearance, a speciality of Lombardy, but enjoyed across Italy; often served as an ANTIPASTO, sliced thin and drizzled with olive oil and lemon. A SALUME.

bricchetti [brik-**ket**-ti] 'little sticks', pasta from Liguria served in MINESTRONE.

bringoli [**brin**-go-li] 'twisted ones', pasta from Val di Pierle, Tuscany, served with a variety of local sauces.

brioche [bri-**osh**] a French term borrowed to describe a broad variety of semi-sweet breakfast pastries.

broccoletti, broccoli [broc-co-**let**-tt, **broc**-co-li] broccoli.

broccolo romanesco see ROMANESCO.

brodetto [bro-**det**-to] soup, a diminutive of BRODO (broth) but nonetheless fairly substantial. *Brodetto di Pasqua* is chicken soup thickened with eggs and lemon, served at Easter in Florence and Lazio. In Italy's fishing ports, strikingly different fish-based *brodetti* have developed over the centuries, their ingredients dependant on what is readily available.

brodo [**bro**-do] broth, a meat, poultry or fish stock, slowly reduced, often used as the basis for RISOTTO or heavier pasta dishes in which the pasta is cooked in the meat juices as opposed to being boiled in water.

brodo consumato [**bro**-do con-su-**ma**-to] clear chicken soup, consommé, also known as *brodo ristretto*.

brodosini [bro-do-**zi**-ni] 'the watery, soupy ones' (pasta shapes), noodles served in broth, especially around Chieti in Abruzzo.

brodoso [bro-**do**-zo] runny, in a creamy, wholesome, slightly glutinous sense.

broeto [bro-**e**-to] stock (Venetian dialect).

bros see BRUSS.

brossa [**bros**-sa] a runny RICOTTA, traditionally eaten with POLENTA, from Valle d'Aosta.

brovada [bro-**va**-da] pickled turnips, fermented under grape marc (pressed skins, stems etc), then grated and lengthily cooked with a SOFFRITTO and pork, a DOP speciality of Friuli-Venezia Giulia. *Brovada* is often served with FRICO cheese or MUSÈT, a typical Friulan sausage.

Brunello [bru-**nel**-lo] a clone of the SANGIOVESE grape grown around Montalcino in Tuscany. It produces one of Italy's finest DOCG wines.

bruscandoli [brus-**can**-do-li] the shoots of the hop plant, used in soups and as a flavouring in sauces.

bruschetta [brus-**ket**-ta] toasted bread rubbed with garlic, drizzled with olive oil and garnished with tomatoes, onions and other toppings depending on the region or the imagination of the cook. Sometimes known as FETT'UNTA or PANUNTA in Tuscany and Umbria. See also CROSTINI and CROSTONI. *Bruschetta di fegatini* are *bruschetta* topped with sautéed chicken liver pieces, sometimes with a hint of chilli. A *bruschetteria* [brus-ket-te-**ri**-a] is an establishment specialising in *bruschette*, often with many types of unusual topping.

bruss [broos] a pungent Piedmontese cheese spread made of fermented RICOTTA enlivened with pepper, herbs and sometimes chilli. Also known as *bros* or *brus*.

brustenga [brus-**ten**-ga] Carnival dish from the Marche, consisting of egg custard thickened with breadcrumbs or cornflour, flavoured with MISTRÀ, lemon zest or rum, and cooked in a frying pan like an omelette.

brustolini, bruscolini [brus-to-**li**-ni, brus-co-**li**-ni] toasted pumpkin seeds.

brutti ma buoni [**brut**-ti ma **buo**-ni] 'ugly but good', almond biscuits.

bruzzo [**bruts**-zo] fermented sheep's RICOTTA from the Ligurian alps.

bucaniera, alla [bu-can-i-**e**-ra] 'pirate style', see CARRETTIERA.

bucatini [bu-ca-**ti**-ni] 'pierced ones', hollow pasta strands, in eastern parts of Italy (Abruzzo, Marche) often served with a fish sauce. The best-known variant is *bucatini all'*AMATRICIANA, which takes its name from the town of Amatrice in northern Lazio.

bucato [bu-**ca**-to] 'pierced', the generic name for the many kinds of long pasta pierced down the centre, e.g. BUCATINI.

buccellati [bu-chel-**la**-ti] ring-shaped pastries filled with nuts and figs (Sicily).

buccellato [bu-chel-**la**-to] sponge cake with raisins, flavoured with aniseed. A speciality of Lucca, Tuscany.

buccuni [buc-**cu**-ni] see MURICE.

budella [bu-**del**-la] offal, intestines, the plural form of *budello*. In the Tuscan dish *budella alla sestese*, these are pig's intestines.

budellacci [bu-del-**lat**-chi] (in Umbria) smoked, spiced pig intestines, usually spit-roasted or broiled.

budelletti [bu-del-**let**-ti] very thin intestines, either the real thing or pasta shapes. The latter are often served in PANCETTA-based sauces or, in Ascoli Piceno in the Marche, in a tuna sauce.

budino [bu-**di**-no] pudding; *budino di riso* is rice pudding; *budino di ricotta* is a soufflé with RICOTTA cheese, lemon and cinnamon.

bue [**bu**-e] beef, a more colloquial word than the genteel *manzo*, as in a no-nonsense rural dish such as *bue brasato con gnocchi di polenta* (braised beef with polenta gnocchi).

bufalo, bufala [**bu**-fa-lo, **bu**-fa-la] the water buffalo, the meat of which is eaten in some southern areas and whose milk is used for MOZZARELLA.

bugie [bu-**jee**-e] 'lies', Piedmontese nickname for a type of fried pastry made at Easter, the name alluding to the dishonest weakness of snacking on the sly during Lent.

buglossa [bu-**glos**-sa] bugloss, used in salads and soups.

bukë [bu-cu-e] ARBËRESH bread made with local hard-grain flour in antique wood-burning ovens,

---

Bufalo, the water buffalo

Some say buffalo were introduced to Italy in the 6th century AD by the invading Goths, others that the Normans brought them to the mainland from Sicily c. AD 1100, still others that they were progressively introduced over time by pilgrims, crusaders and Arab merchants. They are hardy, versatile animals, having unusually large hooves that prevent them from sinking in muddy soil and therefore enable them to thrive in watery terrain. Though Neapolitan buffalo herds were slaughtered by the retreating Nazis during the Italian Campaign, the industry soon picked up after the Armistice. Buffaloes have an efficient digestive system that enables them to transform indifferent vegetation into protein-rich milk, high in mineral content and more nutritious than cow's milk.

traditionally eaten with olive oil and RICOTTA.

buridda [bu-**rid**-da] 1. seafood stew (Liguria); 2. the Sardinian method of serving flat fish such as skate or ray cold, after simmering in stock and marinading in vinegar.

burrata [bur-**ra**-ta] a creamy cheese from Puglia, made from buffalo milk.

burrino [bur-**ri**-no] a creamy, piquant, salted cheese, often filled with an inner core of butter, from Molise and Basilicata.

burro [**bur**-ro] butter.

burroso/a [bur-**ro**-zo] buttery, ripe; *una pera burrosa*: a ripe ('buttery') pear.

busa, busiata [**bu**-za, bu-zi-a-ta] twisted pasta from Sardinia, made by winding a strand of dough around a thin stick or spike (the *busa*). *Busiata* is a robust Sicilian version of *busa*, described in the 15th-century *Libro de arte coquinaria* by Martino da Como, where he calls them '*maccaroni siciliani*': 'These *maccaroni* should be dried in the sun, and will last for two or three years, especially if done in the month of August; and cook them in water or meat broth; and put them on platters with a goodly quantity of grated cheese, fresh butter and sweet spices...' Today you can still find hand-made *busiata* in Sicily, often served with *sugo alle sarde*, a sardine and wild fennel sauce.

busaki [bu-**za**-ki] festive FETTUCCINE from Sardinia, served at Easter.

busara, alla [bu-**za**-ra] in a sauce of tomato, parsley, garlic, white wine and seasoning. Sometimes spelled *buzara*, this sauce probably originates in Friuli-Venezia Giulia and is popular in the Veneto. On menus you will often find *spaghetti alla busara* or *scampi alla busara*, pasta or prawns dressed with this sauce.

busecca [bu-**zec**-ca] a thick tripe with vegetables and beans.

bussolà [bus-sol-**a**] doughnut-shaped biscuit or ring-shaped cake, typically baked for Easter but now available year-round. A speciality of the Veneto.

bussùl [bus-**sool**] the traditional short-stemmed shot-glass used for drinking GRAPPA.

bustrengo [bus-**tren**-go] a central Italian baked pudding made with breadcrumbs soaked in milk, eggs, spices, dried figs, and sometimes chopped apples. Rimini is the best place to try some.

caccia [**cat**-cha] the hunt.

cacciagione [cat-cha-**jo**-ne] game. If it has not been caught by the *cacciatore* then it will have been commercially farmed; in Italy game includes birds such as woodcock, snipe and quail as well as large animals such as deer and wild boar.

cacciatora, alla [cat-cha-**to**-ra] 'hunter's style': cooked in a rich tomato sauce with mushrooms and sweet peppers.

cacciatorino [cat-cha-to-**ri**-no] a small, hard SALAME, the name indicative of game content such as wild boar rather than domesticated meat.

cacciucco [cat-**chuc**-co] a fish stew of ancient Etruscan origin, native to Livorno, Tuscany. It is often noticeably *piccante* (spicy).

cacio [**ca**-cho] a southern term for cheese, as is the diminutive form *caciotta* [ca-**chot**-ta]. FORMAGGIO is the standard word but *cacio* is frequently used as a prefix. *Caciocavallo* is a southern Italian cow's milk cheese with a mild, slightly salty flavour. The name means 'horse cheese'; the cheeses are hung to mature over a pole known as the *cavallo* ('horse'). *Caciocavallo podolico* is a famously expensive cheese made exclusively from the milk of Podolica cows from Puglia. *Càciofiore aquilano* is cow's milk cheese scented with herbs and grasses, from L'Aquila (Abruzzo). *Cacioricotta*, a piquant sheep's milk cheese, is produced in Puglia and often used for grating when it has matured. *Cacio raviggiolo* is fresh cheese (usually of cow's milk) from the Casentino region of northern Tuscany. First mentioned in the Middle Ages (a present of *cacio raviggiolo* was made to Pope Leo X in the 16th century), it is still produced as a niche product today.

cacio pepe [**ca**-cho **pe**-pe] a typical dish of Rome; long pasta such as spaghetti or BUCATINI dressed with pepper and cheese. Deceptively simple (it's not easy to prepare perfectly), it consists of black peppercorns pounded in a mortar, toasted in a pan with a little olive oil; then abundant grated PECORINO *romano* and the cooked pasta are added and mixed together.

caco [**ca**-co] persimmon (pl. *cachi*). Also known as *kaki*, and as *loto* in Sicily.

cadunsei [ca-dun-**se**-i] PASTA RIPIENA from Lombardy, a type of RAVIOLI filled with meat, salami, herbs and grated cheese. Also known as *cahunei*, this is the traditional dish of the alpine valley of Val Camonica.

caffè [caf-**fe**] coffee.

Coffee in Italy: history and etiquette

Coffee first came to Italy around 1570, entering the port of Venice probably from Ottoman Istanbul. Pope Clement VIII (Ippolito Aldobrandini; 1536–1605) was an early and prominent Italian coffee enthusiast. It is said that when presented with a petition to ban the 'infidel' drink, he promptly 'baptised' a dish of coffee beans.

There are many different ways of making coffee in Italy, all of them falling into two categories: with milk (e.g. *cappuccino*) and without (e.g. *espresso*). The idea that Italians frown on the consumption of *cappuccino* after 11am has entered popular consciousness but the fact is, coffee in itself is regarded as a restorative or an aid to digestion; if taken with milk it becomes a foodstuff, which is why it is fine for breakfast, accompanied by a pastry and a glass or fresh orange juice. Between or after meals, it is better taken black.

Coffee may be ordered either *al banco* (at the bar) or *a tavola* (at the table). If drinking *al banco* you must either remain there, standing up, to drink your coffee and then pay for it, or, in more old-school establishments, order first, then pay at the *cassa* (cash desk), then take the *scontrino* (receipt) back to the bar where you will then be given you coffee. If drinking *a tavola*, find a table and wait to be served or place your order but indicate that you intend to take it sitting down, in which case it will be brought to you. Remember that table service costs more than service *al banco* for a good reason, and it is considered very *brutta figura* (bad manners) to pay bar prices and then make your way to a table and finish your drink sitting down. Most cafés still serve coffee in china cups, although paper beakers of coffee to go are beginning to appear.

A *bar* is an ordinary coffee bar but a *caffè* is something rather more exclusive, an elegant place, usually with a choice of inner, private rooms, and often with a history of famous patrons. Examples are Florian and Quadri in Venice, Pedrocchi in Padua, Giacosa in Florence and Caffè Greco in Rome.

Types of coffee

Espresso is the concentrated, brown-black potion brewed by forcing hot water under pressure through finely ground, roasted coffee beans. It is so called not because it is quick (which it usually is) but because it is made 'expressly' for the person who orders it. A *doppio espresso* or *caffè doppio* is a double *espresso*.

  Ristretto means 'concentrated', and a short shot of *espresso ristretto* is achieved by exposing the coffee grounds to hot water for fractionally less time, giving the caffeine less of a chance to intrude on the natural flavours of the coffee oils.

  Caffè lungo, a 'long coffee' uses more water than a regular *espresso*, and the flavour is thus less intense.

  Cappuccino, named after the cowls of Capuchin monks because of its colour, is prepared with *espresso* and hot milk, the milk being steamed to a froth which gives the *cappuccino* its distinctive surface. *Cappuccino senza schiuma* [**sent**-sa ski-**u**-ma] is *cappuccino* without too much foam and it is perfectly acceptable to ask for this: the *barista* will skim off a layer of *schiuma* with a knife.

  Macchiato ('stained') is *espresso* 'stained' with a dribble of milk. You may also ask for a *latte macchiato* in which a generous slug of milk is 'stained' with a dash of coffee (a form now popular around the world as 'latte'.

  Caffè corretto means 'corrected' coffee, an *espresso* 'corrected' with a shot of GRAPPA, SAMBUCA or brandy. To specify which, order '*caffè corretto a grappa*' or '*corretto a sambuca*', or '*corretto a cognac*'. In simpler bars frequented by artisans you will encounter people, often market traders, drinking *corretto* at breakfast—it is not a good idea to emulate them unless you, too, have been at work since before dawn. An **ammazzacaffè** is a 'coffee killer', a small glass of liqueur drunk after coffee to dull its taste. There is a variation on this theme in the Veneto and Trentino, where it is customary to rinse out an empty coffee cup with grappa and pour the liquid into a glass. The resulting drink in known as a *resentin*, literally a 're-feeling' of the original coffee experience. In Piedmont this drink is known as *pussacaffè*.

An *americano* is black coffee prepared by adding hot water to *espresso*. *Caffè instantaneo* or *solubile* is instant coffee and to ask for it in an Italian bar would be a breathtaking solecism. *Caffè di cicoria* is chicory coffee or camp coffee, an acquired taste, as is *caffè d'orzo*, coffee made with barley. *Bicerin* is a Torinese mixture of *cappuccino* and hot chocolate, sometimes served with whipped cream and decorated with chocolate powder. *Caffè alla turca* is Turkish coffee.

caglio [cal-yo] rennet, used to divide curds and whey in the cheese-making process.

cahunei [ca-hoo-**ne**-i] see CADUNSEI.

caicc [ca-**itch**] large RAVIOLI originally from Breno in Val Camonica (Lombardy) with a rich filling of meat, greens, macaroons, currants and cheese, made for special occasions and often accompanied by a dish of polenta dressed with butter and cheese.

cajubi [ca-**yu**-bi] short MACCHERONI from Puglia, usually served *alla* RICOTTA.

Calabria [ca-**la**-bri-a] peninsula forming the toe of Italy, site of the 7th-century BC Greek settlement of Sybaris, renowned for its citizens' devotion to the pursuit of pleasure, and ancient Croton, famous for healthy athletes such as the wrestler Milo, who won the Olympic olive wreath six times. According to legend, after a contest he would run around the track carrying an ox on his shoulders, which he then roasted and devoured. This ancient exuberance is annually reawoken at festival time, evident in the elaborate pastries and sweet RAVIOLI typical of the area. The cuisine is notably spicy. Famous Calabrian produce includes bergamots, mountain mushrooms, aubergines (reputedly the finest in Italy), chilli pepper and onions (notably the red onions of Tropea). Its most highly-regarded wine is CIRÒ. It has lent its name to calabrese, a type of broccoli.

calamari [ca-la-**ma**-ri] 1. squid, not to be confused with the cuttlefish (*illustrations on pp. 168–9*). *Calamari* (in the diminutive, *calamaretti*) are mainly deep fried or lightly boiled and served in seafood salads. Their black ink is used to flavour and colour both pasta and RISOTTO. *Calamari ripieni* are stuffed *calamari*; PROSCIUTTO CRUDO is a favourite filling. *Calamari in zimino* is a rich Tuscan stew of squid, garlic, spinach or chard, tomatoes and oil. 2. large macaroni, like sections of hosepipe, slightly smaller than CANNELLONI.

calcioni [cal-**cho**-ni] PASTA RIPIENA from the Marche, filled with RICOTTA and herbs. There is also a deep-fried, sweet version, dusted with sugar, the filling flavoured with lemon zest and cinnamon.

caldo/a [**cal**-do] warm, hot.

calhù [cal-**hoo**] in Alpine dialect, 'trousers': PASTA RIPIENA from Lombardy, named after the traditional baggy breeches of the Val Camonica.

calia see SIMENZA.

calice [**ca**-li-che] wineglass.

calzoncelli [calt-zon-**chel**-li] traditional sweet pastries filled with RICOTTA, chestnut purée and/or chocolate.

calzone [calt-**zo**-ne] 'trousers' or 'stockings'; in gastronomic terms a 'turnover', a crescent-shaped pasty with a savoury filling, often MOZZARELLA and tomato. In Sicily they are known as *scacciate* and have a variety of fillings including onion, potatoes, broccoli and sausage in addition to the usual cheese and tomato.

calzonicchi [calt-zo-**nik**-ki] pasta filled with brains, onions and spices, a delicacy of Roman Jewish cuisine.

camera [**ca**-me-ra] room, e.g. *servito in camera*: served in your room.

camicia, in [ca-**mi**-cha] poached (lit. 'in a shirt').

camionista, alla [ca-mi-o-**ni**-sta] 'lorry driver style', a term applied to a variety of robust dishes. See also CARRETTIERA.

camomilla [ca-mo-**mil**-la] camomile.

camoscio [ca-**mo**-sho] chamois.

campanelle [cam-pa-**nel**-le] 'little bells', a pasta shape.

Campania [cam-**pa**-ni-a] region of southern Italy, the location of important towns and cities including Naples, Salerno, Sorrento, Amalfi, Positano, Ravello and the islands Ischia and Capri. The region has been famous for its bounty since the days of the ancient Roman, who called it *Campania felix*, the 'happy land'. Campania is known for the quality of its fruit: *Annurca* apples, red and sweet, are ripened on straw; called the 'Queen of Apples', they can be seen in some of the wall paintings at Herculaneum. Plum tomatoes and strawberries are renowned; fine lemon trees grow in and around Sorrento and the Costa Amalfitana, traditional home of LIMONCELLO. Campania is also the land of buffalo-milk MOZZARELLA, and PIZZA, which Naples claims to have invented. TAURASI is probably the region's finest red wine. Its most famous white is FIANO di Avellino.

campanilismo [cam-pa-ni-**lis**-mo] *See box overleaf.*

Campari [cam-**pa**-ri] a popular bitter aperitif, invented in the 19th century in Piedmont, by Gaspare Campari. It is usually served with soda and is also a key ingredient of the popular NEGRONI cocktail.

campo [**cam**-po] the countryside, a source of wild herbs and vegetables, e.g. *asparagi di campo*, wild asparagus.

Campofilone [cam-po-fi-**lo**-ne] little town in the Marche renowned for very fine egg noodles, called *maccheroncini di Campofilone*. 'Campofilone' is synonymous for angel's hair egg noodles in Italy.

candele [can-**de**-le] long, pierced pasta, similar to BUCATINI or ZITI (the larger versions).

canditi [can-**di**-ti] candied fruit.

canederli [ca-**ne**-der-li] bread dumplings, the Italian South Tyrolean version of Austrian and German *knödel*, a speciality of Trentino-Alto Adige. *Canederli* are made with stale bread mixed with milk and eggs, flavoured with a SOFFFRITTO of cheese or SPECK, onion and parsley. They are typically cooked and then served in meat broth.

canestrato pugliese [ca-ne-**stra**-to pul-**ye**-ze] Hard sheep's milk cheese with DOP status native to the province of Foggia in Puglia. The cheese is left to mature in traditional reed baskets (*canestre*), the ribs of which give the rind its distinctive corrugated appearance. Sicilian PECORINO is sometimes called *canistratu* in dialect.

cannacce [ca-**nat**-che] long pasta designed to resemble reeds, commemorating the burning at the stake of St Apollonia, patron saint of Ariccia in Lazio. On her feast day (9th Feb) a public feast is held where *cannacce* are served, along with other local delicacies, notably the town's famous

---

Campanilismo, the key to Italy's regional diversity

Italy is a land of regions. This is obvious from the landscape, the architecture, political attitudes and linguistic variations. But nowhere is it more marked than in what you see on *trattoria* menus. Partly this diversity is a result of tradition. Today, however, when ingredients and ideas can and do travel great distances, regionalism owes its survival more to the will of the people and to their *campanilismo*, 'bell-tower thinking', the belief that the bell-tower or *campanile* [cam-pa-**nee**-le] of one's own town or village occupies the centre of the universe and that one's community produces the best cheese, wine and pasta in the world, has the prettiest girls, the handsomest men and the best restaurants. In gastronomic terms *campanilismo*, far from resulting in complacency and stagnation, is a vigorous commercial stimulant, each village, town, city, province and region competing with next for international recognition of its hospitality and produce, all proud of the uniqueness and low mileage of their recipes.

SALSICCIA. *Cannacce* are very similar to (and sometimes also known as) ZITI.

cannariculi [can-na-**ri**-cu-li] a Calabrian Christmas speciality: gnocchi-shaped pieces of dough, fried and then coated in honey or MOSTO COTTO. *Struffoli* and *cicirate* are other versions of the same thing.

cannella [can-**nel**-la] cinnamon.

cannellini [can-nel-**li**-ni] small white beans, similar in shape to kidney beans, bought dried and then soaked before being used in soups and stews.

cannelloni [can-nel-**lo**-ni] large, tube-shaped pasta typically filled with minced meat or RICOTTA and spinach, and often topped with cheese or béchamel sauce. CRESPELLE are similar but in pancake form. *Cannelloni alla partenopea* is a Neapolitan speciality, filled with a mixture of RICOTTA and MOZZARELLA and topped with tomato sauce.

cannizzu [can-**nits**-zu] in Sicily, a woven reed mat, used for drying tomatoes, figs or grapes.

cannolicchi [can-no-**lik**-ki] 1. 'little tubes', a hollow pasta shape used in casseroles or vegetable soups; 2. razor clams. See CANNOLICCHIO.

cannolicchio [can-no-**lik**-ki-o] the razor clam, a bivalve often cooked and served in one half of its shell with oil, garlic and parsley, garnished with lemon.

cannolo [can-**no**-lo] exquisite Sicilian confection (pl. *cannoli*), consisting of a crisp sweet pastry cylinder filled with fresh ricotta, decorated at both ends with glacé cherries, chopped hazelnuts, candied orange, chopped dark chocolate, or pistachio. Recipes vary from town to town.

Cannonau [can-no-**na**-u] Sardinian name for Grenache or Garnacha, the red-wine grape of Châteauneuf du Pape. As vinified in Sardinia, it is very dark in colour, and pleasingly rustic on the palate.

cannoncino [can-non-**chi**-no] a cream horn.

canocie, canocchie [ca-no-che; ca-**nok**-ki-e] mantis shrimps (*Squilla mantis*), also known as *cicale di mare* ('sea cicadas'), an essential ingredient in many fish soups of the Adriatic as well as Sicily. They

Canocie, mantis shrips, on sale from a fishmonger in Venice. The label notes that they are freshly caught, not frozen, and specifies the fishing zone.

are frequently found on menus in Venice.

canoe di mele [ca-**no**-e di **me**-le] pastry 'canoes' filled with rum-laced cream and glazed apples. *Canoe salate* are the savoury version, with meat or fish fillings, slightly similar to a vol-au-vent.

cantarelli [can-ta-**rel**-li] fragrant yellow mushrooms; chanterelles. A native of beech and oak woods, they are found fresh in season (autumn) or dried. Also known as *finferli* or *gallinacci*.

cantucci, cantuccini [can-tu-chi, can-tu-**chi**-ni] hard, almond-flavoured biscuits that can be dipped into coffee or vinsanto.

capelli d'angelo [ca-**pel**-li **dan**-je-lo] 'angel hair' pasta, so called because of its fine texture and appearance, in little curled bundles. It is also known as *capellini* or campofilone.

capellini [ca-pel-**li**-ni] 'little hairs', long pasta strands, thin, fine pasta often used in soups. Essentially a synonym for capelli d'angelo.

capesante [ca-pe-**san**-te] the scallop, seen in a variety of spellings including *cappasanta*, *capa santa*. The scallop's other Italian names, *pellegrina* (pilgrim) and *conchiglia di San Giacomo* (St James's shell), allude to its religious symbolism. Pilgrims would often stitch a shell-shaped patch on their travelling capes before setting off for St James's major shrine in

Spain, Santiago de Compostela. Many would carry shells as scoops, useful for helping oneself to the food provided by religious foundations along the route, or for drinking from rivers. Scallops are cooked in a variety of ways. They can be simmered simply with lemon and parsley, or served *au gratin*, with saffron sauce, or with pasta.

capicola SEE CAPOCOLLO.

caplaz SEE CAPPELLACCI.

capocollo [ca-po-**col**-lo] lit. 'head-neck', a dry-cured SALUME originating in Calabria (*Capocollo di Calabria* has DOP status). It is flavoured with different seasonings according to region. Similar to COPPA.

caponata [ca-po-**na**-ta] a Sicilian sweet-sour appetiser or side dish, made with aubergines, onions, celery, tomatoes or tomato purée, capers and green olives. When nearly cooked, a spoonful of wine vinegar mixed with sugar or orange-blossom honey rounds off the flavour. Other versions call for pine nuts, unsweetened cocoa, sultanas and peppers, and yet other kinds are made with courgettes or artichokes.

capone [ca-**po**-ne] 1. Sicilian name for LAMPUGA. *Capone apparecchiato* is *lampuga* in a sweet and sour sauce; 2. gurnard (fish).

cappa liscia [**cap**-pa li-sha] the smooth Venus clam.

cappalunga [cap-pa-**loon**-ga] lit. 'long hat', the razor clam; see CANNOLICCHIO.

cappasanta [cap-pa-**san**-ta] see CAPESANTE.

cappellacci [cap-pel-**lat**-chi] 'little hats', a PASTA RIPIENA from Emilia-Romagna, particularly Ferrara, where they are known as *caplaz*. They are filled with a mixture of pumpkin, cheese and grated nutmeg. The dish is similar to TORTELLI *di zucca*.

Capesante, the scallop.

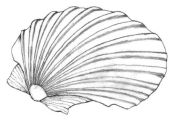

cappelletti [cap-pel-**let**-ti]
small CAPPELLACCI; pasta 'hats',
similar to TORTELLINI, stuffed
with a variety of fillings,
typically RICOTTA or PARMIGIANO
REGGIANO. They are a speciality
of Emilia-Romagna.

cappello del prete [cap-**pel**-
lo del **pre**-te] 'priest's hat': 1. a
pork meat sausage; 2. a shoulder
cut of stewing beef.

capperi [**cap**-per-i] capers,
the intensely-flavoured flower
buds of the wild Mediterranean
shrub *Capparis spinosa*, usually
preserved in vinegar or salt.
The best are said to be those
from the island of Pantelleria. If
allowed to mature, the resulting
fruits, like little gherkins, are
called *cucunci*

cappon magro [**cap**-pon **mag**-
ro] a Ligurian dish, a sort of
seafood and vegetable trifle. The
main ingredient is the CAPONE,
though sometimes sea bass is
used instead.

cappone [cap-**po**-ne] capon, a
castrated rooster.

cappuccio [cap-**pu**-cho] 1.
a cabbage; 2. short, informal
name for a CAPPUCCINO.

cappuccino [cap-pu-**chi**-no]
see COFFEE.

capra [**cap**-ra] goat, e.g.
formaggio di capra: goat's cheese.

caprese [cap-**re**-ze] in the style
of Capri, commonly used of the
simple salad *insalata caprese*,
made with MOZZARELLA, tomato
and basil.

capretto [cap-**ret**-to] a kid,
ideally a young milk-fed goat
between 4 and 8 weeks old.

Capri [**ca**-pri] island off the coast
of Campania, traditionally the
retreat of sybarites and literati.
Traditional Capri food is plain:
cheese, pasta and fish, notably
PEZZOGNA. The island gives its
name to the CAPRESE salad.

capricciosa [ca-pri-**cho**-za] the
chef's 'caprice'.

caprini [ca-**pri**-ni] generic term
for cheeses made with goat's
milk.

caprino degli Alburni [cap-**ri**-
no del-yi al-**boor**-ni] quick-
maturing goat's milk cheese
from Campania.

capriolo [cap-ri-**o**-lo] roe buck
venison.

capunsei [ca-pun-**se**-i] bread
gnocchi from Mantua. The
Capunsel di Solferino is a
variant that includes crumbled

AMARETTI in the mix.

carabaccia [ca-ra-**bat**-cha] an onion soup occurring in many variations, sometimes with almonds and cinnamon. An ancient Tuscan dish.

carapigna [ca-ra-**peen**-ya] (Sardinia) a type of sorbet.

carasau [ca-ra-**sa**-u] thin sheets of Sardinian flatbread, traditionally eaten by shepherds when away from home with their flocks.

caratello [ca-ra-**tel**-lo] a barrel (up to 200 litres capacity).

Caratelli of 50 litres are traditionally used to make VINSANTO.

carbonara [car-bo-**na**-ra] pasta sauce made with finely sliced pig's cheek bacon (*guanciale*), gently fried (sometimes in red wine) and then stirred into the spaghetti along with beaten eggs, PECORINO, and a generous sprinkle of freshly-ground black pepper (*see box*). Some people add a little chopped onion but cream is a no-no.

The origins of *carbonara*

The sauce is said to take its name from the *carbonari*, the itinerant charcoal burners of Lazio and Abruzzo, who welcomed the hearty dish as a relief from their rigorous and lonely lifestyle. Others maintain it originated after WWII (it is unrecorded before then) as an Italian variant on the ham and eggs favoured by American soldiers. Another theory claims invention by, or in honour of, a secret society of 19th-century revolutionaries, known as the *Carbonari* because their quasi-masonic initiation rites bore similarities to charcoal-burning traditions. Upholders of this theory maintain that the recipe went unrecorded for so long because it had been veiled in secrecy to protect its originators. Yet another theory claims that *carbonara* is derives from the Austro-Czech *schinkenfleckerl*, a ham and pasta dish with a breadcrumb topping that found its way to Italy during the post-Napoleonic Habsburg era.

The artichoke (*carciofo*), particularly popular in Rome and in the Veneto, though cooked in very different ways in the two regions.

carbonata [car-bo-**na**-ta] see CARBONNADE.

carbonade [car-bo-**nahd**] a rich beef and red wine stew from Valle d'Aosta, sometimes known as *carbonata*.

carbonizzato [car-bo-nits-**za**-to] char-grilled or barbecued.

carciofi [car-**cho**-fi] artichokes; there are several types, green or purple, with leaves terminating with a thorn or without, all equally delicious and particularly nutritious.

Italy provides 30 percent of the world's production, more than any other country, and Sicily (especially Gela, Niscemi and Cerda) accounts for 60 percent of the national crop. The variety from Paestum, near Salerno, bears the IGP seal. They are also grown around the Venetian lagoon. Apicius, the Roman gourmet, was the first to document their use in the kitchen. Older artichokes must be braised or boiled but young, tender specimens, known as *carciofini*, can be cut up and eaten raw in a salad or preserved in olive oil. *Carciofi alla giudea* (*or giudia*)are deep-fried, and typical of Roman Jewish cooking. *Carciofi alla romana* are served braised, stuffed with mint, garlic and breadcrumbs. *Carciofi alla veneziana* are braised in oil and white wine.

cardi [**car**-di] cardoons, a vegetable related to the thistle but actually part of the artichoke family. The part most used in cooking is the stem. Cardoons are in season in winter, and chopped stems are typically found braised or baked as a side dish or added to soups and stews. In Catania (Sicily) the flower heads are gathered before they open, boiled in big vats and sold as street food.

cardinale, alla [car-di-**na**-le] 'cardinal style', in a white sauce made with cream and fish bouillon.

Cardini, Cesare (1896–1956) Italian-Mexican restaurateur, inventor of the Caesar Salad. The salad is named after Mr Cardini, not after one of the Roman emperors as is sometimes supposed.

carnaroli [car-na-**ro**-li] a medium-grain rice from Lombardy, used for RISOTTO.

carne [**car**-ne] meat, e.g. *carne ai ferri* (grilled meat), *carne cruda* (raw meat), *carne di maiale* (pork), *carne di manzo* (beef), *carne ovina* (lamb or mutton). *Carne cruda all'Albese* is steak tartare with truffle sauce, *albese* alluding to Alba, the truffle capital of Italy. *Carne di cavallo* or *carne equina* is horse meat.

carne salada [**car**-ne sa-**la**-da] salt beef, a speciality of Trentino-Alto Adige. It is either eaten cold, or as a hot dish with

BORLOTTI beans: *carne salada e fasoi*.

carnesecca [**car**-ne **sec**-ca] a salted and smoked bacon, much used in Tuscan cuisine.

caro [**ca**-ro] caraway.

carota [ca-**ro**-ta] carrot, along with onions and celery one of the 'Holy Trinity' of Italian cooking. See SOFFRITTO.

carpa [**car**-pa] carp.

carpaccio [car-**pat**-cho] thin-sliced raw beef (*see box overleaf*).

carpione [car-pi-**o**-ne] 1. freshwater fish native to two Italian lakes, Garda and Posta Fibreno (Lazio), and endangered in both; 2. a marinade: *in carpione* means soused in a mixture of lemon juice, salted anchovy, chopped parsley and vinegar, with a hint of dry mustard.

carrettiera, alla [car-ret-ti-**e**-ra] 'cart-driver style' in reference to a simple, hearty spaghetti sauce. Various recipes exist: tuna and cheese are staple ingredients; tomatoes, mushrooms and chilli are sometimes added. Compare BUCANIERA and ZAPPATORA.

carsenta lunigianese [car-**sen**-ta lu-ni-ja-**ne**-ze] a Tuscan bread, traditionally baked on a fire of chestnut leaves.

carta da musica [**car**-ta da **mu**-zi-ca] a large, circular, thin, crisp flatbread some 40cm (16 inches) in diameter, resembling an outsized poppadum and similar to the Sardinian CARASAU. The name, 'music sheet', is a reference to its unusual size and paper-thin consistency, though its antecedents may be rooted even more deeply in antiquity. Virgil refers to the *orbem fatalis crusti* (*Aeneid* VII:115), the circular flatbreads 'of destiny', eaten by Aeneas and his men when they disembarked at Italy for the first time, in what today is Lazio. These were very likely the forebears not only of today's *carta da musica* but of all other circular flatbreads and *pizze* in Italy.

The invention of beef *carpaccio*

The term *carpaccio* is now widely used for any thin-sliced raw meat or fish, served with a vinaigrette or mayonnaise and (sometimes) with shavings of PARMESAN or similar cheese on top, often couched on a bed of RUCOLA. In order to slice the meat to the required wafer-thinness, the meat must be cold and the knife sharp. The original beef *carpaccio* is said to have been invented in 1950 by Giuseppe Cipriani, founder of Harry's Bar in Venice. He devised it for Countess Amalia Nani Mocenigo, who had been advised by her doctor to eschew cooked meat. Today's champions of Raw Foodism, also known as the Paleo Diet, would have applauded. Raw products, after all, give stimulus to the digestive enzymes: anyone who embraces the diet can hope to recapture the get-up-and-go spirit of their cave-dwelling forebears. Cipriani added sophistication to this raw elementality with a mustard mayonnaise and then completed the effect by naming it after the 16th-century Venetian painter Vittore Carpaccio, whose gentle and luminous palette, dominated by cream and red, are echoed in the tints of the raw meat and mayonnaise.

cartellate [car-tel-**la**-te] thin strips of puff pastry from Puglia, fried in oil and often coated with honey.

cartoccio [car-**tot**-cho] parchment, used to wrap meat and fish together with herbs and vegetables, prior to baking. *Cartoccio di pesce spada* = swordfish baked in this way.

carvi [**car**-vi] caraway.

casalinga [ca-za-**lin**-ga] a housewife; *cucina casalinga* [cu-**chi**-na ca-za-**lin**-ga] is home cooking.

casarecce [ca-za-**ret**-che] short lengths of pasta resembling a rolled and twisted tube or scroll. The name refers to their home-made (*casereccio*), rough-and-ready quality.

casatiello [ca-za-ti-**el**-lo] a Neapolitan Easter pie with a filling of PARMESAN and PECORINO cheese, eggs, SALAME, bacon and pepper.

casciotta d'Urbino [cash-**ot**-ta dur-**bi**-no] soft cheese from the Marche, made of a mixture of sheep and cow's milk. Michelangelo loved it and had it regularly sent.

Casella, Cesare (b.1960)

Casarecce, short pasta twisted in order to catch and retain the sauce.

Tuscan-born chef, Dean of Italian Studies at the Italian Culinary Academy in New York. His company Republic of Beans has done much to popularise Italian food in the USA. He helped set up a project to raise Italian breeds of cattle and pigs on farms in upstate New York and is the author of a number of cookbooks.

casereccio/a [ca-ze-**ret**-cho] home-made; of bread, home-baked. Applied to any food it suggests comfort, wholesomeness and mother's cooking.

casieddu [ca-zi-**ed**-du] a goat's cheese from Moliterno (Basilicata) that owes its distinctive flavour to the ferns through which the milk is filtered and to the catmint (*nepeta*) which is added to it.

casolèt [ca-zo-**let**] a soft, mild cow's milk cheese from Trentino.

casoncelli [ca-zon-**chel**-li] a type of RAVIOLI popular around Bergamo, Lombardy.

cassa [**cas**-sa] the cash desk in a bar or café.

cassata [cas-**sa**-ta] 1. a rich cake with alternate layers of liqueur-moistened sponge and sweetened RICOTTA, covered with an outer carapace of pistachio marzipan traditionally decorated with green and pink stripes and topped with candied fruit; 2. a Neapolitan ice cream containing candied fruit.

cassateddi, cassatelli [cas-sa-**ted**-di, cas-sa-**tel**-li] sweet *ricotta* turnovers (Sicily), an Easter speciality.

cassoeula [cas-so-**we**-la] a Milanese winter stew of cheap cuts of pork and cabbage. Also known as *bottagio*.

cassola [cas-**so**-la] 1. a thick pancake characteristic of Jewish cuisine, made by beating RICOTTA with eggs and sugar. The pancake mix is fried in olive oil until brown on both sides; 2. in Sardinia, a fish stew.

cassulli [cas-**sul**-li] Sardinian *gnocchi* traditionally served *alla carlofortina*, with a basil and tomato sauce.

castagna [cas-**tan**-ya] chestnut; also known as *marrone* [ma-**ro**-ne]; important in Tuscan, Ligurian and Sardinian cuisine, extensively used either fresh or milled into flour. Fresh chestnuts may poached in wine, roasted, or fried in butter as a garnish. Candied chestnuts are popular in Piedmont.

castagnaccio [cas-tan-**yat**-cho] a sweet, chestnut-flour flatbread from Tuscany, often enriched with pine kernels and raisins.

castagnole [cas-tan-**yo**-le] chestnut-shaped balls of sweet pastry laced with rum or other liqueur.

Castel Ariund [**cas**-tel ari-**oond**] full-flavoured cow's milk cheese from Piedmont, ideally eaten with honey.

Castelluccio [cas-tel-**lu**-cho] village on the border of Umbria and the Marche known for its lentils.

Castelmagno [cas-tel-**man**-yo] type of cow's milk DOP cheese from Piedmont, used for fondues and sauces.

castrato [cas-**tra**-to] a young sheep that has been castrated.

castraure [cas-tra-**u**-re] the first buds of artichokes that grow in the Venetian lagoon, pruned to encourage the plant to produce an abundant crop. They are very tender and tasty, and can be eaten raw or lightly braised.

Cavalcanti, Ippolito, Duca di Buonvicino (1787–1859), Neapolitan author of *Cucina teorico pratica* (*The Theory and Practice of Cuisine*, 1837), a collection of 600 recipes with an inner core of Neapolitan favourites written in dialect.

cavallucci [ca-val-**lu**-chi] Sienese almond biscuits, from *cavalli* ('horses'), supposedly referring to an ancient tradition in which employers supplied coach hands and stable lads with similar biscuits.

cavatappi [ca-va-**tap**-pi] pasta corkscrews.

cavatelli [ca-va-**tel**-li] type of pasta curled over to catch the sauce. Also known as *cavatieddi*. A traditional way to serve them is *con la* RUCOLA.

cavatieddi see CAVATELLI.

cavedano [ca-ve-**da**-no] a freshwater fish, the chub. Good for frying, breading and poaching.

caviale [ca-vi-**a**-le] caviar.

caviale di lumaca [ca-vi-**a**-le di lu-**ma**-ca] snail caviar, a new gourmet food item appearing on the menus of Italy's finest restaurants, tiny white pearls with a delicate earthy flavour (bosky rather than fishy) which lend themselves perfectly to the enhancement and decoration of meat or vegetable dishes; for now this caviar is produced only in a snail farm at Campofelice di Roccella, on the north coast of Sicily.

cavolata [ca-vo-**la**-ta] cabbage soup.

cavoletti see CAVOLINI.

cavolfiore [ca-vol-fi-**o**-re] cauliflower.

cavolini di Bruxelles [ca-vo-**li**-ni di bru-**sell**] Brussels sprouts, also known as *cavoli* or *cavoletti*.

cavolo [**ca**-vo-lo] cabbage, much used in winter soups. Popular varieties include the *cavolo nero*, the dark-leaved cabbage of Tuscany.

cavolo broccolo [**ca**-vo-lo

broc-co-lo] broccoli, particularly the pale green, pointy kind.

cavolo con le fette [**ca**-vo-lo con le **fet**-te] 'cabbage with slices': toasted bread with oil and garlic, topped with warm Tuscan cabbage.

cazzaregli [cat-sa-**rel**-yi] in Molise, STROZZAPRETI.

cazzellitti [cat-sel-**lit**-ti] gnocchi-like pasta from Abruzzo.

cazzilli [cat-**sil**-li] potato croquettes.

cecamariti [che-ca-ma-**ri**-ti] 'husband blinders', food so delicious that it blinds a husband to the misdemeanours of his wife. In Puglia the term refers either to a kind of pasta or to a rich pea soup.

cecatelli [che-ca-**tel**-li] short pasta, similar to CAVATELLI.

ceci [**che**-chi] chickpeas.

cecina [**che**-chi-na] chickpea bread from Volterra, Tuscany.

cecinelli [che-chi-**nel**-li] 1. small chickpeas; 2. in Naples, smelt, small fish.

cedro [**che**-dro] citron, a large citrus fruit resembling a monster lemon, excellent for the preparation of candied peel.

Also known as *citro* to avoid confusion with the word for a cedar tree or cedar wood, which is also *cedro*.

cefalo [**che**-fa-lo] grey mullet. *Cefalo calamita* is thin-lip mullet, a fish of shallow seawaters. *Cefalo dorato* is golden grey mullet.

cena [**che**-na] dinner, supper, evening meal.

cenci [**chen**-chi] deep-fried pastries, fritters.

cencioni [chen-**cho**-ni] 'little rags', a pasta shape, either in strips or ovals.

centerbe [chen-**ter**-be] vivid green herbal DIGESTIVO from Abruzzo made by macerating a herbs and plants (the name means '100 herbs') in alcohol.

centopelli [chen-to-**pel**-li] see OMASO.

cerasa [che-**ra**-za] cherry.

Cerasuolo di Vittoria [che-ra-su-**o**-lo di vit-**to**-ri-a] DOCG red wine from southern Sicily, named after the town of Vittoria. It is made from NERO D'AVOLA grapes, with some FRAPPATO.

cerfoglio [cher-**fol**-yo] chervil.

cernia [**cher**-ni-a] grouper (saltwater fish).

cervellata [cher-vel-**la**-ta] a Calabrian pork SALAME.

cervello [cher-**vel**-lo] brain (pl. *cervelli*).

cervo [**cher**-vo] stag, venison. *Noce di cervo* is rump of venison. *Spezzatino di cervo* is venison stew.

cespo [**ches**-po] a head of lettuce.

cestello, cestino, cestinetto [ches-**tel**-lo, ches-**ti**-no, ches-ti-**net**-to] a small basket. A *cestino/cestinetto di verdure* is a serving (in a little basket or similar) of vegetables.

cetriolo [chet-ri-**o**-lo] cucumber (pl. *cetrioli*). *Cetriolini* are pickled cucumbers, gherkins.

cheppia [**kep**-pi-a] a freshwater fish similar to the herring, also known as *alosa*.

chiacchiere [ki-**a**-kye-re] 'chatterers', festive fried pastries,

---

Cervio, Vincenzo

Carver-in-chief (*trinciante*) to Cardinal Alessandro Farnese in Rome. His 1582 treatise on carving, *Il trinciante*, established him as the high priest of theatrical table service, revealing the elaborate ceremonial of his craft and the stamina required to practise it successfully. The elaborately liveried carver, prominently in sight of high table, would secure the heavy joint of meat on a dagger or trident and hold it aloft at arm's length above the carving dish. Then, often to an orchestral or choral accompaniment, he would bestow horizontal and vertical slashes to the surface of the flesh, a final *coup de grâce* resulting in a cascade of morsels onto the dish below. Whilst Cervio was the acknowledged master, the first treatise on the Italian art of carving was the *Refugio del povero gentilhuomo* (*The Refuge of Poor Gentlemen*, 1520) by Giovanni Francesco Colle, *trinciante* to the Court of Ferrara. The title reflects the tradition that master-carvers were frequently men from noble families who had fallen on hard times. Cervio was unusual in that he began as a menial in the court of Urbino, working his way up to be steward and later master-carver.

strips or ribbons of fried or baked pastry, often cut with a zigzag ('pinked') edge, and dusted with powdered sugar, a favourite at carnivals. They go by a variety of names according to region, including *fiocchetti* ('little bows'), *frappe*, *cenci* and *bugie*.

chiancaredde [ki-an-ca-**red**-de] flattened chunks of pasta from Puglia, somewhat resembling coins. The Taranto-born photographer and writer Lorenzo Manigrasso has written a hymn in their honour, where he speaks of the 'generations of hands' who have made them, and of the 'humble value of an existence when computers didn't exist'. Also *chiancarelle*.

Chianina [ki-a-**ni**-na] breed of cattle from the Val di Chiana region of Tuscany. They supply the beef used in the traditional BISTECCA *alla fiorentina*.

Chianti Classico [ki-**an**-ti **clas**-si-co] wine-growing area between Siena and Florence, whose producers may use the GALLO NERO emblem on their labels. Chianti is the most famous wine of Tuscany, a youthful red, made mainly or entirely from the SANGIOVESE grape. If other grapes are added to the blend, these may only (since a ruling of 2006) be red-wine grapes. Earlier wines which used white MALVASIA would not now qualify as Chianti Classico. TIGNANELLO is a famous wine made in the Chianti region, though it does not label itself a Chianti.

Chianti Rufina [ki-**an**-ti ru-**fi**-na] respected Tuscan winery lying outside the boundaries of the Chianti Classico area that brought Chianti to the international scene in traditional straw-covered bottles. These flasks, that would have been slung across the saddles of medieval hunters and warriors, were widely seen in *trattorie* in the UK and USA throughout the '60s and '70s. Once the wine was finished, the bottles often enjoyed an afterlife as candlesticks, the straw jacket becoming ever more encrusted with trickling wax.

chiarello [ki-a-**rel**-lo] light-coloured red wine.

chiaretto [ki-a-**ret**-to] a pale red

wine, a rosé. Historically such wines came from the Bardolino region of Lake Garda, made from a very brief contact with the grape skins, imparting only a slight tinge of red.

chiccara [**kic**-ca-ra] a cup. The name derives from the Spanish *jícara*, a drinking gourd.

chicche, chicche di patata [**kic**-ke, **kic**-ke di pa-**ta**-ta] tiny potato GNOCCHI.

chicco [**kic**-co] a grain, a (coffee) bean.

chifferi [**kif**-fe-ri] small, curved, tubular PASTA CORTA widespread in Italy, named after the *Kipferl*, the little Austrian pastry it resembles.

chinato [ki-**na**-to] describes a red wine, typically made from NEBBIOLO, fortified with botanicals and quinine.

chinotto [ki-**not**-to] 1. fruit of the myrtle-leaf orange (*Citrus myrtifolia*), a small, bitter citrus grown in Liguria, Calabria, Tuscany and Sicily. A mutation of the sour orange, it is native and endemic to Italy. Most citrus fruits may stay on the branches for months before harvesting, without consequences; but the chinotto can remain on the tree even for two years. The normal annual harvest is in July; 2. a soft fizzy drink made from this orange.

chinulille [ki-nu-**lil**-le] sweet RAVIOLI served at Christmas and other feasts (Calabria). Also known as *chinuliddri*.

chiocciole [ki-**ot**-cho-le] 1. snails; 2. snail-shaped pasta, also known as PIPE.

chiodi [ki-**o**-di] cloves.

chitarrine [ki-tar-**ri**-ne] slender noodles made on the *chitarra*, a board strung with wires like a guitar. Also known as *pasta alla chitarra*. When coloured with squid ink, they are *chitarrine nere*.

chiummenzana, alla [ki-um-ment-**za**-na] tomato-and-herb pasta sauce from Capri and the Amalfi Coast.

chiuso [ki-**oo**-zo] closed, for a variety of reasons including: *per ferie* (for the holidays); *per restauro* (for restoration); *per lutto* (due to bereavement); *per ristrutturazione* (for redevelopment); *per motivi di sicurezza* (for security reasons); *per azione sindacale* (because of industrial action).

chivarzu [ki-**vart**-zu] coarse-textured bran loaves from Sardinia.

ciabatta [cha-**bat**-ta] lit. 'the carpet slipper'; internationally popular bread with a crisp crust and a soft interior with air pockets (*see box below*).

ciaccia [**cha**-cha] in Tuscany, a FOCACCIA, also known as *schiacccia*, *schiacciata*.

cialda [**chal**-da] a fine crisp or wafer, a waffle.

cialdona [chal-**do**-na] see CIARDUNA.

ciambella [cham-**bel**-la] a ring-shaped cake, loaf or biscuit.

ciambotta, cianfotta [cham-**bot**-ta, chan-**fot**-ta] vegetable stew with potatoes, tomatoes, aubergine, onion and peppers.

ciapinabò [cha-pi-na-**bo**] Jerusalem artichoke.

The story of *ciabatta*

Ciabatta was the brainchild of Arnaldo Cavallari, a retired rally driver from the Veneto who later took over his family's flour mills. By the early '80s, Cavallari had become alarmed at what he saw as disproportionately high imports of French bread, especially baguettes, into Italy. In his days as a rally driver Cavallari had shown the rest of Europe, including the French, that he was a force to be reckoned with. In 1966, for example, he and Dante Salvay had conclusively won the Mitropa Rally Cup, speeding to victory in their Alfa Romeo Giulia GTA. Determined to apply the unwavering spirit of the race track to the ovens of the Veneto, in 1982 Cavallari patented the *ciabatta*. The shrewdly-judged act of entrepreneurial patriotism paid off richly and today the *ciabatta* is famous all over the world. As to variations on the original theme, *ciabatta integrale* is made with wholemeal flour, while *ciabatta al latte* is the result of adding milk to the dough. Ciabatta dough has many regional seasonings and the possibilities are nearly infinite. Romans favour a simple formula of olive oil, salt, and marjoram. Small, filled *ciabatte* are the archetypal quick lunch.

ciapole [**cha**-po-le] in Piedmont, slices of apples, pears, apricots, peaches, figs or plums, sun-dried then set aside for winter. The consistency is chewy, but they can be soaked overnight in water to tenderise them.

ciaramicola [char-a-**mi**-col-la] a simple cake from Umbria covered with white icing and hundreds-and-thousands.

ciarduna [char-**du**-na] or *cialdona*, a Sicilian pastry from Agrigento with a RICOTTA filling and chopped almond topping.

ciauscolo [cha-**oo**-sco-lo] or *ciabuscolo*, a soft spreadable SALAME from the Marche, made from the belly and shoulder of pork with half the weight again in pork fat, the mixture well seasoned, stuffed into an intestine, smoked in juniper wood and then air-dried.

cibo [**chi**-bo] food.

cibreo di rigaglie [chi-**bre**-o di ri-**gal**-ye] chicken livers and cock's combs fried in butter, then simmered in a broth thickened with egg yolks and lemon.

cicale di mare [chi-**ca**-le-di-ma-re] see CANOCCHIE.

cicatelli see CECATELLI.

cicc [chik] fried buckwheat FOCACCIA from Lombardy.

ciccheti, cicchetti [chik-**ke**-ti] savoury bar snacks (Venice), typically bite-sized rounds of bread or polenta with a variety of toppings, eaten in the early evening to accompany an OMBRA.

ciccioli [**chi**-cho-li] crispy fragments of pork fat. Also called *siccioli* [**si**-cho-li], and in Palermo (Sicily) *frittula* [**frit**-tu-la] or *frittola*.

cicerchiata [chi-cher-ki-**a**-ta] traditional carnival sweet of the Marche, Abruzzo and Molise, in the form of a ring or mound of fried dough balls doused with honey.

cicerchie [chi-**cher**-ki-e] the seeds of the chickling vetch, a legume from Central Italy. Once a popular peasant food, it is now difficult to find outside the Marche. The seeds look very much like chickpeas and are used in a similar way, in soups and stews.

ciceri e tria [**chi**-che-ri e **tri**-a] pasta with chickpeas (Puglia). The ancient Roman orator

Cicero got his name from the fact that one of his ancestors is said to have had a nose shaped like a chickpea.

cicione [chi-**cho**-ne] a small GNOCCHI-shaped pasta from Sardinia, resembling a chickpea and coloured and flavoured with saffron; also known as *malloreddus*.

cicirate see CANNARICULI.

cicoria [chi-**co**-ri-a] chicory. The leaves are used for salads or are boiled and served as a side dish or in soups and stews. The roots are ground up and used as a coffee substitute or additive. Wild chicory is boiled and served with lemon or sautéed with garlic; bitter but very nutritious.

ciliegie [chil-i-**e**-je] cherries.

cima [**chi**-ma] a Ligurian speciality (generally known as *cima alla genovese*) consisting of a thin cut of veal formed into a pocket and stuffed with a mixture of vegetables, pine nuts and cheese. The pocket is tightly sewn and boiled. It is served in slices, either hot or cold.

cime di rapa [**chi**-me di **ra**-pa] turnip tops, the leaves of field mustard (*Brassica rapa*). They have a pleasant, nutty flavour and are often sautéed with garlic and olive oil and served over pasta, typically ORECCHIETTE.

cinesi rigati [chi-**ne**-zi ri-**ga**-ti] ridged pasta, similar to CONCHIGLIE.

cinghiale [chin-ghi-**a**-le] the wild boar, popular in northern and central Italy, particularly Tuscany, and cooked in a variety of ways. *Cinghiale in agrodolce* (in sweet and sour sauce) is cooked with herbs and spices such as ginger and cloves; *cinghiale alla cacciatora* is wild boar 'huntsman style', simmered slowly in white wine with onion, carrot and parsley. Wild boar sausages are also made during the hunting season.

cinta senese [**chin**-ta se-**ne**-ze] an ancient breed of long-haired Tuscan pig (literally 'the Sienese belt') that narrowly escaped extinction in the European agricultural reforms of the 1980s. Small herds now thrives in the Tuscan countryside, little changed in appearance since the 14th century when they were depicted by the Sienese artist Ambrogio Lorenzetti in his cycle of frescoes *Gli Effetti del Buon Governo* (Siena, Palazzo Pubblico). Here a stalwart little black pig, with the distinctive broad white band around its middle and down the foreleg, is seen being used as a truffle-hunter. Today, the breed is highly prized; the black hind hooves are often left untrimmed on the finished PROSCIUTTO as a mark of authenticity.

Cinzano [chint-**za**-no] a popular aperitif, a vermouth flavoured with a blend of herbs and spices, created in the mid-18th century in Turin by the Cinzano brothers. Cinzano Rosso was the original type; since then Cinzano Bianco, Cinzano Extra Dry and Cinzano Rosé have appeared.

ciocchetti [choc-**ket**-ti] a curled, tube-shaped pasta.

cioccolato [choc-co-**la**-to] chocolate.

cipolla [chi-**pol**-la] onion (pl. *cipolle*).

cipollaccio [chi-pol-**lat**-cho] also known as *lampascioni* [lam-pa-**sho**-ni], these are grape-hyacinths, with an onion-like

edible bulb.

cipolline [chi-pol-**li**-ne] spring onions.

Cipriani, Giuseppe (1900–80) inventor of CARPACCIO and founder of Harry's Bar in Venice.

cipudduzzi [chi-po-**doot**-si] the bulbs of grape-hyacinths, see CIPOLLACCIO.

ciriola romana [chi-ri-o-la ro-**ma**-na] a bread roll typical of Rome, so-called because its elongated shape is supposedly reminiscent of a type of young eel (*ciriola*) once fished in the Tiber.

ciriole [chi-ri-**o**-le] 1. 'little eels', spaghetti-type pasta typical of Umbria, where it is prepared *alla Ternana* (with garlic and chilli) or *alla norcina* (with truffles); 2. young eels, a speciality of Lazio, steamed in white wine with peas. Recipes usually call for live eels, since their flesh deteriorates rapidly. Eels are known to put up a fight and leap from the pan.

Cirò [chi-**ro**] town in Calabria which prides itself on its wine tradition, one of the oldest in the world. Both red and white wine is made. The reds are tannic and fruity, made largely from the Gaglioppo grape.

citro [**chit**-ro] see CEDRO.

ciufele [**choo**-fe-le] a type of pasta from Molise, similar to CAVATELLI.

ciuppin [choo-**pin**] a hearty fish stew (Liguria). There is no set recipe: whatever the boats had brought in, or any fish left over at the end of market day, would be used, cooked together with tomatoes and other vegetables.

civreo [chi-**vre**-o] see CIBREO.

cjarsons [ki-ar-**sons**] 'trousers' in local dialect, sometimes called *cjalsons*, PASTA RIPIENA from Friuli-Venezia Giulia, made with a variety of fillings, typically smoked RICOTTA and spinach (never meat) and served with melted butter.

clementina [cle-men-**ti**-na] seedless mandarin orange.

cobeletti [co-be-**let**-ti] (also *gobeletti*), Ligurian cakes filled with jam, traditionally served on 5th Feb, the feast of St Agatha; they are symbolic of her breasts, severed during her martyrdom.

cocciolette see ABISSINI.

cocco, noce di cocco [**coc**-co, **no**-che di **coc**-co] coconut.

coccoli [**coc**-co-li] Tuscan bread fritters. Also known as *coccole*.

cocomero [co-co-me-ro] in southern Italy, a watermelon.

cocuzza [co-**coot**-za] regional word for a pumpkin or squash; can also mean a person's head or 'nut', e.g. *la moglie* (his wife) *ha colpito* (bashed) *la sua cocuzza* (his nut) *con un mattarello* (with a rolling pin). See also CUCUZZA.

coda [**co**-da] tail. *Coda alla vaccinara* is oxtail stew, literally 'the tail' (*coda*) cooked in the manner of the *vaccinaro* (butcher). In ancient times and well into the Middle Ages it was customary to pay the butcher in kind by allowing him the hide, entrails and tail of the animal.

coda di rospo [**co**-da di **ros**-po] monkfish, literally 'toad's tail'. *Coda di rospo fumegada* is a Venetian speciality where the fish is soused in a black pepper marinade and wrapped in smoked PANCETTA before being cooked.

coffee see CAFFÈ.

cognà [con-**ya**] a spicy Piedmontese preserve made with grape must and various fruits and nuts.

coj [coy] Piedmontese dialect for cabbage.

colazione [co-lat-zi-**o**-ne] literally a collation, a meal that you piece together from a selection of different elements on offer. This usually refers to breakfast (usually presented as a buffet in Italian hotels), which is correctly *prima colazione*, the 'first' such meal of the day.

colla de pesce [**col**-la di **pe**-she] sheet gelatin.

colomba pasquale [co-**lom**-ba pas-**qua**-le] a dove-shaped Easter loaf (*colomba* = 'dove') from Lombardy, studded with sugar and almonds.

colombaccio [co-lom-**bat**-cho] wood pigeon.

comino [co-**mi**-no] cumin.

companatico [com-pa-**na**-ti-co] (pl. *companatici*) something to accompany bread, e.g. olives, ham or salami.

composta [com-**pos**-ta] a *compôte*, usually of fruit.

composto [com-**pos**-to] a mixture, a blend.

con, col with.

concentrato [con-chen-**tra**-to] a concentrate or purée.

conchiglie [con-**kil**-ye] shell-shaped pasta widespread throughout Italy. Also known as *conchigliette*.

conchiglioni [con-kil-**yo**-ni] the larger version of *conchiglie*, enormous pasta shells with a distinctive grooved surface.

condigiun, condiglione [con-di-**joon**, con-dil-**yo**-ne] a substantial Ligurian salad made with tomatoes, cucumber, black olives, basil, garlic, hard boiled egg, oregano and tuna or anchovies.

condimento [con-di-**men**-to] a condiment, dressing or seasoning.

confetti di pistoia [con-**fet**-ti di pis-**to**-ya] aniseed comfits made in the town of Pistoia, Tuscany.

confettura [con-fet-**tu**-ra] jam, also called *marmellata*. If in need of marmalade, ask for *confettura di arancia* or *marmellata di arancia*.

confortini [con-for-**ti**-ni] little biscuits, typically made of hazelnut and aniseed.

congelato/a [con-je-**la**-to] frozen.

coniglio [co-**nil**-yo] rabbit.

conservanti [con-ser-**van**-ti]

preservatives.

contenuto calorico [con-te-**nu**-to ca-**lo**-ri-co] calorific content, e.g. *piatti con moderato contenuto calorico* (moderate-calorie dishes).

contorno [con-**tor**-no] side dish (pl. *contorni*).

controfiletto [con-tro-fi **let**-to] sirloin or entrecôte.

coperto [co-**per**-to] the cover charge for a meal, covering the cost of bread and water.

coppa [**cop**-pa] 1. cured sausage made from the neck or shoulder of pork, often sliced for use in sandwiches or as an ANTIPASTO. Varieties include: *coppa di Parma* and *coppa piacentina* (from Piacenza); 2. a cup, e.g. *coppa di gelato*, ice cream in a cup.

coppiette [cop-pi-**et**-te] salted dried strips of meat, once horse, now usually pork. A speciality of Frascati and Ariccia (Lazio), once served to accompany wine in taverns.

coque, uovo alla [**wo**-vo al-la **cock**] soft-boiled egg.

coralli, corallini [co-**ral**-li, co-ral-**li**-ni] tiny sections of pasta tube named after the beads in a coral necklace.

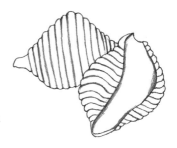

Conchiglie, pasta shells.

coratella d'agnello [co-ra-**tel**-la dan-**yel**-lo] lamb's offal.

corbezzola [cor-**bet**-zo-la] arbutus, tree-strawberry.

corbo [**cor**-bo] Venetian name for OMBRINA.

cordelle [cor-**del**-le] pasta 'ropes'. Long pasta similar to LINGUINE.

coregone [co-re-**go**-ne] whitefish, freshwater fish found in the Lombardy lakes; also known as *lavarello*.

coriandolo [co-ri-**an**-do-lo] coriander. Not to be confused with *coriandoli*, which is confetti.

cornetto [cor-**net**-to] 1. a croissant; 2. *Cornetto de mà*, see MURICE.

corniola [cor-ni-**o**-la] the dogwood or cornel cherry, a bitter fruit used to make relishes and meat sauces in northern Italy.

corno di bue [**cor**-no di **bu**-e] 'ox horn', *peperoni corno di bue* are sweet yellow or red peppers from Carmagnola in Piedmont, excellent for stuffing.

corposo [cor-**po**-zo] full-bodied (wine).

corto [**cor**-to] 1. short; 2. a *ristretto*, see CAFFÈ.

Corvina [cor-**vi**-na] red grape which along with Rondinella and MOLINARA is used to produce the wine of the Lake Garda region, notably the famous VALPOLICELLA.

corvina [cor-**vi**-na] saltwater fish (*Cilus gilberti*), also known as *corvo*, cooked like sea bass. In English it is also known as corvina drum and is related to OMBRINA.

Corvinone [cor-vi-**no**-ne] red wine grape from the Veneto, used in VALPOLICELLA and BARDOLINO.

corzetti [cort-**zet**-ti] thin, circular pasta 'coins' from Liguria embossed with patterns (traditionally made by wooden stamps) including flowers and coats of arms.

cosacavaddu [co-za-ca-vad-du] a pungent Sicilian cow's milk cheese.

coscia [**cosh**-a] in anatomy, the thigh. As a cut of meat, the leg, usually small in size, e.g *coscie di rana* (frog's legs) or *coscia di pollo* (chicken drumstick).

cosciotto [co-**shot**-to] a larger COSCIA, or leg, as in *cosciotto d'agnello*, leg of lamb.

costa, costata [**cos**-ta, cos-**ta**-ta] 1. a chop, e.g. *costa di maiale alla griglia*: grilled pork chop; 2. e.g. *costata di manzo* = rib-eye steak or entrecôte.

costarelle [cos-ta-**rel**-le] spare ribs.

costicine [cos-ti-**chee**-ne] ribs, rib chops.

costoletta [cos-to-**let**-ta] a cutlet or chop of pork, lamb or veal, also called *cotoletta*. *Costoletta milanese* is a thinly breaded veal chop, very similar to a Wiener Schnitzel (*see box*). *Costoletta a orecchia di elefante*, the 'elephant-ear cutlet', is a larger incarnation.

cotechino [co-te-**ki**-no] a large, spiced pork sausage.

cotognata [co-ton-**ya**-ta] a

dense jam made from quince, left to set in moulds; quince comfits.

cotoletta [co-to-**let**-ta] a chop, see COSTOLETTA.

cotto/a [**cot**-to] cooked.

cotturo [cot-**tu**-ro] copper cauldron (Abruzzo); *al cotturo* describes a dish cooked in such a cauldron, typically a stew.

couscous [**coos**-coos] a durum wheat staple popular throughout southern Italy, one of the contributions of the North African Maghreb to Italian cuisine. Some of the traditional dishes that use couscous are strikingly reminiscent of the Maghrebi tradition that uses spiced lamb and vegetables. There is an annual couscous fair in San Vito Lo Capo (Sicily) in Sept. The *cuscussu* of Tuscan Jewish cuisine, served with meatballs on the feast of *Tu B'Shvat* (the 'New Year of the Trees', Feb) was probably the import of Spanish Jews who fled

---

Schnitzel or *costoletta*?

Culinary historians disagree about the origins of the *costoletta all milanese*, the famous dish of golden brown fried breaded veal. Some claim ancestry in Milan (hence *alla milanese*); others claim that it is originally Viennese (*Wiener Schnitzel*). Austria and Northern Italy were closely linked in the 19th century, however, so it is highly likely that the dish was introduced from one to the other. During the Habsburg occupation of Lombardy, which came about after the fall of Napoleon in 1815, Milan was home to a large Austrian garrison, and it has been suggested that Field Marshal Radetzky (for whom Strauss wrote the *Radetzky March*) so loved the dish that he took the recipe back with him to Austria.

Cheap establishments might serve breaded beaten pork in the guise of *costoletta alla milanese*. However, the real article is always tender veal, and to be a true *milanese*, it should still be on the bone. The Austrian version is always veal fillet.

to Livorno in the 15th century to avoid persecution. See also FREGULA.

coviglia [co-**vil**-ya] a soft ice cream (Naples), usually coffee or chocolate-flavoured.

cozza [**cot**-za] mussel (pl. *cozze*).

crafi see KRAFI.

crastuni [cras-**tu**-ni] Sicilian word for large snails, *Helix aspersa*.

crauti [**craŭ**-ti] sauerkraut, common in the north, especially in Trentino-Alto Adige.

crema [**cre**-ma] 1. a creamy sauce or purée. *Crema di legumi* is creamed vegetables or vegetable cream soup; 2. custard pudding made with eggs and milk. *Crema frangipane* is custard made with egg yolks, milk, crushed almonds and vanilla; *crema inglese* is custard made with egg yolks and milk, omitting flour; *crema pasticcera* is confectioner's custard, thickened with flour and eggs.

cremolata [cre-mo-**la**-ta] a soft GRANITA, a smoothie.

cremoso/a [cre-**mo**-zo] creamy or thick.

cren [kren] in the northern

Cozza, a mussel.

regions, horseradish.

crescentina, crescenta [cre-shen-**ti**-na, cre-**shen**-ta] a flatbread that puffs up when fried into small pillows of dough. The name comes from the Latin *crescere*, to grow. In and around Modena a similar flatbread is baked between *tigelle* [ti-**jel**-le], traditional stone moulds.

crescenza [cre-**shent**-za] a soft, creamy, fresh cow's milk cheese, also known as *stracchino*, typical of Lombardy, though it is also made elsewhere.

crescia [**cre**-sha] a type of soft bread, typical of the Marche, studded with pieces of cheese and/or salami.

crescia al testo [**cre**-sha al **tes**-to] a circular bread of pizza-type dough from the Gubbio area of

Umbria, sliced in half and eaten with a variety of fillings. Also known as *torta al testo*.

cresc' tajat [cresh ta-**yat**] originally a peasant dish from the Marche, a way of using up leftover POLENTA that had stuck to the sides of the pot. Added to flour and water to make pasta, and traditionally served with *sugo finto*, 'mock sauce', little cuts of GUANCIALE and diced tomatoes.

crescione [cre-**sho**-ne] cress.

crespelle [cres-**pel**-le] crêpes, pancakes.

creste di galli [**cres**-te di **gal**-li] cocks' combs; also a short-cut pasta suitable for salads or soups.

crispelle, crispelli see CRESPELLE.

crispigno [cris-**pin**-yo] sow thistle, a wild herb similar in appearance to a dandelion, said by Pliny the Elder to have been eaten by Theseus prior to his battle with the Bull of Marathon.

croccante [croc-**can**-te] (pl. *croccanti*) crispy, e.g. *crosta croccante*: a crispy crust.

crocchette [croc-**ket**-te] croquettes. *Croquette di pesce* [di **pe**-she] are fishcakes.

Crodino [cro-**di**-no] a non-alcoholic aperitif, golden yellow in colour, made of an infusion of spices and other (never-divulged) ingredients. Invented in 1965, it now belongs to the CAMPARI group. It is typically served with ice, a slice of orange and a green olive.

crosta [**cros**-ta] crust, e.g. of a pie.

crostata [cros-**ta**-ta] (pl. *crostate*) a pie or tart, either sweet or savoury, e.g. *crostata di frutta*, a fruit tart.

crostini [cros-**ti**-ni] miniature slices of bread, toasted and spread with a variety of toppings, e.g. anchovies, tomatoes etc, often served as bite-sized canapés; see also CROSTONI.

crostoli [**cros**-to-li] pastry strips or ribbons fried and sprinkled with powdered sugar.

crostoni [cros-**to**-ni] large CROSTINI, sometimes sufficient to bear an entire pork chop, in effect, 'rustic' canapés.

crudo [**cru**-do] 1. raw, rare; 2. cured, in the case of SALUME, fish or ham.

crumiri [cru-**mi**-ri] half-moon-shaped biscuits from Piedmont.

crusca di frumento [**crus**-ca di fru-**men**-to] bran.

cubbaita [coob-**baï**-ta] Sicilian nougat of Arab origin.

cubetti [cu-**bet**-ti] cubes, *cubetti di ghiaccio* [ghi-**a**-cho], ice cubes.

cuccìa [cu-**chi**-a] a dessert of boiled grains of wheat and RICOTTA sweetened with candied fruit, eaten on 13th Dec in Syracuse (her birthplace) for the feast of St Lucy, and in Palermo on that day to commemorate the delivery of the city from famine in 1646. The dish derives from the pagan *panspermia*, a ritual porridge of unmilled grains eaten in honour of Apollo at the summer and winter solstices.

cucina [cu-**chi**-na] kitchen, cuisine, style of cooking.

cucina povera [cu-**chi**-na po-ve-ra] so-called 'poor' cuisine, the fashionable reincarnation of low-budget rustic staples as venerable regional dishes. Though the phenomenon has its pretensions, it has done much to stimulate international interest in regional Italian cooking.

cuculo calabrese [cu-co-lo ca-la-**bre**-ze] called *cudduru* in Sicily, an Easter cake from Calabria made of sweet bread woven in the form of a nest around hard-boiled eggs, glazed with sugar and decorated with hundreds-and-thousands.

cucunci [cu-**cun**-chi] see CAPPERI.

cucuzza [cu-**coot**-sa] In Sicily, a word used indiscriminately to describe pumpkin, green squash, courgette or marrow, nourishing vegetables which have the reputation of being tasteless, hence the popular saying: *Preparala come vuoi, sempre cucuzza è!* (However you cook it, it's still squash!).

cuddhurite [cood-du-**ri**-te] ring-shaped PASTINA from Sicily.

cudduru see CUCULO CALABRESE.

cuddurune [cood-du-**ru**-ne] 1. see CUCULO CALABRESE. 2. In the Hyblaean Mountains of Sicily, a simple pizza of bread dough studded with sun-dried tomatoes, black olives and pecorino cheese.

culaccio [cu-**lat**-cho] rump.

culatello [cu-la-**tel**-lo] a very lean, pear-shaped ham made with pork rump, seasoned with salt, pepper, and sometimes dry white wine and garlic; the DOP Culatello di Zibello is said to be one of Italy's finest hams. It comes from the area centred on the village of Zibello in the Parma lowlands (Emilia-Romagna), where the conditions for its production are perfect: cold, damp, foggy winters and sultry summers; such an important product has an annual spring festival and its own website (*www. consorziodelculatellodizibello.it*).

culurgiones [cu-lur-**jo**-nes] Sardinian RAVIOLI resembling mini pasties, typically filled with potatoes, local cheese, garlic and mint. Also known as *culurzones*.

cumino [cu-**mi**-no] cumin; *cumino tedesco* is caraway.

cuoco [cu-**o**-co] cook, chef.

cuore [cu-**o**-re] the heart, e.g. of an artichoke, as opposed to its *fondo* (base).

curcuci [**cur**-cu-chi] a popular snack in Calabria, bacon rind or pork crackling.

cuscus see COUS COUS.

cuzzetielle [coot-ze-ti-**el**-le] type of pasta from Molise, hollowed in the centre or curled like CAVATELLI, traditionally served with meat (particularly hare) RAGÙ.

cuzzi [**coot**-zi] irregular pasta shapes, 'cuts', popular in Lazio. As with many staples once humble peasant fare, *cuzzi* now have a niche following; there is a festival in their honour held every July in Roviano.

cuzzupe [coot-**zu**-pe] sweet Easter breads from Calabria, made in a variety of shapes, often featuring a hard-boiled egg.

Cynar [chee-**nar**] a popular bitter liqueur, drunk either as an APERITIVO or DIGESTIVO, made with artichokes and a variety of herbs.

dadi [**da**-di] cubes.

dalle and **alle** with opening times, from and to: e.g. *dalle ore 9:30 alle 14:30*: from 9.30am to 2.30pm.

damigiana [da-mi-**ja**-na] a demijohn or carboy, large container from which *vino* SFUSO is dispensed..

datteri [**dat**-te-ri] dates.

datteri di mare [**dat**-te-ri di **ma**-re] 'sea dates', large shellfish once considered a great delicacy.

They burrow into rocks, making tunnels for themselves to live in, with the result that fishing them required destruction of marine habitats. It has now been outlawed in most EU states.

datterino [dat-te-**ri**-no] a *pomodoro datterino* is a small, elongated tomato particularly good for sauces.

decaffeinato [de-caf-fe-i-**na**-to] decaffeinated.

degli see DEL.

degustazione [de-gu-stat-si-**o**-ne] tasting, e.g. a 'tasting menu', where a number of dishes in a restaurant's repertoire are offered for a set price.

del, dello, della, delle, degli of, any, some e.g. *delle acciughe*: some anchovies; *del bosco:* of (from) the forest.

denocciolato/a [de-no-cho-**la**-to] pitted, with the stone removed. *Olive denocciolate* are pitted olives.

dental [**den**-tal] Venetian dialect name for DENTICE.

dente, al [**den**-te] firm (of pasta). The opposite of *al dente* is *stracotto*: soggy.

dentice [**den**-ti-che] dentex (fish).

denti di cavallo [**den**-ti di ca-**val**-lo] 'horse's teeth', a short, narrow pasta tube. Also known as *denti di pecora* ('sheep's teeth').

denti di leone [**den**-ti di le-**o**-ne] dandelions.

denti di pecora [**den**-ti di pe-co-ra] see DENTI DI CAVALLO.

diavoletti [di-a-vo-**let**-ti] 'little devils', pasta in the form of slim curved tubes.

diavolicchio [di-a-vo-**lik**-ki-o] chilli (Abruzzo).

diavolillo [di-a-vo-**lil**-lo] the 'little devil', an intensely hot chilli (*peperoncino rosso*) from Abruzzo and Molise.

digestivo [di-jes-**ti**-vo] an alcoholic drink thought to have health-giving properties and to aid the digestion if taken after meals. A number of *digestivi* are found throughout Italy, many of them herbal infusions.

dindo, dindio [**din**-do, **din**-di-o] a dialect word for turkey (*tacchino*).

dischi [**dis**-ki] discs, circular pasta shapes; variants include MESSICANI and *dischi volanti* [**dis**-ki vo-**lan**-ti], 'flying saucers'.

disponibilità [dis-pon-i-bi-li-**ta**] availability. On menus, you will often see fish listed as '*secondo disponibilità del mercato*', subject to market availability.

distillati [dis-til-**la**-ti] spirits, e.g. gin, vodka, whisky, brandy, GRAPPA.

dita degli apostoli [**di**-ta del-yi a-**po**-sto-li] 'Apostles', fingers': miniature pancakes filled with RICOTTA flavoured with chocolate or citrus zest.

ditali [di-**ta**-li] small pasta 'thimbles' (also *ditalini* or *ditaletti*). Suitable for soups.

DOC/DOCG see VINO.

dolce [**dol**-che] 1. sweet (adjective); 2. a sweet or dessert course (singular noun; pl. *dolci*).

dolcelatte [dol-che-**lat**-te] a smooth blue cheese, strong but milder than GORGONZOLA.

Dolcetto [dol-**chet**-to] red-wine grape of Piedmont producing dark-coloured but lighter-drinking wines than the signature BAROLO.

dolci [**dol**-chi] desserts.

dolciume [dol-**choo**-me] sweets, candy, confectionery.

donderet [don-der-et] GNOCCHI from Piedmont served with butter and cheese.

donzelline [dont-zel-**li**-ne]

deep-fried pasta, a Tuscan recipe (sweet and savoury versions exist, but the favourites are filled with salted anchovies or sausage.

DOP (*Denominazione di Origine Protetta*), the equivalent of an *appellation contrôlée* for food products, particularly cheese such as PARMIGIANO REGGIANO.

doppio/a [**dop**-pi-o] double.

dragoncello [dra-gon-**chel**-lo] tarragon.

durke [**dur**-ke] sweet (Sardinian).

duro/a [**du**-ro] hard.

durone [du-**ro**-ne] cherry.

e, ed and.

ecco! [**ec**-co] behold! here it is! often said by waiters with impressive theatricality upon the presentation of even the most modest dish.

edule [**e**-du-le] edible.

eliche [**e**-li-ke] 'propellers', a pasta shape.

elicoidali [e-li-co-i-**da**-li] spiral pasta shapes.

Emilia-Romagna [e-**mi**-li-a ro-**man**-ya] a populous region of central Italy dominated by the Po valley and delta. The capital is Bologna; but the

From a greengrocer's in Trieste: *asparagi di bocso* (wild asparagus), *aglio orsino* (wild garlic) and *sclopit*, all sold by the *etto*.

emiliani consider their spiritual capital to be Modena, while the *romagnoli* are intensely proud of Ravenna, the city which in 402 became capital of the Byzantine empire. Other main centres are the coastal town of Rimini, and inland, Ferrara, Parma, Reggio and Piacenza. Said to have the finest cuisine in the country, specialities include egg pasta, such as tagliatelle, and balsamic vinegar (see ACETO), PARMA ham, PARMESAN cheese and BOLOGNESE sauce. The name can be written with or without the hyphen, because there is considerable rivalry between *emiliani* and *romagnoli*, who sometimes object to being united in this way.

enoteca [e-no-**te**-ca] a wine shop.

eperlano [e-per-**la**-no] smelt (fish).

equina [e-**qui**-na] as in *carne equina*: horse meat. Horse meat is much less commonly found that it once was. In the 19th and early 20th centuries, it was readily eaten as a sort of poor man's beef. However, it has always courted controversy: in 8th-century Italy its consumption was associated with pagans from Germania and it came under papal interdict. In Jewish cuisine, it is forbidden.

erba [**er**-ba] a herb (pl. *erbe*).

erba cipollina [**er**-ba ci-pol-**li**-na] chives.

erba San Pietro in Liguria, another name for rock samphire (see FINOCCHIO MARINO). In other parts of Italy it refers to *Tanacetum balsamita*, or costmary, a bitter, slightly lemony herb.

erbaggi [er-**bad**-ji] cooked vegetables.

erbazzone [er-bats-**zo**-ne] or *scarpazzone*, a spinach and cheese pie from Emilia-Romagna. *Erbazzone dolce* is the sweetened version, a Jewish speciality.

erbe aromatiche [**er**-be a-ro-**ma**-ti-ke] aromatic herbs.

espresso see CAFFÈ.

esse buranei [**es**-se bu-ra-**ne**-i]

S-shaped butter cookies from the island of Burano, a Venetian speciality. They are very similar to the circular BUSSOLÀ (the difference is in the shape, not so much in the ingredients). Made with flour, egg, vanilla, sugar, lemon and an optional dash of rum.

Est! Est!! Est!!! light white wine from Montefiascone, Lazio, usually a blend of MALVASIA and TREBBIANO. Its name comes from the story of a bishop's servant

Example of the little biscuits known as *Esse buranei*, 'S-es from Burano', butter cookies popular in and around Venice.

told to leave chalk messages on tavern doors where good wine was to be had ('est' being the Latin for 'is'; in other words, 'it's here'). On one particular tavern he wrote it in triplicate, as if to say, 'This place serves it in spades!'

estivi [es-**ti**-vi] summer dishes.

estragone [es-tra-**go**-ne] tarragon.

estratto [e-**strat**-to] extract.

etto [**et**-to] Italian equivalent of the prefix hecto-, meaning 100. A price per *etto* is a price per 100g.

evo [**e**-vo] as in *olio evo*, extra virgin olive oil.

Fabriano [fa-bri-**a**-no] town in the Marche renowned for its excellent salami, which even graces the dining table of Buckingham Palace, where an order is placed for it every year.

fagiano, fagianello [fa-**ja**-no, fa-ja-**nel**-lo] pheasant.

fagiano di monte [fa-**ja**-no di **mon**-te] black grouse.

fagiolata [fa-jo-**la**-ta] bean soup.

Types and grades of Italian flour

Flour for baking is usually obtained from *grano tenero* (*Triticum aestivum*). It is graded according to how finely it is milled. '00' or *doppio zero*, the 'flower of flours' is a snow white powder with no bran at all. It makes the lightest of dainty cakes, but its nutritional value is minimal. Other grades, less purely white because some bran remains, are '0' and '1'. Then comes '2' (*semi-integrale* or semi-wholemeal) and '*integrale*' (wholemeal).

For pasta-making, flour is obtained from durum wheat (*grano duro; Triticum durum*). This is a hard-grained variety which when milled reduces to a fine meal called *semola* or *semolino*, which allows the cooked pasta to remain *al* DENTE. Not all Italian soil and terrain is suitable for wheat-growing, and in the past other flours, made of rye (*segale*), millet (*miglio*) and chickpeas (*ceci*) were widely used. They are still found today in traditional recipes

fagioli [fa-**jo**-li] haricot beans, brown or white, usually bought dried, soaked, and then stewed slowly. *Fagioli di pollo* are rooster testicles.

fagiolini [fa-jo-**li**-ni] French beans, long green beans.

fagiolini rigati [fa-jo-**li**-ni ri-**ga**-ti] pasta shapes, curved tubes approximately shaped like French beans.

fagiolone [fa-jo-**lo**-ne] runner beans.

fainà [fa-i-**na**] Ligurian dialect for FARINATA.

fainelle [fa-i-**nel**-le] leaf-shaped Puglian pasta, often cooked with potato and RUCOLA and served with a bacon or anchovy SOFFRITTO.

falloni [fal-**lo**-ni] 'big phalluses', a pasta resembling a thin pancake, stuffed with vegetables.

falso magro [**fal**-so **ma**-gro] in Sicilian *farsu magru*, 'false lean', a Sunday delight consisting of a large slice of beef, beaten thin, and rolled up on a filling of minced meat with ham, salami or MORTADELLA (whatever is handy), peas, cheese, breadcrumbs and hard-boiled eggs, bound with string, and

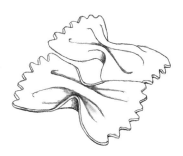

Farfalle, 'butterfly pasta'.

cooked in a tomato sauce.

faraona [fa-ra-**o**-na] guinea fowl.

farcito/a [far-**chi**-to] stuffed.

farfalle [far-**fal**-le] pasta shaped like butterflies. Often prepared with a tomato sauce, with a salmon and cream sauce or used cold in salads.

farina [fa-**ri**-na] flour.

farina gialla [**jal**-la] 'yellow flour', a name for polenta, as in the recipe *zuppa di cavolo nero e farina gialla* (cabbage and cornmeal soup).

farinata [fa-ri-**na**-ta] thick pancake somewhat resembling a Mexican *tortilla*, usually made of chickpea flour. Typical Ligurian street food.

farinata di zucca [fa-ri-**na**-ta di

tsoo-ca] a Ligurian pie made of pumpkin and cheese.

farro [**far**-ro] emmer wheat, an ancient, hard-grained variety. Thoroughly soaked before cooking, it is often used in soups and salads and is common in Tuscany and the Marche.

Fassona [fas-**so**-na] a Piedmontese breed of cattle, known for its extremely lean meat.

fasui see FAGIOLI.

fasul, fasule [fa-**zul**, fa-**zu**-le] dialect form of FAGIOLI.

fattisù [fat-ti-**soo**] a stuffed pasta from Emilia-Romagna typically with a filling of cabbage (*fattisù di verza*); the resulting parcel is 'done' or sealed (*fatti*) up (*sù*).

fava [**fa**-va] broad beans, eaten fresh in spring and early summer when small and tender; popular around Rome. *Favata* is a bean stew; *fave dei morti*, literally, 'beans of the dead', are little sweetmeats traditionally baked for 2nd Nov, All Souls Day or the Day of the Dead.

favata [fa-**va**-ta] see FAVA.

fazzoletti [fats-zo-**let**-ti] 'handkerchiefs', pasta sheets folded around a filling or topped

Menù del giorno offering three main dishes made with *Fassona* beef: *filetto* (fillet), *tagliata* (sliced sirloin) or *costata* (entrecôte).

with sauce.

fecata [**fe**-ca-ta] liver (Naples).

fecola [**fe**-co-la] starch, such as corn starch, used for thickening and baking.

fedde del cancelliere [**fed**-de del can-chel-li-**er**-e] 'chancellor's buttocks', a dessert invented by some 12th-century nuns of Trapani (Sicily) made of semolina and pistachios or almonds, formed into a patty and served split down the middle so as to resemble the prosperous buttocks of the founder of their convent.

fegatazzo di Ortona [fe-ga-**tats**-zo di or-**to**-na] a liver sausage from the Abruzzo.

fegatelli [fe-ga-**tel**-li] diced pig's liver wrapped in strands of OMENTO; faggots.

fegatini [fe-ga-**ti**-ni] chicken livers.

fegatino [fe-ga-**ti**-no] liver sausage from the Marche.

fegato [**fe**-ga-to] liver.

fermo [**fer**-mo] of wine, not sparkling. In parts of Lombardy and Emilia-Romagna, where LAMBRUSCO is the house red wine, you will need to specify if you want a still wine with your meal.

Fernet Branca [fer-**net** bran-ca] a bitter DIGESTIVO made of roots and spices macerated in alcohol. It is manufactured in the Branca family distillery in Milan. The name Fernet is a combination of the French *fer* ('iron') and *net* ('clean'), a reference to the traditional process of stirring the liquor with a red-hot iron rod. Its supposed curative properties (in the early 20th century it was marketed as an effective safeguard against cholera) hark back to medieval times when monasteries and mountebanks would market herbal tonics and potions.

ferrazzuoli [fer-rats-**zwo**-li] long, thin pasta ribbons, slightly twisting, an effective way of trapping the sauce.

ferri [**fer**-ri] the grill. Anything cooked '*ai ferri*' is grilled or barbecued.

fesa [**fe**-za] for beef and veal, the rump; for turkey, the breast.

fetta [**fet**-ta] a slice, e.g. *una fetta di pane*: a slice of bread (pl. *fette*).

fettina [fet-**ti**-na] a thin slice; *fettine di vitello* are veal escalopes.

fettucce, fettuccelle [fet-**too**-che, fet-too-**chel**-le] 'ribbons', a pasta shape.

fettuccine [fet-too-**chi**-ne] 'little ribbons', a long, flat egg-and-flour pasta similar to TAGLIATELLE.

fett'unta [fet-**toon**-ta] in Tuscany, dry bread rubbed with olive oil and garlic, also known as *panunta*.

fiadi [fi-**a**-di] a type of ribbon pasta.

Fiano [fi-**a**-no] ancient white-wine grape from Campania, used to produce the excellent Fiano di Avellino.

fiasco [fi-**as**-co] a flask. The Tuscan FAGIOLI (or CANNELLINI) *al fiasco* are beans stewed over charcoal with garlic and sage in a traditional straw-protected flask.

ficatu [fi-ca-tu] liver (Sicily).

fico [**fi**-co] (pl. *fichi*) fig. Warning: make sure you get the gender right. The feminine form, *fica*, is a slang word for female genitalia.

ficodindia [fi-co-**din**-di-a] prickly pear; introduced by the Spanish in the 15th century from Central America to provide their seamen with a ready source of vitamin C (in which they are even richer than lemons), to prevent scurvy. The finest are grown around the village of San Cono, in central Sicily.

fideg, fidic [**fi**-deg, **fi**-dic] Lombard and Piedmontese forms of *fegato*, liver.

fidelini [fi-de-**li**-ni] very thin pasta strands.

fieno di canepina [fi-e-no di ca-ne-**pi**-na] 'hay from Canepina', long pasta noodles, a speciality of Viterbo in Lazio,

traditionally served with a sauce of chicken giblets.

figà [fi-**ga**] liver (Venice).

filateddi [fi-la-**ted**-di] a long ribbon-like pasta, a Sicilian and Calabrian variant of FETTUCCE.

filato/a [fi-**la**-to] 'spun'. *Zucchero filato* is spun sugar. *Formaggio a pasta filata* is a cheese such as MOZZARELLA, SCAMORZA or PROVOLONE, where the curds have been stretched and kneaded to an elastic consistency.

fileja [fi-**le**-ya] rolled pasta from Calabria.

filetto [fi-**let**-to] fillet (UK), tenderloin (US).

filindeu [fi-lin-**de**-u] the 'threads of God', a thin sheet of pasta resembling a rush mat or piece of gauze, traditionally 'woven' by hand. It is a speciality of Nouro in Sardinia, where it is made on the feast of St Francis of Lula. The *filindeu* is broken up, cooked in mutton broth and served with a sheep's cheese.

filone [fi-**lo**-ne] 1. an elongated bread roll, a short baguette; 2. see SCHIENALE.

finferli see CANTARELLI.

finanziera [fi-nant-si-e-ra] a Piedmontese stir-fry of cocks' combs and veal sweetbreads with mushrooms and MARSALA.

fino/a [**fi**-no] fine.

finocchio [fi-**noc**-ki-o] fennel. The bulbous base of the stem is popular, but all of the plant is used in various ways, from flowers and leaves to roots.

finocchio marino [fi-**noc**-ki-o ma-**ri**-no] rock samphire (*Crithmum maritimum*), a shrub that grows on cliffs and seashores. Its aromatic leaves are eaten raw or pickled. Also known as *erba di San Pietro* or *critamo*.

finocchiona [fi-noc-ki-o-na] Tuscan SALAME flavoured with fennel seeds.

fiocchetti see CHIACCHIERE.

fiocchi d'avena [fi-**oc**-ki da **ve**-na] oat flakes.

fiocchi di mais [fi-**oc**-ki di **ma**-is] cornflakes.

fior di latte [fi-or di **lat**-te] a MOZZARELLA made from cow's, not buffalo's, milk. See also GELATO.

Fiore Sardo [fi-o-re **sar**-do] hard Sardinian sheep's milk cheese.

Fiore Sicano [fi-o-re si-**ca**-no] delicate cheese from the high-

Fennel (*finocchio*). The plant's stem, leaves and seeds are all edible.

pastures of Sicily's Monti Sicani, still made using raw milk in spite of European Union rules (it was saved by the regional government which declared it to be a historic treasure and thus exempt from the rule).

fiore di zucca [fi-o-re di **tsoo**-ca] courgette/zucchini flowers, usually fried in light batter.

fiorone [fi-o-**ro**-ne] fig (pl. *fioroni*).

fiscariedd' [fis-ca-ri-**ed**] irregularly-shaped offcuts left over from RAVIOLI-making, served in soup, originating in the poorer areas of Basilicata.

fischiotti, fischioni [fis-ki-**ot**-ti, fis-ki-**o**-ni] tubular pasta from Abruzzo.

fiyat [**fee**-yat] liver (Friuli).

focaccia [fo-**cat**-cha] savoury flatbread baked in a variety of ways: *alla salvia*: with sage; *alle olive*: with olives; *alle noci*: with walnuts; *al rosmarino*: with rosemary. The word originates from the Latin *panis focacius*, 'bread from the hearth' (*focus* in Latin means hearth, the 'focal' point of the home).

foglia [**fol**-ya] a leaf (pl. *foglie*).

fojade [fo-**ya**-de] wide noodles from Lombardy.

folletti [fol-**let**-ti] elves, a pasta shape.

fondo [**fon**-do] base, bed.

fonduta [fon-**du**-ta] 1. a fondue, a mixture of melted cheese and wine, sometimes with truffles, into which bread or vegetables may be dipped, typical of the alpine regions; 2. any 'melted' dish, e.g. *fonduta di cioccolato*.

fongadina [fon-ga-**di**-na] a stew made of lamb, calf or kid's offal, richly flavoured and seasoned.

fontina [fon-**tee**-na] a cow's milk cheese from the Valle d'Aosta.

formagella [for-ma-**jel**-la] a delicate cow's milk cheese, a little like Brie.

formaggio [for-**mad**-jo] cheese. In Italy it is made from the milk of goats, sheep, cows and, in the case of MOZZARELLA, buffalo. The taste and texture depend on several factors, including the plants on which the animals graze. *Formaggio a pasta dura* [**pas**-ta **du**-ra] is firm-textured cheese; *formaggio a pasta molle* [**mol**-le] is soft. There are many different types and consistencies of cheese in Italy. *Formaggi freschi* are young, fresh, delicate-tasting cheeses such as MOZZARELLA and MASCARPONE. *Formaggi duri* and *semiduri* are made by taking smaller portions of the coagulated whey and compressing it to varying degrees. PROVOLONE is a *semiduro*, PECORINO and PARMIGIANO are *duro*. Many cheeses go through a number of mutations in their life cycle. There might be a young, fresh version and a harder, aged version of the same cheese.

formaggio di fossa [for-**mad**-jo di **fos**-sa] *see box*.

Formaggio di fossa

Literally 'pit-cheese', a strong cheese, made with mixed cow's and sheep's milk, originating in Emilia-Romagna and the Marche; the most famous is from Talamello, where it is called *ambra di Talamello*, 'Talamello amber'. At the end of summer the round cheeses are wrapped in cloth and left in deep, circular pits or ditches hewn out of tufa, the volcanic rock of the area. Quantities of straw are burnt in the ditches to dry them out before they are lined with chalk. When the cheeses are stacked in place, the ditch is firmly sealed until 25th Nov, St Catherine's Day, when a mini festival is held to celebrate the new batch of *formaggio*. The tradition has its roots in a medieval scheme for evading papal tax. Well in advance of the tax agent's visit, the citizens of Sogliano al Rubicone would conceal their valuables—wine and imperishable food as well as cash—in the inner recesses of volcanic caves or in specially dug pits or ditches (*fosse*). Over time it became clear that these hiding places provided excellent refrigeration and that their internal humidity could be manipulated by careful sealing, lining and part-ventilation. Similar evasive measures were taken in the Veneto, where peasants hid their cheese in barrels of grape must. This was found to hasten the ripening process and increase longevity, and thus *formaio embriago* (*see below*) was born.

formai de mut [for-**ma**-i de **moot**] a tangy cow's milk cheese from the Alta Val Brembana near Bergamo, Lombardy.

formaio embriago [for-**ma**-yo em-bri-**a**-go] literally 'drunken' cheese, originating in Treviso (Veneto), so called after the practice of immersing a cheese in red wine or grape must.

forno [**for**-no] oven, bakery; *forno a legna*: wood burning-oven; *al forno*: baked.

fragola [**fra**-go-la] (pl. *fragole*) 1. strawberry; *fragola di bosco* or *fragola selvatica*: wild strawberry;

2. *uva fragola*, the Concord grape.

fragolino [fra-go-**li**-no] 1. sea bream; 2. still or sparkling red wine from north Italy, made from FRAGOLA grapes.

Franciacorta [fran-cha-**cor**-ta] the premier Lombard DOCG, known for its white Chardonnay and red PINOT NERO, as well as for sparkling wines.

frantoiana [fran-to-**ya**-na] e.g. *zuppa frantoiana*: a soup into which olive oil has been drizzled; from FRANTOIO.

frantoio [fran-**to**-yo] the mill or press where olive oil is manufactured, often a family-run operation tucked away in the hills. Finer olive oil is often referred to as *olio di frantoio* to distinguish it from mass-produced oil.

Frappato [frap-**pa**-to] red-wine grape from southeast Sicily. On its own it makes a light-bodied wine. It is often blended with NERO D'AVOLA to make the prized CERASUOLO DI VITTORIA.

frasca [**fras**-ca] in Friuli, a traditional tavern run by wine producers as a showcase for the latest vintage, also serving food

to go with it. *Frasca* means a branch or twig. To show that the tavern was open, a branch was stuck up outside. The same tradition survives today in the *Buschenschänke* of Austria.

frascarelli [fras-ca-**rel**-li] irregularly-shaped lumps of pasta, popular in central Italy. The dough is traditionally moistened by flicking it with water from a small switch ('*frasca*'). *Frascarelli* are also known as '*nsaccaragatti*, 'cats in the bag'.

Frascati [fras-**ca**-ti] light white wine from the Alban Hills, south of Rome.

frascatielle [fras-ca-ti-**el**-le] see FRASCARELLI.

frattaglie [frat-**tal**-ye] offal.

fregnacce [fren-**yat**-che] pasta triangles from Lazio, Abruzzo and the Marche, served in piquant, meaty sauces.

fregula, fregola, freula [**fre**-gu-la] Italian couscous, originating in Sardinia. The semolina spheres are large, about 2–3mm in diameter, and toasted in the oven. Fregula is particularly good when made into soup with clams or other fish.

Freisa [**fray**-za] red-wine grape from Piedmont that produces DOC-quality red and rosé wines, both 100 percent varietal and in blends.

fresco/a [**fres**-co] fresh, cool.

fricassea [fri-cas-**se**-a] fricassée.

friccò [fric-**co**] from Gubbio (Umbria), a dish of lamb, chicken and rabbit braised together in a wine and tomato sauce.

frico [**fri**-co] fried potato pancake from Friuli, with an outer layer of cheese.

frico balacia [**fri**-co ba-**la**-cha] a cheese with a high melting point, ideal for grilling or frying (Friuli-Venezia Giulia). Also known as *balacin*.

frigulozzi [fri-gu-**lots**-zi] lengths of leavened bread dough boiled and served with tomato sauce and PECORINO. A speciality of Lazio.

friselle or **frisedde** [fri-**zel**-le, fri-**zed**-de] bread rings half-baked, cut in half and baked again (Puglia). They provide a quick and simple meal, slightly dampened with water and topped with chopped tomatoes,

onions, black olives, oregano and a dribble of olive oil.

frisse [**fris**-se] in Piedmont, pork meat minced with the offal, mixed with egg and parmesan, formed into small balls and fried in pieces of pig's bladder.

fritedda [fri-**ted**-da] in Sicily, a springtime dish of fresh peas, broad beans and artichokes, cooked together with a few spring onions, and served tepid, with a spoonful of wine vinegar stirred in at the last moment.

fritole [**free**-to-le] see FRITTELLE.

frittata [frit-**ta**-ta] egg-based dish like a thick omelette or soufflé, made with a variety of flavourings such as chopped meat and vegetables. In Friuli and northeast Italy, cut-up pieces of *frittata* are often served as a small snack to accompany an evening drink.

frittelle [frit-**tel**-le] small Carnival doughnuts (Venice). Also called *fritole*.

fritto/a [**frit**-to] fried; *fritto misto* = a mixed fry-up; *fritto misto alla fiorentina* = a Florentine fry-up of meat, vegetables and offal; *fritto misto alla milanese* = a Milanese fry-up of brains,

frittola, frittula see CICCIOLI.

frittura [frit-**too**-ra] a fried dish, a fry-up. *Frittura di pesce*, a fish fry.

Friuli-Venezia Giulia northeastern region of Italy reaching deep into Central Europe. The cuisine shows strong Austrian and Central European influence. There is a rich variety of cheese, soups and SALUMI: *Prosciutto di San Daniele* is famous. The staples are POLENTA and rice. The region also produces good fish, and some interesting wines, including PICOLIT.

frizzante [frits-**zan**-te] of wine or water, sparkling.

frocia [**fro**-cha] or *froscia* (Sicily), a thin omelette with cheese, breadcrumbs and parsley.

frolla see PASTA FROLLA.

frollino [frol-**li**-no] a shortbread biscuit (pl. *frollini*).

fromadzo [fro-**mad**-zo] DOP cow's milk cheese from Valle d'Aosta.

froscia see FROCIA.

frullato [frul-**la**-to] a milkshake or smoothie.

frumento [fru-**men**-to] wheat.

frumentone [fru-mun-**to**-ne] sweetcorn, maize.

frustega [fru-**ste**-ga] a pastry from the Marche cooked with grape must.

frustenga [fru-**sten**-ga] a cornmeal fruitcake, known as *frustingo* in the Marche, where it is a speciality of the province of Fermo.

frustingo see FRUSTENGA.

frutta [**frut**-ta] fruit.

frutti [**frut**-ti] *frutti di mare* ('fruit of the sea') = seafood; *frutti di bosco* = 'fruit of the forest', i.e. mixed berries.

funghetti [foon-**ghet**-ti] 'little mushrooms', a PASTINA.

funghetto, al [al foon-**ghet**-to] 'mushroom style', sliced and cooked as you would a mushroom, in other words sautéed or stir-fried so that it sweats but does not burn.

funghi [**foon**-ghi] mushrooms, hugely popular in Italy and widely available fresh in season (*see box*).

funghi porcini [**foon**-ghi por-**chee**-ni] *Boletus edulis*, the cep or penny bun, a mushroom with a brown cap and a chunky white stem. Good for eating and highly prized. *Tagliatelle ai funghi porcini* is a popular autumn dish. A number of towns and villages in Italy grow hold an annual *Sagro del fungo porcino*, a porcini festival.

Italian mushroom mania

Principal varieties of Italian mushroom include *colombina* (Columbine), *colombina dorata* (golden Columbine), *chiodino* (honey mushroom), *prataiolo* (meadow mushroom), *lattario delizioso* (milk cap), *mazza di tamburo* (parasol mushroom), *spugnola* (morel), *porcino* (perhaps the best-known outside Italy) and the *vescia* (the puffball). A *trun* [troon], meaning 'thunder' in Piedmontese dialect, is a plump, apricot-coloured mushroom; a *gallinaccio* [gal-li-**nat**-cho] is a chanterelle; *famiglioli* [fa-mil-**yo**-li] are red, flat-topped mushrooms with yellow rays on the underside of the cap; the ruffled fungus known as *grifola* [**gri**-fo-la] requires prolonged boiling and baking to make it edible.

Funghi secchi [**sec**-ki] are dried mushrooms. Edible funghi are known as *funghi buoni*, 'good mushrooms'. Poisonous funghi are *funghi velenosi*, the deadliest of which are known as *funghi mortali*: consumption of these is almost certain to be fatal. Novice mushroom gatherers should beware. The edible *ovolo buono*, for example, looks very like its poisonous cousin the *ovolo malefico*, also known as Satan's boletus. One of the most fearful of the *funghi velenosi*, it resembles the typical storybook mushroom, red-capped and plump-stemmed, the seat of fairies and pixies. When eaten, it provokes infernal hallucinations and agonising muscular spasms. A *fungaiolo* [foon-ga-i-**o**-lo] is a mushroom hunter. There is a significant mortality rate among intrepid *fungaioli*, occasioned not by poisonous mushrooms but by climbing accidents. The rarer species grow in out-of-the-way places and many a *fungaiolo* has been found at the bottom of a deep crevasse, limbs broken but heroically clutching the prize.

fuori [**fwo**-ri] outside. Waiters will commonly ask if you would like to sit *fuori* (on the terrace) or *all'interno* (indoors). *Fuori stagione* means out of season. *Fuori servizio* is out of order, not working.

furn [foorn] = FORNO.

fusi istriani [**fu**-zi is-ti-**a**-ni] 'Istrian spindles' pasta from Friuli-Venezia Giulia and Istria, often served with a filling RAGÙ of chicken or game.

fusiddi [fu-**zid**-di] southern dialect for FUSILLI.

fusilli [fu-**zil**-li] corkscrew-shaped pasta; *fusilli bucati* are *fusilli* with holes running down the middle; *fusilli stretti* are tightly wound *fusilli*; *fusilloni* are larger. Before machine production took over, the shapes were made by laboriously winding strips of dough around thin knitting needles.

fusto [**fus**-to] barrel, often of oak, used for ageing wine.

Gaglioppo [gal-**yop**-po] grape variety imported to Calabria from Greece, the main constituent of red Cirò.

galani [ga-**la**-ni] fried pastries from northeast Italy, made for Carnival.

galantina [ga-lan-**ti**-na] galantine, cold meat stuffed with forcemeat.

galba [**gal**-ba] in Milan and Lombardy, a popular name for a hearty vegetable soup.

galletto [gal-**let**-to] a pullet, in other words a young hen, under a year old.

Galliano [gal-li-**a**-no] a sweet liqueur, flavoured with anise and vanilla, either drunk as a DIGESTIVO or used for cocktails. Invented in Livorno in Tuscany in 1896, it shot to prominence in the mid-20th century with the invention of the Harvey Wallbanger cocktail (vodka, orange juice and Galliano). Galliano comes in slim,

Fusilli ('little spindles'), one of the most familiar of Italian pasta shapes, its tight whorls ideal for catching and retaining sauce.

tapering, very tall bottles (higher than most shelves, which makes them difficult to store).

gallina [gal-**li**-na] a hen (older than a POLLO), a stewing fowl, an old broiler.

gallinacci see CANTARELLI.

gallinella [gal-li-**nel**-la] 1. gurnard (fish); 2. see POLLANCA.

gallo [**gal**-lo] a cock, rooster.

gallo cedrone [**gal**-lo ched-**ro**-ne] grouse, literally the 'cedar cock', from its habitat.

gallo forcello [**gal**-lo for-**chel**-lo] black grouse.

Gallo Nero [**gal**-lo **ne**-ro] 'black cockerel'. The emblem of the black rooster on a yellow background is used as a mark of quality and authenticity by producers of CHIANTI CLASSICO.

gallurese [gal-lu-**re**-ze] 'Gallura style', named after an area of northern Sardinia.

gamberelli [gam-be-**rel**-li] small prawns.

gamberetti [gam-be-**ret**-ti] shrimps.

gamberi [**gam**-be-ri] prawns.

gamberi di fiume [**gam**-be-ri di fi-**oo**-me] also *gamberi d'acqua dolce*, crayfish.

Four Italian mixers: Italicus, Galliano, Punt e Mes and Cynar. The height of the Galliano bottle (43.5cm) is one of its distinctive features.

gambero imperiale [**gam**-be-ro im-pe-ri-**a**-le] large prawn.

Gambero Rosso [**gam**-be-ro **ros**-so] influential food and wine publishing group. Its guides and listings are a good source of information on gastronomic developments in Italy. The name means 'The

Red Prawn', after the inn in the Pinocchio story.

garbanzo [gar-**bant**-zo] chickpea.

Garganega [gar-**ga**-ne-ga] white grape from the Veneto, used to produce SOAVE.

garganelli [gar-ga-**nel**-li] ridged pasta squares curled over on themselves into a tube shape, resembling a gullet or *garganel*.

gargati [gar-**ga**-ti] PASTA CORTA from the Veneto, usually served with a vegetable sauce.

garofalato [gar-o-fa-**la**-to] beef or lamb cooked in red wine and cloves.

garofano [ga-**ro**-fa-no] *chiodi di garofano* are cloves.

garusolo SEE MURICE.

gassata [gas-**sa**-ta] carbonated.

gasse [**gas**-se] bow-shaped PASTINA from Liguria.

gattafin [gat-ta-**fin**] deep-fried pasta parcels from Levanto in Liguria, filled with greens, eggs and cheese.

Gattinara [gat-ti-**na**-ra] long-lived red wine from Piedmont, made mainly from NEBBIOLO, in good years capable of rivalling a BAROLO.

gattò [gat-**to**] a Neapolitan potato pie with ham and cheese.

gattuccio [gat-**tu**-cho] dogfish.

gè in preixun [**je** in pre-**zhun**] 'chard in prison', Genoese slang for PANSOTTI.

gelatina [je-la-**tee**-na] gelatin, jelly, aspic.

gelato [je-**la**-to] ice cream.

Italian *gelato*

Ice cream was invented in Italy. In AD 62 the emperor Nero, with characteristic panache, ordered relays of slaves along the Appian Way to ferry buckets of ice and snow from the Apennine mountain ranges to Rome. This, mixed with honey and berries, was the forerunner of modern ice cream and made a kind of sorbet similar in texture to those that had been popular in the Mediterranean since the 5th century BC, when the Greek physician Hippocrates had promoted the health-giving properties of ice to his patients.

Throughout the Arab world sorbets of a similar kind developed along parallel lines. The fertile exchange of ideas among Jewish, Arabic and Christian scholars throughout the Middle Ages brought about dramatic changes in gastronomy as well as in mainstream science and art. To the great benefit of gastronomy, the aggressive expansionism of the Crusades stimulated rather than inhibited that exchange of ideas, all of which helped bring the ancient sorbet closer in form to the ice cream we enjoy today. The Arab occupation of Sicily, followed by the intermingling of Arab and Christian culture under Norman rule, had a profound influence on all southern Italian dishes including the sorbet; among other things, they introduced the cultivation of sugar cane which gave a much better flavour and a smoother result than honey. The Renaissance saw innovations by Bernardo Buontalenti (1536–1608), a Florentine engineer in the service of the Medici and a notable pioneer of refrigeration. In the Baroque era there were further developments set in motion by Francesco Procopio dei Coltelli (fl.1650–1720), a Sicilian fisherman who foresaw the gastronomic possibilities of the snow he was bringing down from Mt Etna to keep his fish fresh. He emigrated to Paris, became a confectioner, and developed an early ice cream-making machine; he was the first to add cream to his mixtures, which became immensely popular. Procopio became purveyor of ice cream to Louis XIV, who was enthusiastic. In 1686 he opened the first coffee house in Paris, the Café Procope, which still flourishes today.

Gelato today is served in a cup (*coppa*) or cone (*cono*) and comes in a variety of *gusti* (flavours). These include a variety of fruit flavours, many kinds of chocolate, coffee, spices and some others, including: *bacio* [**ba**-cho], 'a kiss', a chocolate hazelnut mix; *cioccolato all' azteca* [cho-co-**la**-to al az-**te**-ca] with cinnamon and chilli pepper; *fior di latte* [fi-**or** di **lat**-te], sweet, creamy, milk ice cream; *gianduja* or *gianduia* [jan-**doo**-ya], chocolate and hazelnut; *malaga* [**ma**-la-ga], rum and raisin; *riso* [**ri**-zo], rice, somewhat like rice pudding; *puffo* [**puf**-fo], a sort of bubblegum flavour; *stracciatella* [stra-cha-**tel**-la], chocolate chips in a *fior di latte* base; *Viagra*, a curiosity, not containing the drug itself but, instead, various herbs that are said to be used in Viagra and to have an aphrodisiac effect; *zabaione* [za-ba-**yo**-ne], a foundation of egg and custard with a MARSALA *leitmotif.*

Granita siciliana is a kind of crushed water ice; *semifreddi* are soft ice cream confections; *torta gelata* is ice cream cake.

gelo di mellone [je-lo di mel-**lo**-ne] a sweet, decorative dessert probably of Arab origin, made only in Palermo (Sicily), consisting of watermelon juice thickened with corn starch, to which bits of chocolate to represent the seeds, and pistachio, cinnamon and candied pumpkin (optional) are added before it sets; jasmine flowers (edible) are scattered over it before serving.

gelone [je-**lo**-ne] oyster mushroom.

gelso [**jel**-so] mulberry.

gemelli [je-**mel**-li] 'twins', two short pasta strands twisted together.

genepì [je-ne-**pi**] a liqueur from the Valle d'Aosta and Savoy region made from herbs of the wormwood family.

geretto [je-**ret**-to] shank, the cut used for OSSO BUCO.

geriebenes Gerstl [gu-**ree**-be-nes **ger**-stl] a pasta GRATTUGIATA from northern Friuli.

germogli [jer-**mol**-yi] sprouts, sprouted seeds.

ghiacciato/a [ghi-a-**cha**-to] ice-cold, chilled.

ghiacciolo [ghi-a-**cho**-lo] an ice lolly, popsicle.

ghianda [ghi-**an**-da] acorn.

ghiotta, alla [ghi-ot-ta] *pesce spada alla ghiotta* is swordfish cooked in a sauce of tomatoes, olives and capers.

ghiozzo [ghi-**ots**-zo] goby, a small fish, eaten in RISOTTO.

gianduia, gianduiotto,

gianduja [jan-**doo**-ya, jan-doo-**yot**-to] a Piedmontese speciality, hazelnut and chocolate.

gigli [**jil**-yi] 'lilies', PASTINA slightly resembling a calla lily flower.

ginepro [ji-**ne**-pro] juniper, used in marinades and stews and to season ham.

Gingerino [jin-je-**ri**-no] a ginger-flavoured non-alcoholic aperitif.

gioddù [jod-**du**] Sardinian yoghurt.

giorno [**jor**-no] day, e.g. *specialità* [spetch-ah-lee-**tah**] *del giorno*: today's special.

giovane [**jo**-va-ne] young.

Giovedì Grasso [jo-ve-**di gras**-so] 'Fat Thursday', the last Thursday in Lent.

girello [ji-**rel**-lo] topside or silverside of beef or pork, suitable for stews.

giudea, giudia, alla [ju-**de**-a] in the Jewish style. In the case of artichokes, this means flattened and fried whole.

giuggiulena [ju-ju-**le**-na] sesame seeds.

giuncata, giuncà [joon-**ca**-ta, joon-**ca**] an unsalted fresh cheese.

gizzoa [jits-**zo**-a] a flatbread pouch ideal for meat or vegetable fillings (Liguria).

Glera [**gle**-ra] a white-wine grape, originally from Slovenia and originally called Prosecco, renamed by the EU in 2009 to avoid confusion with the famous sparkling wine of the same name. Glera is a neutral variety and is typically cultivated for use in light sparkling wines. It is grown in northeast Italy.

gloria patri [**glo**-ri-a **pa**-tri] 'Glory be to the Father', a ring-shaped PASTINA, the name being an allusion to the widespread practice of reciting short prayers to time cooking in the days before people had clocks.

gnocchetti [nyoc-**ket**-ti] little GNOCCHI.

gnocchi [**nyoc**-ki] thick, soft dumplings made from a variety of ingredients, which can include semolina, wheat flour, potato and breadcrumbs; a single example is a *gnocco*; they may be eaten as a starter or as the pasta course. Traditionally they are served with tomato sauces, pesto, and in melted butter, with sage (*see box*).

Gnocolar see Venerdì.

gnomirelli [nyo-mi-**rel**-li] faggots or sausages, usually of lamb's offal.

gnudi [**nyu**-di] see *Some types of gnocchi*, below.

gnumareddi [nyu-ma-**red**-di] see GNOMIRELLI.

gò [go] the Venetian dialect name for GHIOZZO.

gobeletti [go-be-**let**-ti] see COBELETTI.

gobbo [**gob**-bo] alternative name for the cardoon (see CARDI), from the Italian *gobbo*, a dwarf.

gocce di cioccolato [**got**-che di choc-co-**la**-to] chocolate chips.

goccio [**got**-cho] a drop.

gogotto [go-**got**-to] leg of lamb.

Gorgonzola [gor-gon-**zo**-la] a veined blue DOP cheese, of cow's or goat's milk, widely made in Piedmont and Lombardy.

Some types of *gnocchi*

Gnocchi can be round, ovoid, elongated or flat. They can be smooth or ridged. They are always cooked for a very short time, in boiling water, removed as soon as they float to the surface. *Gnocchi di zucca* [**tsoo**-ca] are dumplings made with squash, typically served with butter and cheese. *Gnocchi ossolani* [os-so-**la**-ni], from Piedmont, are made with chestnut flour, mashed potato and pumpkin purée. *Gnocchi ricci* [**ree**-chi], from Amatrice in northern Lazio, made with two doughs, one made of flour and eggs and the other of flour and water. The doughs are kneaded together, then pieces are broken off and dragged and pressed through flour to make the distinctive, flattened *gnocchi*.

The **gnocco gigante** is a giant dumpling; a potato *gnocco* from Parma weighing 58.5 kg entered the Guinness Book of Records in May 2010. **Gnudi** are dumplings made of RICOTTA and flour, called *gnudi* ('naked') because they look like RAVIOLI filling without the ravioli coat.

It is named from the town of Gorgonzola, now a suburb of Milan, which was an early centre of production. The penicillin spores that create the blue mould are added to the milk, and when the curds have coagulated, metal nails (formerly made of hardwood) are inserted to create ventilated channels in which the mould can grow (if you cut open a cheese, you can see the tracks of these very clearly). In the past, cheeses were left to mature in ice-pits in the hills. Today's refrigeration technology makes these obsolete, though some producers still cling to the old techniques.

graffe [graf-fe] ring-shaped Neapolitan doughnuts, sprinkled with sugar.

gramigna [gra-**min**-ya] short pasta curls.

grana [gra-na] fine-grained cheese, e.g. PARMIGIANO REGGIANO (parmesan) and *Grana Padano*, both DOP and both hard cheeses originating in the Po Valley in Emilia-Romagna. *Grana Padano* matures faster than *Parmigiano*, and there are fewer rules about what the cows may eat, making it a more economical option. Another *grana* cheese is *Granone lodigiano* [gra-**no**-ne lo-di-**ja**-no] from Lombardy.

granchio [**gran**-ki-o] (pl. *granchi*) crab.

grandinine [gran-di-**ni**-ne] 'little hailstones', a pasta shape.

granelli [gra-**nel**-li] testicles.

granita [gra-ni-ta] an iced refreshment like a Slush Puppie or snow cone, made with crushed fruit, ground almonds or coffee, mixed with sugar and stirred constantly while freezing in order to keep its consistency soft.

grano arso [**gra**-no **ar**-so] literally, 'scorched wheat' (in Puglian dialect *gren iars*). After threshing, arable fields were burnt in order to fertilise the ground. The *grano arso* was the grain that had escaped the attention of the gleaners and survived the fire. It was gathered up and made into flour by the needy. Today the smoky flavour that it imparted to traditional dishes is much sought-after, and grain is specially toasted to recreate the effect. *Grano arso* flour is also available.

grano duro [**gra**-no **du**-ro]
durum wheat (*Triticum durum*),
a hard grain high in gluten, used
for making pasta.

Granone lodigiano see GRANA.

grano saraceno [**gra**-no sa-ra-
che-no] buckwheat.

granoturco [gra-no-**tur**-co]
sweetcorn, maize.

granseola [gran-**se**-o-la] spider
crab. They are common on
menus in the northern Adriatic
region.

granum paradisi [**gra**-num
pa-ra-**di**-zi] 'grains of paradise',
see AFRAMOMO.

grappa [**grap**-pa] a spirit
steam-distilled from pomace,
the pressed skins and seeds
of grapes left over after wine-
making. *Grappa* exists in many
regional variants, and there is
a broad spectrum of quality
too. Many wineries simply
deliver their pomace to a central
distillery and receive *grappa* in
return. Others follow traditional
artisanal methods, producing
grappa that is accorded the
same status as single-malt
whiskies are in Britain, the
USA and Japan. There is much

Granseola, the spider crab.

gimmickry—oddly-shaped
bottles, exotic flavours—but
there is, nevertheless, excellent
grappa to be discovered
throughout Italy, though its real
home is the north, particularly
Friuli. *Grappa* is drunk as a
DIGESTIVO. The *bussùl* [boos-
sool] is the traditional shot-glass
used for quaffing it; the *quartino*
[quar-**ti**-no] is the jug by
which a measure of *grappa* was
traditionally ordered.

grasso [**gras**-so] fat.

graticola, alla [gra-**ti**-co-la]
barbequed, grilled.

gratinato/a [gra-ti-**na**-to] *au
gratin*, i.e. browned in the oven
or under the grill with a topping
made of breadcrumbs and/or
cheese.

graton d'oca [gra-**ton** do-ca]
Piedmontese goose SALAME, from
Novara and Vercelli

grattoni [grat-**to**-ni] small pasta
lozenges, good for soup.

grattugiato/a [grat-tu-**ja**-to]
grated. *Grattugiata* is used to
describe broken bits of pasta
used in a soup.

graviuole [gra-vi-**wo**-le] pasta
from Molise, traditionally served
with wild boar RAGÙ.

Grechetto [gre-**ket**-to] white-
wine grape grown in Umbria;
blended with TREBBIANO grapes
to produce the pleasant, dry
Orvieto wine.

Greco [**gre**-co] southern
Italian wine grape, possibly
introduced from ancient Greece.
Both white-and red-wine
varieties exist, though the most
celebrated are the white *Greco
di Tufo* (a DOCG from Campania)
and *Greco di Bianco* (a DOC
dessert wine from Calabria).

gremolada [gre-mo-**la**-da] a
seasoning of chopped parsley,
lemon zest, garlic and a touch of
anchovy, added to *ossobuco* just
before serving.

gren iars see GRANO ARSO.

grespino [gres-**pi**-no] see
CRISPIGNO.

gribiche [gri-**bish**] French
mayonnaise with capers and
tarragon.

gricia [**gri**-cha] ancient
condiment for pasta (preferably
RIGATONI) popular in Lazio,
consisting of tiny slices of
crisp GUANCIALE, black pepper
and PECORINO, mixed with the
cooked and drained pasta in the
frying pan.

grigette [gri-**jet**-te] small snails.

griglia, alla [**gril**-ya] grilled.

grigliata [gril-**ya**-ta] grill or
barbecue, e.g. *grigliata mista*: a
mixed grill.

Grignolino [grin-yo-**li**-no]
red-wine grape grown almost
exclusively in the Piedmont
region, producing young-
drinking tannic wines.

Grillo [**gril**-lo] Sicilian white
grape with a high sugar content,
one of the main components of
MARSALA.

grispelle [gris-**pel**-le] see
CRESPELLE.

grissini [gris-**si**-ni] breadsticks,
said to have been invented in
1679 by a Turin doctor for King
Vittorio Amedeo II of Savoy,
who had a weak digestion and

could not tolerate ordinary bread.

grolla dell'amicizia [**grol**-la del a-mi-**chit**-si-a] literally, the 'grail of friendship', in the Valle d'Aosta and Piedmont, a wooden loving cup, shaped like a multi-spouted teapot for serving coffee laced with GRAPPA.

grongo [**gron**-go] conger eel (pl. *gronghi*).

Groppello [gro-**pel**-lo] red-wine grape grown on the Lombard shores of Lake Garda. It makes a medium-bodied wine, sometimes found as a varietal but usually making up a blend. The same grape when grown on the Veneto shores of Garda is known as ROSSIGNOLA.

grostoli [**gros**-to-li] type of fritters in Trentino-Alto Adige, made for Carnival.

Grumello [gru-**mel**-lo] sub-zone of the Valtellina Superiore DOCG in Lombardy, producing fine red wines.

gruviera [gru-vi-**e**-ra] a mild cheese from Northern Italy, the name derived from Gruyère.

guancia, guanciola [**gwan**-cha, gwan-**cho**-la] of an animal or fish, the cheek.

guanciale [gwan-**cha**-le] cured pig's cheek, thought by many to be the ideal ingredient for CARBONARA sauce, and indispensable for pasta all' AMATRICIANA.

guarnizione [gwar-nit-si-**o**-ne] garnish.

guastedda, guastella see VASTEDDA.

guatto see GHIOZZO.

guelfi, gueffus [**gwel**-fi, **gwef**-fus] almond and orange blossom sweetmeats from Sardinia.

guscio [**goo**-sho] a shell. *Frutta a guscio* are nuts.

Hoch Pustertaler [hoh **pus**-ter-**ta**-ler] cow's milk cheese from South Tyrol (Trentino-Alto Adige), also known as *formaggio Alta Pusteria* [**al**-ta pus-ster-**i**-a].

Hugo [**oo**-go] a '*spritz Hugo*' is a SPRITZ made with PROSECCO, elderflower cordial, mint and a small topping of soda water.

ice cream see GELATO.

IGP *Indicazione Geografica Protetta*, a seal of quality awarded to products whose geographical source is considered to be vital to their character or quality. CASTELLUCCIO lentils, for example, are only certainly from Castelluccio if they say IGP on the packet.

IGT Similar to IGP. See VINO.

imbottigliato [im-bot-til-**ya**-to] bottled. See VINO.

imbottito/a [im-bot-**ti**-to] stuffed, filled.

impanadas [im-pa-**na**-das] PASTA RIPIENA from Sardinia in the form of substantial pockets with a variety of fillings such as meat and vegetables or eels and cheese. *Impanadas* are often deep fried but can also be oven baked.

impanato/a [im-pa-**na**-to] breaded.

impanatiglie see 'MPANATIGGHI.

impepata [im-pe-**pa**-ta] a peppery dish, e.g *impepata di cozze*, see PEPATA.

incapriata [in-ca-pri-**a**-ta] Puglian vegetable dish known locally as *'ncapriata* or *maccu*, a *purée* of FAVA beans served with sautéed chicory.

inchiostro di seppia [in-ki-**os**-tro di **sep**-pi-a] cuttlefish ink.

incrocio [in-**cro**-cho] in viticulture, a crossing, for example Manzoni bianco, a grape variety which was created

by crossing Riesling and Pinot Blanc.

indivia [in-**di**-vi-a] endive or curly lettuce. *Indivia riccia* is also called frisée.

indugghia [in-**doog**-ya] a Calabrese pork and offal sausage, known locally as *'ndugghia* or *nuglia*, similar to the French *andouille*.

infornato/a [in-for-**na**-to] baked.

infusioni [in-fu-zi-**o**-ni] infusions, herbal teas.

insaccato [in-sac-**ca**-to] a sausage, literally, 'in the bag', because of the intestine it is stuffed into (pl. *insaccati*) to keep its shape. There are many types, with regional recipes from all over Italy.

insalata [in-sa-**la** ta] salad; *mista* (mixed); *verde* (green); *caprese* (with tomatoes, MOZZARELLA and basil).

insalatina [in-sa-la-**ti**-na] a little salad.

integrale [in-te-**gra**-le] wholemeal; *riso integrale* is brown rice.

intingolo [in-**tin**-go-lo] a sauce or gravy.

intongolo see INTINGOLO.

Mural painting in the *thermopolium*, the bar selling hot food (*tavola calda*) in the ancient port city of Ostia outside Rome. The bill of fare seems to have included carrots, olives (or possibly quails' eggs) and something that could either be a large cheese or else a kind of haggis or *insaccato*.

inv. min. frequently used on menus of cheese, seasoned ham, vinegar, etc., an abbreviation for *invecchiato minimo*, 'aged for at least', e.g. *inv. min. 24 mesi* (aged for at least 24 months).

invecchiato [in-vek-ki-**a**-to] aged, matured.

invecchiato minimo see INV. MIN.

invernali [in-ver-**na**-li] winter dishes.

involtini [in-vol-**ti**-ni] thin slices of meat or fish spread with a filling and then rolled up.

ircano [ir-**ca**-no] Sardinian goat's milk cheese.

issopo [**is**-so-po] hyssop, a strong-tasting herb used in cordials and confectionery.

italico [i-**ta**-li-co] a type of soft cow's milk cheese. Any cheese made in the same way as BEL PAESE is a *tipo italico*.

Italicus [i-**ta**-li-cus] marketing itself as a '*rosolio di bergamotto*', this liqueur is made from Calabrian bergamot. The story goes that this distilled elixir was once the drink of preference at the court of the Savoy kings of Italy. Re-invented in 2016, it can be drunk in a variety of ways: as an ingredient in cocktails; as a mixer for SPRITZ; or on its own on ice, as an apéritif.

IVA *Imposta sul Valore Aggiunto*, the Italian equivalent of VAT (UK); consumption tax.

Jambon de Bosses [jam-**bon** de **boss**] PROSCIUTTO CRUDO flavoured with juniper berries and herbs, from Valle d'Aosta.

jota [**yo**-ta] a stew of beans, bacon and sauerkraut, from Friuli-Venezia Giulia.

kaiserschmarrn [kaï-zer-shmarn] a Trentino-Alto Adige dessert of Austrian origin consisting of fried shredded pancake sprinkled with powdered sugar and served with stewed fruit.

kaminwurzen [ka-**min** voort-sen] smoked pork sausages from Trentino-Alto Adige.

kaki see CACO.

kasher [ka-sher] kosher.

Kerner [**ker**-ner] white-wine grape from the South Tyrol (Alto Adige), making fresh, clean high-acid wines. It is a cross between Riesling and Schiava.

knödel see CANEDERLI.

krafi [**cra**-fi] pasta stuffed with cheese, eggs and sugar, from Friuli and Istria.

lacetti [la-**chet**-ti] see ANIMELLE.

lagane [la-**ga**-ne] broad pasta noodles with an ancient heritage. APICIUS mentions them; so does the 1st-century Latin poet Horace, who speaks of sitting down to a bowl of *lagane*, chickpeas and leeks. The recipe has not much changed. *Lagane e ciceri* (with chickpeas) and *lagane e porri* (with leeks) can still be found on menus in the south. In Puglia they eat CICERI *e tria*.

Lagrein [la-**gre**-in] red-wine grape from the South Tyrol (Alto Adige) province, producing some attractive rosé wines and a number of highly-regarded reds. It is particularly associated with the wine-growing area around Bolzano.

laianelle [la-ya-**nel**-le] RICOTTA-filled RAVIOLI from Molise served with a meat RAGÙ, traditionally goat, but nowadays other meats are often substituted. An unwritten rule specifies that they must be made entirely by hand, without the aid even of a rolling pin.

Lambrusco [lam-**broos**-co] a fizzy red wine mainly made in Emilia-Romagna, from a grape of the same name.

Lamon [la-**mon**] town in the Belluno province of the Veneto, famous for its beans, FAGIOLI *di Lamon*.

lampascione see CIPOLLACCIO.

lampone [lam-**po**-ne] raspberry.

lampuga [lam-**pu**-ga] dolphin-fish.

lampreda [lam-**pre**-da] lamprey, either *lampreda di mare* (sea lamprey) or *di fiume* (river lamprey). In ancient times they were drowned in Malmsey wine (MALVASIA)—incidentally the fate that befalls the Duke of Clarence in Shakespeare's *Richard III*. The custom was widespread throughout Europe and it is reasonable to suppose that the lampreys which caused the English king Henry I's 'fatal surfeit' may also have been prepared in this way. Today they are stewed *alla Bordolese*: in the best Bordeaux vintage you can afford. Young lampreys are also made into a *frittura*: lightly dusted in flour they are tossed into hot oil and fried like whitebait.

lampredotto [lam-pre-**dot**-to] in Tuscany, tripe.

lanzardo [lant-**zar**-do] the Pacific mackerel.

lapistra [la-**pis**-tra] in Calabria, a wild radish.

lardo [**lar**-do] cured pork fat. *Lardo di Colonnata* is a particularly prized type, from a small town near Carrara (Tuscany), matured in caves in the marble quarries. It narrowly escaped extinction under EU hygiene regulations, a near miss with martyrdom that beatified the product and made it a symbol of heroic Italian resistance to bureaucratic tyranny. *Lardo di Arnad*, from Valle d'Aosta, is similarly praised. It too, fell victim to EU legislation when the chestnut-wood barrels in which it was cured were banned. Other regional *lardi* of note include a *lardo al rosmarino* from Piedmont, cured with rosemary and other herbs.

lasagna, lasagne [la-**zan**-ya, la-**zan**-ye] internationally famous pasta dish in which a meat RAGÙ is layered between thin sheets of pasta and béchamel prior to being baked in the oven. See also VINCISGRASSI.

lasagnette [la-zan-**yet**-te] narrow strips of LASAGNA pasta.

lasca [**las**-ca] roach (fish).

lattaiolo [lat-ta-**yo**-lo] a recipe going back to the 17th century, for cinnamon custard or custard tart, once the traditional gift of central Italian peasants (Marche, Tuscany, Umbria and Romagna) to their masters on the day of Corpus Christi in June, and currently enjoying a new-found popularity. Eggs, sugar and rum are added to milk which has lengthily simmered with lemon zest and cinnamon; the mixture is then poured into a pastry shell and baked in the oven (in some areas the pastry case is omitted, and the baking dish is anointed with honey). When cool, it is cut into diamond shapes.

latte [**lat**-te] milk. *Latte scremato* [scre-**ma**-to] is skimmed; *latte intero* [in-**te**-ro] is full fat; *latte condensato* [con-den-**sa**-to] is condensed.

latte di avena [**lat**-te di a-**ve**-na] oat milk.

latte di cocco [**lat**-te di **coc**-co] coconut milk.

latte di mandorla [**lat**-te di man-**dor**-la] refreshing drink of crushed almonds and sugar diluted with water.

latte di soia [**lat**-te di **so**-ya] soya milk.

latte fritto [**lat**-te **frit**-to] milk and sugar thickened with corn starch, left to solidify, then cut in rectangular pieces, breaded and fried; a speciality of Liguria.

latte in piedi [**lat**-te in pi-**e**-di] 'milk standing up', milk jelly; a type of blancmange set with gelatin instead of cornflour.

latterino [lat-te-**ri**-no] the sand smelt, a small fish suitable for frying (pl. *latterini*).

latticini [lat-ti-**chee**-ni] dairy produce.

lattonzolo [lat-**tont**-zo-lo] a suckling pig, no more than six or seven weeks old.

lattosio [lat-**to**-zi-o] lactose. *Senza lattosio* = lactose free.

lattuga [lat-**tu**-ga] lettuce.

lauro [**la**-u-ro] bay. See ALLORO.

lavanda, lavandula [la-**van**-da, la-**van**-du-la] lavender, widely used in baking and confectionery.

lavarello [la-va-**rel**-lo] see
    COREGONE.

Lazio [**lat**-zi-o] central region
    of Italy, site of ancient Etruscan
    settlements and eventually of
    the rise, decline and fall of
    Imperial Rome followed by
    the steady growth of Christian
    Rome. Despite all this world-
    shaping history, the cuisine is
    simple and local. Bread, cheese,
    lamb, artichokes and offal are
    the staples of Lazio cooking.
    Even the wines are humble,
    with FRASCATI probably the best
    known.

lecca-lecca [lec-ca-**lec**-ca] an
    ice lolly, popsicle.

leccia [**let**-cha] the leerfish or
    garrick.

leggero/a [led-**je**-ro] mild,
    light.

legna [**len**-ya] wood.

lenticchie [len-**tik**-ki-e] lentils.
    Lenticchie di Castelluccio, from
    the village of the same name in
    Umbria, are the most famous of
    all Italian lentils.

lepre [**le**-pre] hare.

lepudrida [le-pu-**dri**-da]
    Sardinian meat and vegetable
    soup of Spanish origin, similar
    to *olla podrida* ('rotten pot').

Lessini Durello [les-**si**-ni
    du-**rel**-lo] sparkling DOC wine
    from the Monti Lessini in the
    Veneto, made mainly (minimum
    85 percent) from the DURELLA
    grape.

lessa fresca [**les**-sa **fres**-ca]
    another name for the leerfish,
    leccia.

lesso [**les**-so] simmered; by
    association boiled meat. *Lesso e
    pearà*, in the Veneto, is a dish of
    mixed boiled meats with a purée
    of vegetables and stale bread.

levistico [le-**vis**-ti-co] lovage.

Liber de Coquina the *Book
    of the Cook*, a 14th-century
    Latin codex thought to have
    been written by a Neapolitan.
    It contains recipes for fish,
    poultry and desserts, and is full
    of examples of contemporary
    gastronomic lore.

licurdia [li-coor-**di**-a] onion
    soup (Calabria).

Liguria [li-**gu**-ri-a] northwestern
    coastal region of Italy (the port
    of Genoa is its principal city)
    known for its fish dishes and
    for the many varieties of fresh
    and dried pasta on offer. There
    is much debate as to what
    constitutes the perfect Genoese

PESTO and many types are on
the market. FOCACCIA is typical
of the region, as is the chickpea
bread known as *farinata*.
Ligurian olive oil is much more
delicate in flavour than Tuscan—
it goes better with fish.

lime [**lee**-me] lime.

limonata [li-mo-**na**-ta]
lemonade, lemon soda.

limoncello [li-mon-**chel**-lo] a
lemon-based DIGESTIVO made
from fragrant southern Italian
lemons (the *amalfitano* variety)
from around the Gulf of Naples,
those from Sorrento being held
to be the best. The Amalfi Coast
tradition is to serve it in a small,
chilled beaker or glass, and this
has spread throughout Italy and
beyond.

limone [li-mo-ne] lemon. IGP
lemons come from the Amalfi
Coast and Syracuse.

lingua [lin-gwa] tongue.

linguattola [lin-**gwat**-to-la] the
spotted flounder.

lingue di gatto [**lin**-gwe di **gat**-
to] cat's tongues, *langues de chat*
biscuits.

lingue di suocera [**lin**-gwe
di **swo**-che-ra] 'mother-in-law's
tongues', crispy flat GRISSINI,

often flavoured with salt and
rosemary.

linguine [lin-**gwi**-ne] 'little
tongues', pasta strands
resembling flattened spaghetti.

Liptauer [**lip**-ta-wa] a spicy,
spreadable sheep's cheese,
popular in Trieste but
originating in the part of old
Austria-Hungary that is now
Slovakia.

liquirizia [lik-wi-**rit**-si-a]
liquorice.

liquore [li-**quo**-re] liqueur.

liquoroso [li-quo-**ro**-zo] of a
wine, fortified.

liscio/a [**lee**-sho] straight. Of
pasta, unridged; of spirits, neat;
of water, still.

locanda [lo-**can**-da] in theory
a simple restaurant, though
the term has been taken up
by high-end restaurateurs. A
locanda may be anything from
a spit-and-sawdust rural set-up
to a sophisticated cosmopolitan
venue.

Lombardy (Lombardia),
northern Italian region well
known for its busy capital city
Milan (home to some of the
most famous restaurants in
Italy) and for the beauties of

its lakes, Como and Maggiore (Lake Garda is split between Lombardy and Veneto). Local produce includes plenty of protein-rich produce, for example GORGONZOLA and TALEGGIO cheese, BRESAOLA (cured beef) and a variety of sausages. The FRANCIACORTA DOCG is the best wine.

lombata, lombo [lom-**ba**-ta, **lom**-bo] loin (e.g. of beef, veal, pork).

lombatina [lom-ba-**ti**-na] loin (usually of veal).

lombrichelli [lom-bri-**kel**-li] 'little earthworms', thick spaghetti-like pasta from Lazio.

lonza [lont-za] 1. pork loin; 2. *Lonza di fichi* is a sweetmeat from the Marche, made of pressed dried figs.

lorighittas [lo-ri-**ghit**-tas] braided pasta from Morgongiori in Sardinia. The traditional dressing is chicken ragout, but they are also good with a sauce based on aubergines and mushrooms.

lotregano, lotregan [lo-tre-**ga**-no, lo-tre-**gan**] golden grey mullet.

lovo [**lo**-vo] in Venice, hake.

luccio [**lu**-cho] pike (fish).

lucioperca [lu-cho-**per**-ca] sometimes called *sandra*, the zander or pike-perch, a freshwater fish particularly popular in Umbria.

Lugana [lu-**ga**-na] white-wine region on the south banks of Lake Garda, producing light, fruity, easy-to-drink wines. See TURBIANA.

luganega [lu-**ga**-ne-ga] (pl. *luganeghe*) a slender pork sausage, sold by length. Its origins are very old: it is recorded in the writings of Latin authors, who call it *lucanica*, after the ancient region of southern Italy corresponding to modern Basilicata.

lumache [lu-**ma**-ke] snails, either the live variety or pasta shapes, also known as *lumachine, lumachelle, lumachette* and *lumaconi. Lumache di vigna* [**vin**-ya] or *lumache di San Giovanni* [san-jo-**van**-ni] are said to ward off evil spirits and are eaten in Rome and Lazio on 24th June, the feast of St John the Baptist. The snails are served in a sauce of garlic and tomatoes, to which anchovies and chilli may also be added.

lunette [lu-**net**-te] half-moon-shaped RAVIOLI.

lunghetti [lun-**get**-ti] semi-long slender pasta from Emilia-Romagna, known in dialect as *lunghètt*, but more commonly referred to as STROZZAPRETI. A traditional recipe serves them with breadcrumbs and cinnamon.

lupini [lu-**pi**-ni] 1. lupin beans, yellow legumes a little like broad beans; 2. *lupini di mare* are small clams, the 'striped Venus', similar to VONGOLE.

lupo di mare [**lu**-po di **ma**-re] sea bass.

luppoli [**lup**-po-li] hops. The new shoots, called *luvertin* in Piedmont, are used for omelettes.

lusso [**lus**-so] luxury; *ristorante di lusso*: a five-star restaurant.

luvertin SEE LUPPOLI.

maccarello [mac-ca-**rel**-lo] mackerel.

maccelleria [ma-chel-le-**ri**-a] a butcher's shop.

maccheroni [mac-ke-ro-ni] a pasta of varying shapes and sizes, mainly but not exclusively tubular in shape, native to Sicily and Calabria but widespread throughout southern Italy.

maccu [**mac**-cu] in Sicily, a thick potage of dried broad beans, sometimes flavoured with wild fennel or borage; once a basic food for farm workers and shepherds. Also see INCAPRIATA.

macedonia di frutta [ma-che-**do**-ni-a di **frut**-ta] fruit salad.

Old-fashioned *macelleria* with a window display of lean veal shoulder, selected cuts of beef, veal *ossobuchi*, roasting beef and veal chops.

macinato/a [ma-chi-**na**-to] minced or ground.

mafalde, mafaldine [ma-**fal**-de, ma-fal-**di**-ne] ribbon-shaped pasta, a kind of LASAGNETTE, widespread in Italy and named after Princess Mafalda, daughter of King Vittorio Emanuele III. Mafalda died in Buchenwald in 1944. 2. In Sicily, braided bread rolls, named after the same unfortunate princess.

maggiorana [mad-jo-**ra**-na] marjoram.

magro [**ma**-gro] lean, not fatty, thin.

maiale [ma-**ya**-le] pig, pork.

maialino [ma-ya-**li**-no] piglet, either a suckling pig (*lattonzolo*), or an animal around a year old, suitable for making PORCHETTA.

maionese [ma-yo-**ne**-ze] mayonnaise, in Italy made with eggs and olive oil, and a squeeze of lemon juice.

maiorchino [ma-yor-**ki**-no] unfortunately quite rare cheese of ancient standing from Novara di Sicilia, in Sicily's Nebrodi Mountains. Compact, delicately flavoured, made of sheep's and goat's milk; a popular feast is dedicated to it in February, when the dark-brown truckles (35cm in diameter) are rolled down the main street, followed by the shepherds, in a mad rush to the finish.

mais [**ma**-is] maize, sweetcorn.

malfatti, malfattini [mal-**fat**-ti, mal-fat-**ti**-ni] 'badly made' little scraps of pasta, resembling medium to small *gnocchetti*, traditionally served in soups.

malga [**mal**-ga] mild, creamy summer cheese from the alpine regions of Friuli-Venezia Giulia; the *malga* is a wooden hut used by cowherds for shelter, storing equipment and for making cheese.

malloreddus [mal-lo-**red**-dus] sturdy southern Italian GNOCCHI, curled over on one side and ridged on the other, the better to trap the sauce. Sardinian *malloreddus* are sometimes coloured and flavoured with saffron.

maltagliati [mal-tal-**ya**-ti] 'the badly cut ones', coarsely cut pasta shapes found extensively in Italy, served with a variety of sauces. They are given different names in different regions (see BLECS). In the province of Ferrara they are known as *sguazzabarbuz* ('beard-splatters') because it is impossible not to eat them messily.

Malvasia [mal-va-**zi**-a] dry white wine made from an ancient grape variety of the same name, prevalent in northeast Italy (and in Dalmatia), perhaps an ancient Greek variety. The old English name is Malmsey. The DOP Malvasia from the Aeolian islands (especially Salina), has a sweet PASSITO version, usually served chilled as an aperitif.

manate [ma-**na**-te] pasta from Vaglio di Basilicata. The paste is kneaded into a ball with egg, then flattened and cut into thin strips.

mandarancio see CLEMENTINA.

mandarino [man-da-**ri**-no] mandarin orange.

mandili 'nversoi [man-di-lin-ver-**soy**] 'reversed handkerchiefs', Piedmontese pasta similar to TORTELLINI but made without egg. They are filled with sausage and sweetbreads.

mandilli di saea [man-**dil**-li di sa-**e**-ya] 'silk handkerchiefs', thin squares of pasta typical of Liguria.

mandorla [**man**-dor-la] almond (pl. *mandorle*). Two varieties are grown: *dolci*, the sweet almonds used in confectionery, and *mandorle amare*, the bitter almonds used in liqueurs.

maneghi [ma-**ne**-ghi] sweet potato GNOCCHI from the Veneto, elongated rather than round.

manfricoli [man-**fri**-co-li] a kind of spaghetti made with spelt flour. In the Marche, *manfrigoli* are tiny gnocchi made from kneading together stale breadcrumbs, flour and eggs.

manicotti [ma-ni-**cot**-ti] 'muffs', pasta in the form of sections of tube.

mantecato/a [man-te-**ca**-to] creamed, as in the BACCALÀ *mantecato* of Venice.

manto [**man**-to] a coating or crust.

manzo [**mant**-so] beef.

Manzoni bianco [mant-**zo**-ni bi-**an**-co] white wine grape, a crossing of Riesling and Pinot Blanc, created in the Veneto by the oenologist Luigi Manzoni, in the early 20th century. It is mainly grown in northeast Italy.

mapo [**ma**-po] dark green, sweet citrus fruit from Sicily, a hybrid of the mandarin orange and the grapefruit.

maraconda SEE MARICONDA.

maracuja [ma-ra-**cu**-ya] passion fruit.

marasche [ma-**ras**-ke] Morello cherries.

Marche [**mar**-ke] central Italian region with an Adriatic coastline, known for its picturesque hilltop towns and cities, the Renaissance splendour of Urbino, the medieval squares and towers of Ascoli Piceno, the splendid Sibylline Mountains, and the great port of Ancona. The coastal cuisine of the Marche centres on *brodetti*, soups that exploit the seasonal variety of fish. Inland, the *marchigiani* are keen carnivores, and avid contenders in Italy's widespread manufacture of SALUMI. Many unusual cheeses and cured sausages of the region are excellent, and chunks of sausage and lard, as well as cheese, are typically stuck into the soft bread called *crescia*, a popular street food. Among the DOC red wines, Lacrima di Morro d'Alba, Rosso Conero and Rosso Piceno take pride of place; the unusual sparkling Vernaccia di Serrapetrona is DOCG. Superb DOC whites include Verdicchio dei Castelli di Jesi, Verdicchio di Matelica, and Bianchello del Metauro. The exquisite 'cooked' wine, *vi' cotto piceno*, can be found at Lapedona and Loro Piceno.

marende [ma-**ren**-de] in the South Tyrol (Alto Adige) a simple meal somewhat similar to the British 'ploughman's': cheese, pickles, cold cuts, radish and bread, usually served on a wooden board, the *Marendebrettl*. Sometimes spelt *merende*.

Margherita [mar-ghe-**ri**-ta] Queen of Italy (1851–1926) consort of Umberto I. The Pizza Margherita is said to have been named after her by its creator, a Neapolitan pizza chef called Raffaele Esposito, who had daringly served the dish to the royal couple at a time when pizza was considered a food of the poor. The ingredients of Esposito's creation, fresh basil, *fiordilatte* (cow's milk mozzarella) and tomatoes, echo the Italian national colours, green, white and red. The queen was delighted with it, and her royal approval is said to have done much for the fame of Esposito's restaurant.

margherite [mar-ghe-**ri**-te] 'daisies', a pasta shape.

mariconda [ma-ri-**con**-da] a bread dumpling, typical of Mantua, often served in broth (pl. *mariconde*).

marinaia, marinara, alla [ma-ri-**na**-ya, ma-ri-**na**-ra] 'sailor style'. Most such dishes would originally have been made by fishermen, and thus use ingredients which they could have taken with them on voyages. Anchovies, capers, olives and other salted items predominate.

marinato/a [ma-ri-**na**-to] marinaded.

Marinetti *see box*.

maritozzi [ma-ri-**tots**-zi] sweet buns (Rome).

marmellata [mar-mel-**la**-ta] jam.

marmitta [mar-**mit**-ta] a pot or stockpot.

marrone [mar-**ro**-ne] sweet chestnut (pl. *marroni*).

Marsala [mar-**sa**-la] a group of DOC wines from Trapani and Marsala in western Sicily, made either with the red Pignatello, Nero d'Avola and Nerello Mascalese grapes (*Marsala Rubino*, or Ruby) or the white Grillo, Catarratto, Inzolia and Damaschino (*Ambra*, or Amber, and *Oro* or Gold). The softly rolling hills covered by the vineyards constitute the largest area under vine in Italy.

Some Marsala wines are fortified, using the Soleras method; the finest kinds can be aged for up to ten years. They have been popular in Britain since the early 18th century, when the pioneer wine merchant John Woodhouse started exporting them, and especially after 1798 when Nelson ordered a large quantity for the Royal Navy. Excellent dessert wines, they are often drunk with cheese. The characteristic rich flavour also makes them useful in cooking. During Prohibition, Marsala was successfully exported to the USA because it was classified as

Marinetti, Filippo (1876-1944)

Italian artist, progenitor of the Futurist movement in Italy, a vigorous debunker of the bourgeois values and habits he thought had infected Italian life over the centuries as a result of foreign, chiefly French, Austrian and British, influence, Marinetti advocated a series of sweeping reforms, not only in art and politics but also in gastronomy. His uncompromising nationalism found favour with Mussolini and for a while his ideas were influential. Though the Futurist recipes devised by Marinetti and his fellow artists were frequently bizarre (e.g. SALAME cooked in black coffee with *eau de cologne*), he gained recognition as one of the first public figures to challenge the time-honoured Italian reverence for pasta. It was 'no food for fighters' he maintained. Furthermore, it was 'anti-virile' and no man with a stomach 'weighty and encumbered' with spaghetti could hope to make love to a woman as a true Italian should. Whatever nutritional merit these proscriptions may have had, they never caught on, though his attempts to revise the language and rid it of foreign contaminants such as 'cocktail' are interesting. Marinetti came up with the neologism *polibibita* ('multi-drink', Italian-sounding enough, although the first part in fact derives from the Greek *poly*). Other Marinettisms include *guidopalato* ('palate-guide', i.e. head waiter) and *guerra in letto* ('war-in-the-bed', i.e. an aphrodisiac).

medicine.

Marsala wine is also used in cooking, to make sauces.

Martini [mar-**ti**-ni] a vermouth first produced by the Martini & Rossi distillery in Turin. The Dry Martini (a cocktail of vermouth and gin) was invented in New York in the early 20th century.

marubini [ma-ru-**bi**-ni] a special-occasions PASTA RIPIENA typical of Cremona, Lombardy.

maruzze [ma-**root**-se] small snails.

marzapane [mart-za-**pa**-ne] 1. marzipan; 2. in Piedmont, a type of pork salami.

Marzemino [mart-ze-**mi**-no] late-ripening red-wine grape grown mainly in Trentino, making dark-coloured wines made famous by Mozart, who has Don Giovanni call for a glass of Marzemino before he is borne away to hell.

marzolino [mart-zo-**li**-no] soft sheep's cheese traditionally made in the month of March (*marzo*) in the Chianti region in Tuscany.

marzotica [mart-**zo**-ti-ca] a Puglian RICOTTA made of a mixture of cow's, sheep's and goat's milk. Used either as a table cheese or for grating.

masaro see MAZORO.

mascarpone [mas-car-**po**-ne] creamy-textured fresh cow's milk cheese used for preparing creams and cakes, especially TIRAMISÙ.

masciddaru [mas-kid-**da**-ru] lamb's cheeks, Sicilian street food.

masculini [mas-cu-**li**-ni] Sicilian name for fresh anchovies, ALICI.

masseria [mas-se-**ri**-a] a wine- or oil-producing farm.

matasse [ma-**tas**-se] 'skeins', long pasta noodles manufactured and packaged in bundles. Also known as *nidi*, 'nests'.

matota [ma-**to**-ta] Piedmontese cheese.

matriciana, alla see AMATRICIANA.

maturazione [ma-tu-rat-si-**o**-ne] the maturing process.

mauru [**ma**-u-ru] Sicilian term for several different types of edible seaweed (mainly *Chondus crispus*), eaten in salad, with olive oil and lemon, or braised with garlic and tomato. Officially forbidden, because if the seawater should be polluted, eating the *mauru* raw in salad could be a health hazard, but in early summer you will see the occasional fisherman surreptitiously offering this rare delight in the fish-markets of Riposto, Acireale and Acitrezza, from a capacious wicker basket covered with a piece of sacking.

mazoro [mat-**so**-ro] wild duck.

mazza di tamburo [mat-za di tam-**bu**-ro] the parasol mushroom. Its Italian name translates as 'drumstick'. It grows in fields and woodland and can be eaten fried, baked or sautéed.

mazzafegati [mat-za-**fe**-ga-ti] pork liver sausages from Umbria, Tuscany and the Marche. The sweet version contains raisins, pine kernels and orange zest. Also known as *sambudello* in Tuscany.

mazzancolla [mat-zan-**col**-la] the giant Mediterranean shrimp (*Penaeus kerathurus*).

mazzarelle [mat-za-**rel**-le] lamb's offal wrapped in lettuce leaves, a speciality of the Abruzzo.

medaglione [me-dal-**yo**-ne] a medallion or circular fillet.

mela [**me**-la] apple (pl. *mele*).

melagrana [me-la-**gra**-na] pomegranate.

melanzana [me-lan-**za**-na] (pl. *melanzane*), aubergine, eggplant.

melassa [me-**las**-sa] molasses.

melegueta [me-le-**gwe**-ta] see AFRAMOMO.

mele cotogna [**me**-le co-**ton**-ya] quince.

melone [me-**lo**-ne] melon.

menietti [me-ni-**et**-ti] a PASTINA native to Liguria; milk and olive oil are added to the flour.

mennuli [**men**-nu-li] almonds (Sicily).

menta [**men**-ta] mint.

Young *mazza di tamburo* (parasol mushroom) before its brown and white scaly cap has fully opened. Large specimens can reach up to 15cm across.

menuzze [me-**noot**-ze] a type of PASTINA typically used in fish broth. Also known as *tretarielle*.

Meraner Leiten [me-**ra**-ner la-i-ten] a light red wine from Merano in Alto Adige.

merca see ZIBBA.

mercato [mer-**ca**-to] market.

meringa [me-**rin**-ga] meringue. *Meringata* is meringue pie.

merlano [mer-**la**-no] whiting

(fish).

merletti [mer-**let**-ti] pasta pieces shaped like lace, used in soups or salads.

merluzzo [mer-**loot**-zo] fresh cod. Also sometimes used to describe hake (*nasello*).

mescciüa [mes-**shoo**-ya] Ligurian soup of chickpeas, beans and wheat grains. La Spezia is famous for it.

mescuetille [mes-cu-e-**til**-le] small square gnocchi from Puglia.

mescuotte [me-scu-**ot**-te] sweet, aniseed-flavoured loaves from Basilicata.

mesi [**me**-zi] months.

messicani [mes-si-**ca**-ni] a pasta shape: 'Mexican hats', resembling sombreros.

mestolone [mes-to-**lo**-ne] shoveler (duck).

metodo Charmat [**me**-to-do shar-**ma**] method of producing sparkling wine wherein the secondary fermentation takes place in a steel tank rather than in individual bottles, as in *méthode champenoise*. Also known as *metodo italiano*, the Charmat technique is usually used for Asti Spumante and Prosecco.

mezzalune [med-za-**loo**-ne] half-moon pasta shapes.

mezzano [med-**za**-no] moderately aged (cheese).

mezze maniche [**med**-ze-ma-ni-ke] 'half sleeves', a short tubular pasta shape.

mezzo/a [**med**-zo] half.

michetta [mi-**ket**-ta] type of bread shaped like a rosette, with 'petals' surrounding a round centre. Also known as *rosetta*.

microonde [mi-cro-**on**-de] microwave oven.

midolline [mi-dol-**li**-ne] fragments of pasta resembling melon seeds.

midollo [mi-**dol**-lo] bone-marrow.

miele [mi-**e**-le] honey. Italy has 51 different types. Among the most prized kinds are acacia and thousand-flower from the north, lavender and sunflower from the Marche, bergamot from Calabria, chestnut from Campania, eucalyptus, cardoon, sainfoin, prickly pear, carob, loquat, thyme, lemon, orange and tangerine from Sicily.

mignaculis [min-**ya**-cu-lis] pasta used in soup (Friuli).

Minni di virgini ('Virgins' breasts'), conical pastries filled with sweet custard, on a pastrycook's counter in Sambuca di Sicilia.

miglio [**mil**-yo] millet.

milanese, alla [mi-la-**ne**-ze]
1. cooked with beef marrow, white wine, saffron and PARMESAN (RISOTTO); 2. breaded veal schnitzel, see COSTOLETTA.

millefanti [mil-le-**fan**-ti] tiny strands of pasta served in broth.

millefoglie [mil-le-**fol**-ye] puff pastry, millefeuille.

milza [**milt**-sa] spleen.

minestra, minestrone [mi-ne-stra, mi-ne-**stro**-ne] a thick soup, usually made with vegetables though it may contain meat or poultry and be based on either a vegetable or meat stock. Rice, pasta or another staple is often used to augment it. The word is derived from the Latin *ministrare*, to serve, and therefore means simply 'that which is served', appropriate given its variety of incarnations, the recipe being usually based on what is in the larder.

minni di virgini [**min**-ni di **vir**-ji-ni] 'virgins' breasts': in Sicily, delicate breast-shaped pies from Sambuca di Sicilia with a filling of confectioner's custard, bits of chocolate and candied pumpkin; in Catania they become *minni di Sant'Aita*, 'St Agatha's breasts', small ricotta-filled, almond-flavoured sponge cakes, covered

with lemon icing and a glacé
cherry, prepared in February for
the feast of the patron St Agatha,
whose breasts were torn off
during her martyrdom.

minuich [mi-nu-**eek**] tubular
pasta from Puglia and Basilicata,
similar to MACCHERONI. Also
known as *minnicchi*.

mirtilli [mir-**til**-li] bilberries,
blueberries.

mirto [**mir**-to] myrtle.

mirtù [mir-**too**] a Sardinian
myrtleberry DIGESTIVO.

mischiglio [mis-**kil**-yo] pasta
from Basilicata, traditionally
made from barley, chickpea,
broad bean and oat flours mixed
with wheat.

missoltini [mis-sol-**ti**-ni] sun-
or wind-dried AGONI from Lake
Como, a little like kippers.

misticanza [mis-ti-**cant**-sa]
mixed leaf salad.

misto/a [**mis**-to] mixed.

Mistrà [mis-**tra**] an aniseed-
flavoured liqueur, a good
AMMAZZACAFFÈ. A reliable Mistrà
is made by Varnelli, from the
Marche.

mocetta [mo-**chet**-ta] cured
beef salami (traditionally
chamois), made in the Valle

d'Aosta.

moddizzosu [mod-dits-**zo**-su]
a soft FOCACCIA-type bread from
southern Sardinia.

Modica [**mo**-di-ca] town in
southeast Sicily famed for its
chocolate, first introduced by
the Spanish in the 16th century
and still manufactured using the
technique of grinding the beans
with sugar on a stone palette,
without heating. This gives a
characteristic grainy consistency.

moeche [mo-**e**-ke] see MOLECA.

moleca [mo-**le**-ca] (pl. *moleche*,
also *moeche*). Crabs caught in
the Venetian lagoon towards
the end of April when they are
changing their shells, which are
therefore soft and succulent.
The crabs are deep-fried whole
in olive oil.

Molinara [mo-li-**na**-ra] red
grape used as part of the
VALPOLICELLA and BARDOLINO
blends of Northern Italy.

Molise [mo-li-ze] the second-
smallest Italian region
(after Valle d'Aosta), mainly
mountainous with a short
coastline (40km) on the
Adriatic. Its gastronomic
heritage is firmly rooted in its

pastoral history, and has much in common with that of Abruzzo (the two were a single region until the mid-1960s). There is a wide variety of sheep's milk cheese and an abundant use of chilli in the preservation and cooking of meat.

molle [mol-le] soft.

mollica di pane [mol-li-ca di pa-ne] breadcrumbs.

molluschi [mol-lus-ki] shellfish.

molo [mo-lo] whiting, a fish similar to (but smaller than) hake.

mondeghili [mon-de-ghee-li] Milanese meatballs, made of stale breadcrumbs, minced roast or boiled meat, sausage, liver sausage, garlic and parmesan or GRANA, formed into patties with the help of a little milk, and fried in butter.

Monica [mo-ni-ca] Sardinian red grape producing light-coloured medium-flavoured reds.

Montalcino [mon-tal-chee-no] town in Tuscany famed for its wine. See BRUNELLO.

Montasio [mon-ta-zi-o] an alpine cow's milk cheese made in the Friuli region.

montasù [mon-ta-soo] a soft, mild-tasting bread roll with an almost creamy-textured crust and scroll-like ends, typical of Venice.

montebianco [mon-te-bi-an-co] a famous Italian dessert made with chestnut pulp and cream.

Montenegro see AMARO.

Montepulciano [mon-te-pul-cha-no] red-wine grape used to produce the fruity, intense Montepulciano d'Abruzzo. It is a grape variety and not to be confused with the Tuscan town of Montepulciano, known for its Vino Nobile.

montone [mon-to-ne] mutton.

mora [mo-ra] blackberry (pl. *more*).

morchella [mor-kel-la] morel mushroom (pl. *morchelle*).

morena [mo-re-na] see MURENA.

Morlacco [mor-lac-co] also known as *morlac*, a creamy cow's milk cheese from the northern Veneto.

moro [mo-ro] blood orange.

mortadella [mor-ta-del-la] a very large, smoked, sweetish, aromatic pork sausage from Bologna and Emilia-Romagna, flavoured with black pepper, myrtle berries, nutmeg, coriander and pistachio nuts; a favourite sandwich filling for summer picnics. *Mortadella di Campotosto* is a hard pork SALUME from the Abruzzo, popularly known as *coglioni di mulo* ('mule's testicles').

morzeddhu SEE MURSEDDU.

moscardino [mos-car-**dee**-no] 1. the musky octopus; 2. a dormouse, eaten with relish in the time of APICIUS (roasted with honey and spices).

Moscato [mos-**ca**-to] the Muscat grape, used mainly to make sparkling or sweet wines. There are many varieties, and

Dessert plate of apple *mostarda* and GRANA PADANO cheese, the way it is served in Mantua, Lombardy.

man has been vinifying them for a long time. The legendary King Midas, who was said to be able to turn everything to gold, apparently drank Muscat. The main varieties grown in Italy are *Moscato bianco* and *Moscato giallo*. The first is grown in Piedmont (where it is used in ASTI SPUMANTE) and the second in Trentino-Alto Adige, where it is used to produce dessert wines. Moscato wines are also produced in Sicily, for example Moscato di Noto (the *Pollium* mentioned by Pliny).

mosciame [mo-**sha**-me] also spelled *mosciamme* and *musciamme*. Originally a cut of dried dolphin meat; today tuna has replaced dolphin.

mostaccioli [mos-**ta**-cho-li] diamond-shaped biscuits, originally cooked with grape must. Today they are often coated in chocolate.

mostarda [mos-**tar**-da] a chutney, made with fruit in mustard-flavoured syrup. A famous example is *Mostarda di Cremona*, from the city of that name in Lombardy. *Mostarda* is typically served with cold boiled meats or hard cheese. NB: *mostarda* is not the Italian for mustard. That is *senape*.

mostardella [mos-tar-**del**-la] a Ligurian beef and pork SALUME.

mosto [**mos**-to] grape must. *Mosto cotto*, lit. 'cooked must', is must that has been heat-reduced to a thick syrup. It forms the basic ingredient for several traditional sweets made for the Feast of the Dead (*Festa dei Morti*) on the 2nd of November, All Souls.

motzetta [mots-**zet**-ta] cured meat, originally mountain goat (see MOCETTA). Nowadays other meats are used. *Motzetta bovina* is cured beef.

mozzarella [mots-za-**rel**-la] a soft, white cheese made from the milk of water buffaloes and preserved in brine. When fresh, the centre is a delectable mix of crumbly and runny textures. It is never rubbery.

'mpanatigghi [im-pa-na-**tig**-ghi] Sicilian pastries from MODICA, filled with nuts, chocolate, sugar, spices and beef.

'mparrettati [im-pa-ret-**ta**-ti] long pasta straws.

muggine [**mu**-ji-ne] grey mullet.

mula [**mu**-la] pork SALUME from Piedmont.

Murazzano [mu-rat-**za**-no] soft, mainly sheep's milk cheese from the Langhe in Piedmont.

murena [mu-**re**-na] the moray eel.

murice [**mu**-ri-che] the murex, a shellfish prized in antiquity as the source of purple dye for imperial robes. *Murici* are eaten today as an ANTIPASTO or with pasta.

murseddu [mur-**sed**-du] also *mursiello, morzeddhu*, Calabrian stewed tripe.

mustica [**mu**-sti-ca] a Calabrian pâté of salted baby sardines and chilli, used for BRUSCHETTA.

muschiata [mus-ki-**a**-ta] the muscovy duck.

muscisca [mu-**shi**-sca] a Puglian speciality consisting of air-dried strips of pork, mutton or beef (formerly goat), well seasoned.

muscolo [**mus**-co-lo] stewing meat from the hind leg.

musèt, musetto [mu-**zet**, mu-**zet**-to] a sausage made of meat from the pig's head (Friuli-

Venezia Giulia).

nasello [na-**zel**-lo] hake.

nastrini [nas-**tri**-ni] 'ribbons', a
pasta shape.

natalin, natalini [na-ta-**lin**,
na-ta-**li**-ni] the 'Christmas
macaroni' of Genoa, long,
smooth PENNE served in broth.

navoni [na-**vo**-ni] turnips.

'ncapriata see INCAPRIATA.

'ncip 'nciap [in-**chip** in-**chap**]
in the Marche, lamb, chicken or
rabbit cut small and braised in a
stewpan.

'ndocca 'ndocca [in-**doc**-ca
in-**doc**-ca] from Teramo in
Abruzzo, a stew of cheap cuts of
pig, including the blood.

'ndugghia see INDUGGHIA.

'nduja [in-**doo**-ya] Calabrian
spreadable sausage made of
pork offal and chilli.

Nebbiola [neb-bi-**o**-la]
Piedmontese grape, one of the
most venerated Italian varieties,
used in BAROLO and BARBARESCO.
The name Nebbiolo means 'little
fog' and refers to the autumn
mists characteristic of the area.

Negroamaro [ne-gro-a-**ma**-ro]
red-wine grape from Puglia used
to produce dark, rustic wines
such as Salice Salentino.

Negroni [ne-**gro**-ni] a cocktail
of gin, vermouth and bitters,
typically CAMPARI. A *Negroni
sbagliato*, a 'bungled Negroni',
is made with PROSECCO instead
of gin.

nepitella [ne-pi-**tel**-la] calamint.

nepitelle [ne-pi-**tel**-le] little
pastry pies filled with nuts and
figs (Calabria)

nero/a [**ne**-ro] black.

Nero d'Avola [**ne**-ro **da**-vo-
la] a red-wine grape native to
southeast Sicily, used to make
rich, plummy wines.

nero di seppia [**ne**-ro di **sep**-
pi-a] cuttlefish ink.

nervetti [ner-**vet**-ti] boiled calf
sinews and ligaments, served
as a snack or salad or as an
ANTIPASTO.

nespola [**ne**-spo-la] loquat,
Japanese plum or medlar.

nettarina [net-ta-**ri**-na]
nectarine.

'nfigghiulata [in-fig-yu-**la**-ta]
a kind of Sicilian pasty, filled
either with sweetened RICOTTA,
or, in the savoury version, with
cheese, sausage and PANCETTA.

'ngritoli [in-**gri**-to-li] a PASTINA
from Lazio.

nidi [**ni**-di] 'nests'.

nocchette [noc-**ket**-te] 1. baked dried figs stuffed with walnuts or almonds (Calabria); 2. a kind of FARFALLE.

nocciola [no-**cho**-la] a hazelnut (pl. *nocciole*).

noce [**no**-che] 1. walnut (pl. *noci*); 2: a cut of meat from the top of the leg.

noce di cocco [**no**-che di **coc**-co] coconut.

noce moscata [**no**-che mos-**ca**-ta] nutmeg.

nocepesca [**no**-che **pes**-ca] nectarine.

Nocino [no-**chi**-no] bittersweet liqueur that purists insist should be made from green walnuts picked by barefooted, bareheaded virgins from Emilia-Romagna on the night of 23rd June, the eve of the feast of St John the Baptist. In the real world Nocino is produced as far afield as New Zealand and the Napa Valley with minimal emphasis placed on either chastity or the cult of St John.

nodini di vitello [no-**di**-ni di vi-**tel**-lo] veal rib chops.

Norcia [**nor**-cha] town in Umbria known for its pork products and its truffles. A butcher's shop is often still called a *norcineria*.

Norma, alla [**nor**-ma] *pasta alla Norma* is a dish created in Catania for the première of Bellini's *Norma* (1831). It consists of spaghetti or macaroni with a sauce of fresh tomato and basil, topped with fried aubergines and coarsely shredded *ricotta salata* cheese. Though he had in mind the appropriately named soprano Giuditta Pasta when he created the title role, Bellini's opera is about love, betrayal and filial loyalty rather than gastronomic ecstasy.

nostrano, nostrale [nos-**tra**-no, nos-**tra**-le] local, e.g. *vino nostrano*: local wine.

novello [no-**vel**-lo] of wine, young, of the new vintage, comparable to the French Beaujolais Nouveau.

'nsacaragatti see FRASCARELLI.

'ntruppicc [in-**trup**-pitch] (Basilicata) a RAGÙ of finely diced pork and lamb.

nuglia see INDUGGHIA.

nunnatu [nun-**na**-tu] in Sicily and Calabria, tiny fish that have only just reached maturity

(the word means 'new-born';
neonato). They are usually
served deep-fried or as fritters.

nuraghe [nu-**ra**-ghe] a conical
megalithic tower house
constructed by the prehistoric
Nuragic tribes of Sardinia.
The name *nuraghe*, *nuraghi*, or
nuraghes is commonly found in
Sicilian dishes, e.g. *zuppa dei
Nuraghi*.

Nuragus [nu-**ra**-gus] light
white-wine grape from southern
Sardinia.

'nzuddi [in-**zud**-di] in Catania
and Messina, chewy almond
biscuits for the Feast of the Dead
(2nd Nov), traditionally made
by the cloistered nuns.

oca [**o**-ca] goose.

occhio di bue [**oc**-ki-o di **bu**-e]
1. a fried egg (lit. 'bull's eye'); 2.
a shortcake biscuit with a jam
centre.

occhi di lupo [**oc**-ki di **lu**-po]
'wolf's eyes', a smooth, tubular
pasta. The size of the cut can
vary, and so can the name: *occhi
di elefante* '(elephant's eyes')
are large tubes; *occhi di passero*
('sparrow's eyes') are tiny ones.

occhiata [oc-ki-**a**-ta] a species of
sea bream.

odori [o-**do**-ri] lit. 'scents', by
association, herbs.

offelle [of-**fel**-le] 1. oval-shaped
shortbread biscuits made with
olive oil instead of butter; 2.
jam-filled shortbread tarts; 3.
in Friuli-Venezia Giulia, RAVIOLI
filled with sausage and spinach.

olio [**o**-li-o] oil; *olio di oliva* =
olive oil (*see box overleaf*).

olio santo [o-li-o **san**-to] literally
'holy oil': olive oil imbued with
chilli.

olive [o-**li**-ve] olives, the fruits
of the olive tree, pickled in
brine to make them edible. *Olive
ascolane* (or *all'ascolana*), with a
meat stuffing, dipped in egg and
breadcrumbs and deep fried, are
a speciality of the Marche.

olivette [o-li-**vet**-te] 1. little
olives; 2. in Catania (Sicily),
tiny balls of green pistachio
marzipan made on the feast of St
Agatha (5th Feb). While being
dragged to her martyrdom, it
is said she insisted on fastening
her sandal, and an olive tree
sprang up on the spot.

omaso [o-**ma**-zo] tripe.

ombelichi di venere [om-
be-**li**-ki de **ve**-ne-re] 'navels of
Venus', TORTELLINI.

Olive oil

Olive groves have been planted throughout the Mediterranean since ancient times, though planting and production in Italy became increasingly intensive and systematic under Roman domination. This partly explains why the Sabine hills in Lazio outside Rome remain Italy's most revered and widely publicised source of fine oils, though it would be a mistake to ignore the many regional oil varieties. Oil is like wine, varying enormously in taste from area to area.

Olives, like grapes, are fruit, and as such they take on characteristics determined by soil, climate and the manner in which they are cared for: Ligurian oils are delicate, Calabrian pungent, Tuscan robust and so on. Competition from other oil-producing countries is strong, but in 2015 an international jury voted three Sicilian farms, all from the area of Syracuse (La Tonda, Terraliva and Agrestis), as producing the finest olive oil in the world. The publisher Slow Food Editore releases an annual guide, *La Guida agli Extravergini*, in which hundreds of Italian oils are reviewed having been tasted by a panel of experts.

The terms 'extra virgin' and 'virgin' refer to the acidity of an oil, extra virgin having no more than 0.8 percent acidity and virgin oil no more than 2 percent. These oils are known as cold-pressed oils, 'cold' because they have not been subjected to the various refining processes essential in mass production, all of which require heat. Heat destroys flavour, which is why a cold pressed extra-virgin or virgin oil from a respected FRANTOIO, replete with a unique regional flavour, is so highly prized. Extra-virgin olive oil is referred to as '*olio evo*' in lists of ingredients.

ombra [**om**-bra] a small glass of wine. The name is said to derive from Venice, where wine sellers set up their stalls in the shadow (*ombra*) of the bell-tower of San Marco. An ombra is traditionally taken with a *ciccheto*, or perhaps several CICCHETI.

ombrina [om-**bri**-na] the bearded umbrine or shi drum

(*Ombrina cirrosa*), a fish slightly similar to sea bass.

ombrina leccia [om-**bri**-na le-cha] the leerfish.

omelette [o-me-**let**-te] a French-style omelette, fried and folded over on itself.

omento [o-**men**-to] caul, the fatty membrane enclosing the intestines of an animal. Also known as *rete* ('net'), it is used for wrapping FEGATELLI.

onda, all' [on-da] of RISOTTO, cooked so that it is neither stiff nor sloppy, and the surface can be made to peak, like a wave ('*onda*').

opa [o-pa] southern name for BOGA.

orata [o-**ra**-ta] gilt-head bream. In Venetian dialect, *orada*.

orecchiette [o-rec-**yet**-te] little ears', a pasta shape.

origano [o-**ri**-ga-no] oregano.

Ornellaia [or-nel-**la**-ya] dry red wine from BOLGHERI, one of the SUPERTUSCANS, made using Bordeaux grape varieties.

orsetti [or-**set**-ti] 'little bears', a pasta or biscuit shape for children.

Orvieto [or-vi-**e**-to] town in Umbria known for its wine. See

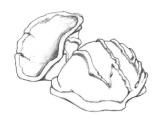

Orecchiette, 'little ears' of pasta.

GRECHETTO.

orzata [ort-**sa**-ta] barley water, almond-milk.

orzo [ort-so] 1. barley. A *caffè d'orzo* is a coffee substitute made with barley, originating from days when coffee was scarce and expensive but now quite popular and offered in most cafés; 2. PASTINA shaped like barley grains, used in soups and salads.

osei [o-**ze**-i] in northern Italian dialect (Lombardy and the Veneto) songbirds, such as the lark or thrush, traditionally served with POLENTA. Shooting and trapping restrictions have meant that nowadays the dish is undergoing a metamorphosis as a dessert. Don't be surprised to see *polenta e osei* served as a mound of sweetened dough topped by chocolate birds. See also UCCELLI SCAPPATI.

ostia [os-ti-a] a wafer. The term derives from the 'Host', or Communion bread.

ossobuco [os-so-**boo**-co] a Milanese speciality, known in dialect as *oss buss*. It consists of sliced veal shank, on the bone with the bone marrow still inside. The name means 'hollow bone' (*osso* = bone, *buco* = hole). True *ossobuco* is cooked *in bianco* (without tomatoes), is braised slowly and flavoured with GREMOLADA towards the end of cooking.

osteria [os-te-**ri**-a] tavern or inn, a simple restaurant.

ostrica [**os**-tri-ca] oyster (pl. *ostriche*). In Venice an oyster is an *ostrega* (pl. *ostreghe*).

ova chi curcuci [o-va ki **coor**-cu-chi] eggs and pork rind fried in dripping (Calabria).

ovino [o-**vi**-no] sheep.

paccheri [**pac**-ker-i] short, fat pasta tubes from Naples, stuffed or served with RAGÙ.

paciugo [pa-**choo**-go] *paciugo di gelato* is an ice cream 'mess' from Liguria, a combination of ice creams of various flavours,

fresh or dried fruit and Morello-cherry syrup.

paccasassi [pac-ca-**sas**-si] in the Marche, a name for rock samphire. See FINOCCHIO MARINO.

paccozze [pac-**cot**-se] in Molise, egg-pasta sheets the size of one's palm (*pacca* = slap), cooked in milk and served with a lamb RAGÙ; a special-occasions dish.

padella [pa-**del**-la] frying pan.

Pagadebit [pa-ga-de-**bit**] light, delicate white wine from Emilia Romagna, made in still and sparkling versions. The name, 'pay your debts', refers to the reliable yields of the grape from which it is made, Bombino bianco, meaning a farmer never had to worry about his revenues.

pagaro [**pa**-ga-ro] red porgy, a type of sea bream.

pagello [pa-**jel**-lo] pandora, a type of sea bream.

paglia e fieno [**pal**-ya e fi-**e**-no] literally, 'straw and hay', a combination of white and green, e.g. TAGLIATELLE made with and without spinach.

pagnotta [pan-**yot**-ta] a loaf of bread. A small one is a *pagnottina*.

pagro [pa-gro] see PAGARO.

pajata [pa-ya-ta] a Roman dish featuring the intestines of an unweaned calf. The milk is left inside and cooked with the intestines, which are chopped

---

Palermo street food

Palermitans are blessed with a superb climate and they love to spend their evenings strolling along, talking to friends and eating at the same time, either in the form of a hefty sandwich, or tasty titbits from a cone of twisted brown paper. It could be boiled octopus (*purpo*); wild artichokes fried in batter (*carduna*); boiled veal offal (*quarume*; meaning 'hot dish', it consists of veal intestines, cartilage and other normally inedible bits, cut up small, cooked with carrots, celery, onions and parsley, dressed with salt, pepper, oil and lemon); olives (*alive*), the black ones dressed simply with dry chilli flakes, the green with coarsely chopped celery, carrot, garlic, parsley and fresh chilli; soft pizza (*sfinciuni*); grilled lamb or kid intestines (*stigghiole*); chickpea fritters (*panelle*); beef spleen in a bread roll (*pani ca' meusa*), sometimes with the addition of ricotta (*pani ca' meusa maritata*); crunchy fried pork crackling and gristle (*frittola*); boiled muzzle of lamb or beef (*musso*), lamb's cheeks (*masciddaru*), or cartilage and sinews from lamb's feet and ankles (*carcagnola*), these last three rather rubbery specialities are usually sold together. These are all very ancient foods, spurned from the rich man's table, and may sound strange to our ears—but when the smoky, aromatic effluvia reach us as we approach the stalls, they become absolutely irresistible. Palermo is not only a city of street food, however; it is also a place where elaborate dishes invented for the 18th–19th-century aristocracy by their French chefs (*monsù*) are still prepared, in all their eye-goggling splendour, and where the cloistered nuns who once spent endless days and even nights creating superb cakes and sweets, especially at Easter-time, still do so—for our delight.

up and served with RIGATONI and a tomato sauce.

Palermo [pa-**ler**-mo] the capital of Sicily, renowned for its street food (*see box on previous page*).

palline [pal-**li**-ne] small pasta pellets, suitable for long cooking.

palline di riso [pal-**li**-ne di **ri**-zo] rice balls, a variant on ARANCINI

pallott' [pal-**lot**] fried cheese balls (Rome and Abruzzo).

palomba, palombaccio [pa-**lom**-ba, pa-lom-**bat**-cho] wood pigeon.

palombo [pa-**lom**-bo] dogfish.

palumma [pa-**loom**-ma] in Sicily, a pigeon.

pampanella [pam-pa-**nel**-la] 1. a fresh goat's or cow's milk cheese, traditionally served on fig leaves (Abruzzo); 2. a spicy pork dish (Molise).

pancetta [pan-**chet**-ta] salt-cured pork belly, either smoked (*affumicata*) or unsmoked.

pancotto [pan-**cot**-to] 'cooked bread', a soup, with different ingredients according to region, but always based on stale bread.

pan di Spagna [**pan** di **span**-ya] sponge cake.

pandolce [pan-**dol**-che] a soft sweet bread made with raisins, pine nuts and candied peel; a fruit loaf.

pandoro, pan d'oro [pan-do-ro] a soft cake, rich in butter, shaped like a flat-topped cone, popular around Christmas and New Year. Originally from Verona but widely produced throughout Italy.

pane [**pa**-ne] bread, a very serious matter in Italy, where people eat more bread than anywhere else in Europe. Every region has its own specialities. The finest are said to be Altamura (DOP) from Puglia; Genzano (IGP) from a village on the outskirts of Rome; Matera (IGP) from Basilicata; and *pagnotta del Dittaino* (DOP) from Sicily.

pane di Spagna see PAN DI SPAGNA.

pane dorato [**pa**-ne do-**ra**-to] literally, 'gilded bread': eggy bread (like French toast but not sweet) or fried bread.

pane grattugiatto [**pa**-ne grat-tu-**ja**-to] 'grated bread'; breadcrumbs.

pane raffermo [**pa**-ne ra-**fer**-

mo] stale bread, the basis of many traditional recipes.

panelle [pa-**nel**-le] Sicilian chickpea fritters.

panera genovese [pa-ne-ra je-no-**ve**-ze] strong coffee-flavoured soft ice cream.

panettone [pa-net-**to**-ne] the well-known Milanese brioche-style loaf, filled with candied fruit and peel and traditionally eaten at Christmas. The name simply means 'big loaf' but a legend has grown up attributing the name to a certain Toni, a scullion in the household of Duke Lodovico Sforza in the 15th century. During an elaborate banquet the planned dessert was overcooked and spoiled. The resourceful Toni threw together a hotchpotch of bread, butter, candied fruit and raisins. The result, served with some trepidation by the butler, was ecstatically received by Lodovico's guests.

panforte [pan-**for**-te] a dense cake filled with dried fruits, nuts and spices, a speciality in Tuscany, particularly Siena.

pangiallo [pan-**jal**-lo] 'yellow' bread, a rich fruitcake from Lazio made with raisins, nuts and spices.

panino [pa-**ni**-no] a small bread roll; by association, a sandwich (pl. *panini*).

panissa [pa-**nis**-sa] 1. in Liguria a kind of POLENTA made of chickpea flour; 2. in Piedmont a risotto with pork and beans.

pan melato [pan-me-**la**-to] a kind of gingerbread, or spiced honey buns.

panelle [pa-**nel**-le] Sicilian chickpea fritters.

pani ca' meusa [pa-ni ca me-**oo**-za] beef spleen served in a bread roll (Sicily).

panna [**pan**-na] cream; *panna montata* = whipped cream.

panna cotta [pan-na-**cot**-ta] 'cooked cream', a popular dessert made by simmering cream, sugar and vanilla, adding gelatin, and pouring into moulds to set.

pannerone [pan-ne-**ro**-ne] creamy cow's milk cheese with a texture similar to GORGONZOLA.

panpepato [pan-pe-**pa**-to] a heavy cake similar to PANFORTE but with the addition of chocolate and black pepper (hence *pepato*; 'peppered'). It is

Small nub of Parmigiano Reggiano, with the bold stencilling on the rind that proves its authenticity.

traditionally claimed by Ferrara but is served throughout Italy during Christmas and Epiphany.

pansotti [pan-**sot**-ti] Ligurian pasta triangles often stuffed with chard and served in a walnut sauce (*salsa di noci*).

panunta [pa-**noon**-ta] stale or dry bread rubbed with olive oil and garlic. Also known as FETT'UNTA.

panuria, in [pa-**noo**-ri-a] breaded.

panzanella [pant-za-**nel**-la] a simple, tasty Tuscan salad of stale bread softened in water, onions, basil and tomatoes dressed with oil and wine vinegar. The tricolor effect of white bread, red tomatoes and green basil imparts a patriotic air to the dish. Count Bettino RICASOLI is said to have served *panzanella* to King Vittorio Emanuele II in 1865, during a royal visit to the Ricasoli estates.

panzerotti [pant-ze-**rot**-ti] filled, deep-fried pasties.

papalina [pa-pa-**lee**-na] sprat (pl. *papaline*).

papero [**pa**-pe-ro] duck.

pappa [**pap**-pa] mush, pottage; in Tuscany, *pappa al pomodoro* is a version of PANCOTTO in which stale sourdough bread is cooked with tomatoes, celery, carrots, onion and basil until it becomes a thick soup.

pappardelle [pap-par-**del**-le] strips or ribbons of egg pasta typically served with a meat or mushroom sauce. Known as *paparele* in the Veneto and *paspadelle* in the Marche.

pappare [pap-**pa**-re] to gobble or 'nosh' in Tuscan dialect.

pappicci [pap-**pi**-chi] sturdy

noodles from the Abruzzo, typically served in a simple tomato sauce with grated cheese.

parago [pa-ra-go] see PAGARO.

paranza [pa-**ran**-za] or *paranzola*, a small rock fish of several varieties, served very fresh, doused in flour and fried.

pardulas [par-**du**-las] sun-shaped sweet cheese cakes from Sardinia, served at Easter and similar to the Greek *kaltsounia*.

Parma [**par**-ma] town in Emilia-Romagna which gives its name to parmesan cheese and Parma ham (see PARMIGIANO and PROSCIUTTO). Acqua di Parma is also a local product, but it is a violet-scented cologne, not a kind of mineral water.

parmesan see PARMIGIANO.

parmigiana [par-mi-**ja**-na] *melanzane alla parmigiana* are layers of sliced fried aubergine, tomato sauce and cheese, baked in the oven.

Parmigiano Reggiano [par-mi-**ja**-no red-**ja**-no] Parmesan, the well-known and liberally-used flaky, hard cow's milk cheese, often grated over pasta but also eaten in shavings with PROSCIUTTO, drizzled with oil.

Genuine *Parmigiano Reggiano* is produced only from cows raised within a defined geographical area and 16 litres of full-cream milk are needed for every kilo of cheese. The cows eat locally-grown feed and no artificial fermenting agents are used to make the cheese. Certified and attested cheese will have the DOP markings on the rind.

partenopea, alla [par-te-no-pe-a] Neapolitan style, from Parthenope, the ancient Greek colony that preceded Naples.

pasimata [pa-zi-**ma**-ta] a Tuscan Easter cake, filled with raisins, a kind of giant hot cross bun; in Lucca they make a savoury version flavoured with aniseed.

passara [**pas**-sa-ra] see PASSERA.

passata [pas-**sa**-ta] a purée, e.g. *passata di pomodoro*.

passatelli [pas-sa-**tel**-li] thick spaghetti made of breadcrumbs, egg and parmesan, shaped by squeezing the dough through a special crusher like a giant garlic press, then cooked in broth; a speciality of central Marche.

passato/a [pas-**sa**-to] mashed.

passera [**pas**-se-ra] flounder. Also known as *passara, passarin*

(Venice), *passera pianuzza* [**pas**-se-ra pi-a-**noot**-sa]

passito [pas-**si**-to] a sweet wine made from grapes that are left to wither on racks before being pressed, thus increasing the sugar content of the must.

passoline [pas-so-**li**-ne] currants.

pasta [**pas**-ta]. The quintessential Italian staple: dough made with a variety of flours mixed with water, sometimes also using egg, the basis of an infinite variety of dishes. More than 500 different kinds of pasta are made, but there are even more names, because they vary from region to region.

pasta corta [**cor**-ta] *see Pasta basics, below.*

pasta e fagioli [**pas**-ta e fa-**jo**-li] a soup of pasta and haricot beans, typical of the Veneto.

pasta filata [fi-la-ta] not pasta, but a cheese-making technique resulting in strings or *file* [**fi**-le], as in MOZZARELLA or PROVOLONE.

pasta frolla [**frol**-la] shortcrust pastry.

pasta grattata, pasta grattugiata [grat-**ta**-ta, grat-tu-**ja**-ta] tiny pasta fragments made by forcing dough through a grater and crumbling it into tiny pieces.

pasta lunga [**loon**-ga] *see Pasta basics, below.*

pasta reale [re-a-le] literally 'royal' pasta, which can be either 1. marzipan; or 2. dumplings

---

Pasta basics

Pasta comes in many variations of the basic forms, which are *pasta lunga* ('long' pastas such as SPAGHETTI and TAGLIATELLE), *pasta corta* ('short', shaped or moulded pastas such as FARFALLE or PENNE) and *pasta ripiena* (filled pastas such as RAVIOLI). Italians call main course pasta dishes *pastasciutta*, 'dry' pasta, to distinguish them from *pasta in brodo*, pasta of a smaller cut and design used in soups: tiny pasta of the kind commonly used in soup is known as *pastina*. *Pasta all'uovo* is made with egg. *Pasta integrale* is wholemeal pasta.

served in broth.

pasta ripiena [ri-pi-**e**-na] *see Pasta basics, opposite.*

pasta sfoglia [**sfol**-ya] puff pastry.

pasta strappata [strap-**pa**-ta] 'torn' pasta, shredded roughly into the cooking pot.

pasta verde [**ver**-de] green pasta, the dough mixed with chopped or puréed spinach.

pastarazzi [pa-sta-**rat**-si] either professionals who take photographs of food for magazines; or amateur bloggers who obsessively post photos of their dinners on social media.

pastasciutta [pas-ta-**shoot**-ta] *see Pasta basics, above.*

paste di mandorle [**pas**-te di **man**-dor-le] delicate pastries made with ground almonds instead of flour.

pastella [pas-**tel**-la] batter.

pasticceria [pas-ti-che-**ri**-a] confectioner's shop, confectionery.

pasticcino [pas-ti-**chi**-no] cake, pastry, tart (pl. *pasticcini*).

pasticcio [pas-**ti**-cho] a pie, in the sense of a shepherd's pie; an oven-baked dish of mixed ingredients, often including pasta. In Venice, *pasticcio di pesce* is pasta baked with fish or served with a fish sauce.

pastiera [pas-ti-**e**-ra] a RICOTTA pie, often with currants or candied fruit, typical of Naples.

pastina [pas-**ti**-na] *see Pasta basics, above.*

pastinaca [pas-ti-**na**-ca] parsnip (pl. *pastinache*).

pastine minute [pas-**ti**-ne mi-**nu**-te] very fine PASTINA.

pastissada [pas-tis-**sa**-da] a stew of the Veneto region, either of horsemeat (*pastissada de caval*), beef (*manzo*) or donkey (*musso*), served with GNOCCHI or POLENTA.

pasto [**pas**-to] a meal, c.f. the English 'repast'; hence *antipasto*, 'before the meal', an *hors d'oeuvre*.

pasutice [pa-**su**-ti-che] wide noodles from Istria, usually served with mussels or cod.

patacuc [pa-ta-**kook**] also known as CRESC' TAJAT, diamond-shaped pasta made with a mixture of corn and wheat flours, often served with beans or with courgettes and fresh cheese.

patanabò [pa-ta-na-**bo**]

Jerusalem artichoke, called thus in Alessandria; elsewhere in Italy, *topinambur*.

patate [pa-**ta**-te] potatoes (sing. *patata*). *Patate fritte* are French fries; *patate novelle* are new potatoes.

patatine [pa-ta-**ti**-ne] crisps, potato chips.

patèca [pa-**te**-ca] watermelon (various dialects).

patellette [pa-tel-**let**-te] flat pasta pieces from Abruzzo often served with a sauce of onions and PANCETTA, or tomato and anchovies.

Paternoster [pa-ter **nos**-ter] the Our Father, a short prayer, traditionally recited to time the cooking of pasta in the days before people had clocks. By association, the pasta itself, typically a short macaroni.

pauro [**pa**-u-ro] see PAGARO.

Pavese, zuppa alla [**tsup**-pa al-la pa-**ve**-ze] a broth with bread, cheese and an egg in the centre, supposedly served to Francis I of France by a poor peasant woman of Pavia in the 16th century. The king was so impressed that he took the recipe back to France.

A *penna* (pl. *penne*), a pasta 'quill'.

pearà [pe-a-ra] see LESSO; a vegetable sauce from Verona, unique to the region and of which the city is extremely proud.

pecora [**pe**-co-ra] mutton.

pecorino [pe-co-**ri**-no] the generic term for hard cheeses made from sheep's milk, of which there are many, varying greatly in flavour and texture and subject to rigorous classification. One of the best known is the DOP *Pecorino romano*, a clean, sharp cheese made in Lazio and parts of Tuscany. *Pecorino sardo* is a strong-tasting Sardinian version. *Pecorino siciliano* is particularly pungent and is studded with grains of black pepper.

pecorone [pe-co-**ro**-ne] 1. a large sheep; 2. a brand of PECORINO from Puglia, marketed as *il pecorino del ghiottone* ('glutton's *pecorino*).

pelati [pe-**la**-ti] peeled tomatoes.

pencarelli [pen-ca-**rel**-li] long, thick spaghetti-like pasta. Also known as *pincarelli*.

penchi [**pen**-ki] wide, flat pasta noodles from Umbria, traditionally served with crumbled sausage and GUANCIALE.

penne [**pen**-ne] 'quills', famous tubular PASTA CORTA distinctively cut on the bias at both ends. *Penne lisce* [**li**-she] are smooth-sided *penne* (not ridged).

pennoni [pen-**no**-ni] large PENNE, also known as *penne a candela*.

pentola [**pen**-to-la] saucepan or cooking pot. Dishes are sometimes described as being *alla pentola*, a term suggestive of home cooking.

peoci [pe-o-chi] mussels (Venetian). The singular is *peocio*. *Peoci in cassopipa* is a dish of mussels steamed with onion, garlic and parsley.

pepata di cozze [pe-**pa**-ta di **cots**-ze] mussels poached in white wine with black pepper.

pepato [pe-**pa**-to] sharp Sicilian PECORINO with black peppercorns.

pepe [**pe**-pe] pepper.

pepe verde [**pe**-pe **ver**-de] green pepper.

peperata [pe-pe-**ra**-ta] a sauce made of thickened beef stock, white wine, butter and pepper.

peperonata [pe-pe-ro-**na**-ta] peppers (often sweet red) braised or sautéed with onion, garlic and tomato.

peperoncino [pe-pe-ron-**chi**-no] the red chilli pepper. Originally introduced to Europe by Columbus, it is a much-loved ingredient in Italian regional cuisine, the best being grown in Calabria and Basilicata. Also known as *diavolillo*, and in Sicily as *pipi ardenti*.

peperone [pe-pe-**ro**-ne] (pl. *peperoni*) red, green or yellow peppers; bell peppers; capsicum.

peposo [pe-**po**-zo] a Tuscan stew of CHIANINA beef cooked slowly in CHIANTI wine with a large quantity of crushed black peppercorns. Peposo was said to be the favourite food of Brunelleschi, who build the dome of Florence cathedral.

pera [**pe**-ra] pear (pl. *pere*).

perchia [**per**-ki-a] perch.

perciatelli [per-cha-**tel**-li] thick strands of spaghetti-like pasta with a hole down the middle.

perlaggio [per-**lad**-jo] from the French *perlage*, the size and longevity of bubbles in sparkling wine. A fine wine has plenty of tiny, rapidly-rising streams of bubbles resembling miniature pearl necklaces. A *vino ordinario*

Notice at the Rialto fish market in Venice, specifying the minimum lengths at which diffferent types of fish may be commercially sold.

has scarce, sparsely-occurring, sluggish bubbles.

pernice [per-**ni**-che] partridge.

persa [**per**-sa] marjoram; in some regions it is called *persia*.

persico [**per**-si-co] freshwater perch. See also SPIGOLA.

pesca [**pes**-ca] peach (pl. *pesche*) [**pes**-ke]

pescanoce [pes-ca-**no**-che] nectarine; in some areas it is called *nocepesca*.

pescatora, alla [pes-ca-**to**-ra] with a fish or seafood sauce.

pescatrice [pes-ca-**tri**-che] monkfish, frogfish or angler fish, a fierce looking predator often used in soups; known as *rospo* in Venice and *boldro* in Tuscany.

Pesce di San Pietro [**pe**-she di san-pi-**e**-tro] John Dory.

pesce [**pe**-she] fish (pl. *pesci*); *pesci d'acqua dolce* are freshwater fish. *Pesce stocco* is dried cod from the Lofoten Islands, requiring long soaking before cooking; popular in the Marche. See also BACCALÀ.

pesce serra [**pe**-she **ser**-ra] the bluefish (*Pomatomus saltatrix*).

pesce spada [**pe**-she **spa**-da] swordfish.

pesce spatola [**pe**-she **spa**-to-la] also known as *pesce bandiera*, *pesce d'argento*, *sciabola* and *spatula*. The silver scabbardfish (*Lepidopus caudatus*), a very slender, long, ribbon-like carnivore, silvery grey in colour. It is popular in Sicily.

pesciolini [pe-sho-**li**-ni] tiny fish, small fry, e.g. whitebait.

pessichi [**pes**-si-ki] peaches (Sicily).

pestariei [pes-ta-ri-**e**-i] 1. little pasta pellets served with RICOTTA or other cheese; 2. a rather liquid POLENTA.

pestazzule [pes-tat-**zu**-le] Puglian pasta also known as PIZZELLE.

pestedo [pes-**te**-do] dry condiment popular in Valtellina, Lombardy, consisting of pepper, salt, garlic, thyme, juniper and musk yarrow.

pesto [**pes**-to] A Ligurian sauce made by pounding fresh basil and other ingredients with a pestle and mortar. The official list of ingredients given by the Consorzio del Pesto Genovese is as follows: fresh basil leaves, extra virgin olive oil, grated cheese (a mixture of PARMESAN and PECORINO), garlic, pine nuts

Ribbon-thin silvery *spatola*, scabbard fish, on sale in Catania, Sicily.

or walnuts, coarse-grained salt. The resulting sauce is used with pasta and to flavour other dishes such as soup, doubling as a garnish or spread.

pesto modenese [**pes**-to mo-de-**ne**-ze] pork fat pounded with garlic and herbs, used as a spread, particularly in a soft bread roll, cut in half and filled with the *pesto*, or on *borlenghi* (see BORLENGO).

pesto rosso [**pes**-to **ros**-so] Sicilian pesto, which uses less

Small shop in Romagna specialising in *piadine*, a tasty, filling, takeaway food that is popular throughout the region.

basil than the Genoese variety, substitutes pine nuts for almonds, and adds tomato.

pestun di fave [pes-**toon** di **fa**-ve] broad bean hash, made with cheese and garlic.

petali [**pe**-ta-li] 'petals', delicate slivers (e.g. of parmesan).

Petit Rouge grape from Valle d'Aosta, used to make light, fruity red and rosé wines.

petronciana [pet-ron-**cha**-na] a dialect word for aubergine.

petti see PETTO.

petto [**pet**-to] breast; *petto di pollo* = chicken breast.

Pezzata [pets-**za**-ta] a festival in Molise when quantities of barbecued lamb and mutton stew are consumed.

pezzetelli [pets-ze-**tel**-li] small, cylindrical, indented chunks of pasta from Puglia, a kind of GNOCCHI.

pezzetti [pets-**zet**-ti] little pieces, morsels.

pezzogna [pets-**zon**-ya] a type of sea bream, much prized in Campania.

piacentinu [pi-a-chen-**ti**-nu] a pepper-and-saffron-infused, semi-hard cheese from Enna, Sicily. The name is derived from the Italian for 'pleasure': it is said that Roger II, king of Sicily in the early 12th century, had the cheese made in an attempt to cheer up his despondent wife. He instructed the cheese-makers to use saffron because of a widely-held belief in its uplifting qualities. Roger was married three times and had a number of mistresses. Which of these women was the intended recipient of the serotonin-rich cheese is unrecorded.

piada, piadina [pi-a-da, pi-a-**di**-na] a type of flatbread, like a thick pancake, sometimes curled round a filling to make a kind of 'wrap' sandwich. Very popular in Romagna, where they come with all kinds of fillings.

piastra, alla [pi-**as**-tra] cooked on a griddle.

piatti freddi [pi-**at**-ti fred-di] cold dishes.

piatto [pi-**at**-to] 1. a dish, plate; 2. a course, e.g. *primo piatto* (first course); *piatto del giorno* (dish of the day).

piave [pi-**a**-ve] a cow's milk cheese from the Veneto.

picagge [pi-**cad**-je] Ligurian noodles, served with anchovy sauce, PESTO, etc.

piccante [pic-**can**-te] hot, piquant, spicy.

piccata [pic-**ca**-ta] a slice or cutlet.

picchiettini [pic-yet-**ti**-ni] Umbrian pasta resembling matchsticks, traditionally served with tomato sauce or a meat RAGÙ.

piccione [pi-**cho**-ne] pigeon.

piccolo/a [pic-co-lo] little.

pici [**pee**-chi] thick Tuscan noodles, typically made by hand.

piciocia [pi-**cho**-cha] Sicilian chickpea POLENTA, sometimes with the addition of the chickling vetch.

Picolit [**pi**-co-lit] late-harvest and PASSITO dessert wine from Friuli-Venezia Giulia.

Piedirosso [pi-e-di **ros**-so] red-wine grape grown in Campania, producing rich, bold wine.

Piemonte [pi-e-**mon**-te]
Piedmont, in northwestern
Italy, the heartland of the
Risorgimento, the 19th-century
movement for Italian unity, the
first seat of Italy's monarchs,
home of some of the country's
heaviest industry, and birthplace
of some of its finest cuisine.
Much tourism to Piedmont
is gastronomic: not only is
the food excellent, but the
region also produces some of
Italy's finest wines, and many
of its most enduring aperitifs
and mixer drinks (Cinzano,
Martini) were invented here. It
was in Piedmont that the dry
breadsticks known as GRISSINI
were invented. The region is
also internationally famous for
its truffles, produced in the
provinces of Alba and Mondovì.
Of the excellent wines, the best
known are BARBERA, BARBARESCO
and BAROLO. This is a land of
butter, not of olive oil. Cuisine
is rich, with much emphasis on
fine sausages, dairy produce,
duck and goose.

Pigato [pi-**ga**-to] a white grape
from Liguria, producing young-
drinking wines that pair well
with seafood.

pignato grasso [pin-**ya**-to
gras-so] Neapolitan winter
soup of pork and green leaf
vegetables.

pignoccata, pignolata [pin-
yoc-**ca**-ta, pin-yo-**la**-ta] little
cakes similar to STRUFFOLI; coated
in chocolate and lemon icing, or
honey.

pignolate [pin-yo-**la**-te] little
balls of crushed almonds and
pine nuts.

pignoli [pin-**yo**-li] see PINOLI.

pimenta dioica [pi-**men**-ta di-
o-i-ca] allspice.

pimpinella [pim-pi-**nel**-la]
Mediterranean salad burnet
(*Poterium verrucosum*), a wild
plant sometimes used in salads:
*non c'è insalata bella se non c'è la
pimpinella* ('it's not a good salad
if it doesn't have *pimpinella*').

pincarelli see PENCARELLI.

pincinelli another name for
PENCARELLI.

Pinella, Pinello [pi-**nel**-la,
pi-**nel**-lo] white wine grape
indigenous to the Veneto. Not
much is grown and what there
is is usually used for blends.
However, the Euganean Hills,

near Padua, produce sparkling varietal Pinellas.

pinoli [pi-**no**-li] pine nuts.

Pinot Bianco [**pi**-no bi-**an**-co] Pinot Blanc, a white wine grape grown quite widely in northeast Italy.

Pinot Grigio [**pi**-no **gree**-jo] white-wine grape which produces a popular, easy-drinking wine. Its homeland is in Lombardy, Friuli-Venezia Giulia and Trentino.

Pinot Nero [**pi**-no **ne**-ro] Italian name for Pinot Noir, the great red-wine grape of Burgundy. It Italy is it grown in the north and produces light, fruity wine.

pinzimonio [pint-zi-**mo**-ni-o] an ANTIPASTO of raw vegetables (crudités) and/or bread served with a selection of dressings or simply with olive oil, salt and pepper.

piombi see ANCHELLINI.

piovra [pi-**ov**-ra] in Venice, an octopus.

pirciati [pir-**cha**-ti] pasta similar to BUCATINI.

pipe [**pee**-pe] short lengths of pasta shaped like bent tubes.

pirlo [**pir**-lo] in Brescia, a SPRITZ made with Campari.

Pipe, pasta pipes.

pisarei e fasò [pi-za-**re**-i e fa-**zo**] GNOCCHI and BORLOTTI beans in an onion and tomato sauce (Emilia-Romagna).

pisci spata [**pi**-shi **spa**-ta] swordfish (Sicilian).

piscialandrea [pi-sha-lan-**dre**-a] FOCACCIA with tomatoes and anchovies (Liguria). The name is said to derive from the great Genoese nobleman and sea captain Andrea Doria.

piselli [pi-**zel**-li] peas; *pisellini* are *petits pois*, small or baby peas, received with great enthusiasm at the court of Louis XIV when they were first exported from Genoa to France in 1660.

pistacchio [pi-**stack**-yo] pistachio. The only place in Italy where these trees are cultivated is on the northern slopes of Mt Etna, in Sicily, close to the town of Bronte; the strangely contorted trees produce a crop of the prized green nuts only once every two years.

pistingolo [pis-**tin**-go-lo] a rich fruit cake from the Marche.

pitta [**pit**-ta] in Catanzaro (Calabria), a thick bread ring, about 40cm across, traditionally served in sections with MURSEDDU or sliced to make a *murseddu* sandwich. Otherwise, the word can denote any kind of flatbread.

pitta 'mpigliata [**pit**-ta im-pil-**ya**-ta] baked pastry rosettes filled with nuts, raisins, cinnamon, cloves, laced with a liqueur (e.g. STREGA) and drizzled with honey.

pizza [**pits**-za] probably the most internationally famous dish of Italy: a flat, circular, leavened bread with a variety of toppings. It is a very ancient food (*see box*). Pizzas come in two main forms: the thin, circular hand-tossed pizza of Naples, baked in a wood-fired oven; and Roman pizza, which has a thicker base and is cut into square portions.

Deep pizzas with high outer walls, ideal for rich fillings and runnier sauces, are baked in pans rather than directly on the over floor. Some of the most common types of pizza are listed below.

pizza al formaggio [**pits**-za al for-**mad**-jo] not a pizza, but a dome-shaped Easter cake from the Marche, using several type of cheese.

pizzaiola [pits-za-**yo**-la] a tomato and garlic sauce.

pizzelle [pits-**zel**-le] Puglian pasta similar to PACCOZZE but made without egg.

pizzoccheri [pits-**zoc**-ker-i] buckwheat TAGLIATELLE served with potatoes, cabbage, spinach or Swiss chard, butter, sage and BITTO cheese; a famous dish of the Valtellina.

platessa [pla-**tes**-sa] plaice.

plin [plin] see RAVIOLI and AGNOLOTTI.

polenta [po-**len**-ta] a maize flour hash prepared in one of two main ways: 1. as a savoury porridge topped with sauces, meat, fish, etc.; or 2. cut into squares and fried or grilled. This style is common in the

A short digression on pizza

Pizza has existed in various forms since ancient times. In Book VII of the *Aeneid*, Virgil's epic poem recounting the founding of Rome, Aeneas and his men picnic on the Lazio shore after their voyage from Troy. They are so ravenous that they eat the circular flatbreads upon which their food was served. '*Heus! etiam mensas cosumimus?*' cries Iulus: 'Oh no! Have we even eaten the plates?' It might be said that these flatbreads were the first true pizzas eaten on Italian soil.

The first reference to pizza by that name comes in the 10th century, in a document known as the *Codex Diplomaticus Caietanus*, from Gaeta, near the border of Lazio and Campania (the two regions, with Rome and Naples as their capitals, that claim pizza as their own) where '*duodecim pizze*' (a dozen pizzas) are among many comestibles ordered for the Easter festivities. Over the centuries, Naples established itself as the most imaginative producer of *pizze*. The increasing popularity of tomatoes meant that by the mid-19th century pizzas were beginning to resemble the familiar product we know today. Finally in 1889, in honour of Margherita of Savoy, Queen of Italy, the Neapolitan pizza maker Raffaele Esposito created the first *tricolore*, a tomato, basil and cheese pizza celebrating the red, white and green flag of the newly unified Kingdom of Italy. Since then, the Margherita has become the simple template upon which all other pizzas are based.

Some common types of pizza

- *bianca*: 'white' pizza, without tomato; in Rome, pizza bread topped with olive oil, salt and rosemary sprigs;
- *capricciosa*: MOZZARELLA, tomato, mushrooms, artichokes, ham, olives, oil (in Rome, PROSCIUTTO and hard-boiled egg are added);
- *fritta* popular street food in Abruzzo, where the pizza is folded over its filling and fried;

- *funghi e salsicce* (or *boscaiola*): MOZZARELLA, mushrooms and sausages, with or without tomato;
- *marinara*: tomato, garlic, oregano and olive oil;
- *Margherita*: tomato, MOZZARELLA, basil and olive oil;
- *Napoli*: in Rome, the name for a pizza topped with tomato, MOZZARELLA, anchovies and oil;
- *quattro formaggi*: four different cheeses, melted together or in decorative sectors;
- *quattro stagioni*: 'four seasons', with tomatoes, MOZZARELLA, mushrooms, ham, artichokes;
- *romana*: the Neapolitan name for what the Romans call *Pizza Napoli*;
- *siciliana*: tomato, MOZZARELLA, capers, olives and anchovy.

Veneto. Regional polentas made of other flours also exist and the Valtellina (Lombardy) is famous for *polenta taragna*, made with buckwheat flour and cheese.

polipo [po-li-po] octopus.

pollame [pol-la-me] poultry.

pollanca, pollastra, pollastrella [pol-**lan**-ca, pol-**las**-tra, pol-la-**strel**-la] a young fattened hen.

pollo [**pol**-lo] chicken; strictly speaking a young hen which has not begun to lay; *pollo all diavola* is roast chicken with PEPERONCINO; *pollo in porchetta* is chicken stuffed with ham; *pollo*

novello is spring chicken; *pollo ruspante* is free-range chicken.

polmone [pol-**mo**-ne] lung. Usually this is calf's lung (*polmone di vitello*), cooked *in umido*, in other words in a rich casserole.

polpa [pol-pa] pulp, flesh. *Polpa di pomodoro* is finely chopped tomato, not as liquid as a pureé. When talking about meat, *polpa* refers to a lean cut.

polpetta [pol-**pet**-ta] (pl. *polpette*) a rissole; *polpette di carne* are meatballs.

polpettone [pol-pet-**to**-ne] meatloaf.

polpo [**pol**-po] see POLIPO.

pomarola [po-ma-**ro**-la] *salsa pomarola*, tomato sauce.

pomelo [po-**me**-lo] a very large, pale green citrus fruit, sweeter than grapefruit, often used in salads.

pomo [**po**-mo] apple.

pomodoro [po-mo-**do**-ro] tomato. *pomodori secchi*: sun-dried tomatoes; *pomodori perini*: plum tomatoes; *pomodori San Marzano*: a variety of plum tomato with DOP status, grown on Mt Vesuvius; *pomodorini di Pachino*: IGP cherry tomatoes grown near Pachino in southeast Sicily; *'pachino'* is now synonymous with 'cherry tomato' in Italy.

pompelmo [pom-**pel**-mo] grapefruit.

porceddu [por-**ched**-du] Sardinian roast suckling pig.

porcellana [por-chel-**la**-na] purslane, a wild plant used for salads, also known as *portulaca*.

porcellino di latte [por-chel-**li**-no di **lat**-te] suckling pig. Also known as *porcello*.

porchetta [por-**ket**-ta] a whole young pig, boned and stuffed with herbs and roasted over an open fire or in a wood-burning oven; known in Sardinia as *porcetto* or *porceddu*.

porcinelli [por-chi-**nel**-li] brown and pink wild mushrooms; red boletus.

porcini [por-**chi**-ni] *Boletus aedulis* (penny bun or cep); said to be the most delicious

How *pomodori* became safe to eat

The tomato was introduced to Europe in the 16th century as an ornamental plant, its seductive colour suggesting to many that it might be posionous. It was not until well into the late 17th century that cooks began to experiment with the food, encouraged by the activities of pet monkeys (there were many in the princely courts of Europe) who made no bones about seizing and eating the fruit and suffered no ill effects as a result. Today the tomato is a cornerstone of Italian gastronomy.

mushroom to be found in Italy. Dried *porcini*, along with other dried FUNGHI, are widely available.

porco [**por**-co] pig, also known as *maiale*.

porrata [por-**ra**-ta] bacon and leek tart, a kind of quiche.

porro [**por**-ro] leek.

portafoglio [por-ta-**fol**-yo] a dish where ingredients are placed in a 'portfolio', an outer wrapping, e.g. *portafogli di vitello alla salvia*: veal cutlets stuffed with sage.

portaluca SEE PORCELLANA.

portare via [por-**ta**-re **vee**-a] take away. *Un caffè per portare via* is a coffee to take away. In traditional Italian coffee bars, this is almost never done. The coffee is still served in a china cup, at the counter (*al banco*) or at a table (*a tavola*).

Portoghese [por-to-**ghe**-ze] Portuguese.

pottaggio [pot-**taj**-jo] a thick soup or stew.

pranzo [**prant**-so] the midday meal; lunch.

prataioli [pra-ta-**yo**-li] field mushrooms, meadow mushrooms; *Agaricus campestris*.

preboggion [pre-boj-**jon**] in Liguria, a mixture of wild herbs used for risotto and as a filling for ravioli.

presnitz [pres-**nits**] a shortcrust pastry coil filled with dried fruits (Trieste).

prezzemolo [prets-**ze**-mo-lo] parsley.

prezzo fisso [**prets**-zo **fis**-so] 'fixed price'; set menu.

prima colazione [**pri**-ma co-lat-zi-**o**-ne] breakfast.

primi piatti [**pri**-mi pi-**at**-ti] main courses.

Primitivo [pri-mi-**ti**-vo] red-wine grape introduced into Puglia in the 18th century, a cousin of the Californian Zinfandel, used to produce dark, intense wines.

primizie [pri-**mit**-si-e] 'first fruits'; young vegetables.

propria [**pro**-pi-a] own, e.g. *produzione propria*: local ('our own') produce.

prosciutto [pro-**shoot**-to] ham; cured meat from the hind leg of a pig. There are two main types of *prosciutto*: *cotto* (cooked) and *crudo* (raw). All *prosciutto*, whether destined to be cooked or left raw, is first dried (the name *prosciutto* means 'dried out'). *Prosciutto cotto* is then usually deboned and steamed. *Prosciutto crudo*, raw ham that has been cured and air-dried, is what many people think of as typically Italian. The most famous type is *Prosciutto di Parma* ('Parma ham') but there are important regional variants, their flavour determined by factors such as the pigs' diet and the method and length of preparation, such as the DOP *Prosciutto di Carpegna* from the Marche (the ideal type for eating with melon or figs). Another prized variety is the DOP *Prosciutto di San Daniele* from Friuli, which has lent its name to a popular restaurant chain, Pane Vino e San Daniele. *Prosciutto* is commonly eaten as an ANTIPASTO. *Prosciutto crudo* is also an important component of SALTIMBOCCA.

Prosecco [pro-**sec**-co] a popular sparkling white wine made from grapes grown almost exclusively in the Veneto region.

provola [**pro**-vo-la] fresh cow's milk PASTA FILATA cheese. *Provola delle Madonie* is a famous variety from the Madonie mountains of Sicily. In Campania and Puglia they make a *provola* from buffalo milk.

provolone [pro-vo-**lo**-ne] firm, creamy cheese mainly produced in the north of Italy, though a notable example from the south is *Provolone del Monaco*, made from the milk of *Agerolese* cows, a breed from the Monti Lattari, the 'milky mountains', of Campania. Another is *Provolone Valpadana* from the Po basin.

prugna [**proon**-ya] plum (pl. *prugne*).

Prugnolo Gentile [prun-**yo**-lo jen-**tee**-le] grape grown in the Montepulciano region of Italy, a clone of the SANGIOVESE Grosso. It is used to make Vino Nobile di Montepulciano.

puccia [**poo**-cha] 1. a bread roll (pl. *pucce*). 2. *Puccia di Cortina* is a kind of FOCACCIA from Cortina d'Ampezzo, in the Veneto, made partly of rye flour and flavoured with fennel and cumin seeds or wild oregano. 3. *Puccia piemontese* is a firm POLENTA cooked with chopped pork and cabbage leaves.

pucce e uliate [**poo**-che e u-li-

a-te] small bread rolls (Puglia) made with black olives.

Puglia [**pul**-ya] the fertile region in the heel of Italy. Puglia has always grown wheat, and this has made it historically wealthy. Its breads are excellent, as are its fruit and vegetables. Puglia also has 500 miles of coastline and a correspondingly varied and sophisticated fish cuisine. Puglia's wines, particularly those from the Salento peninsula, are becoming increasingly well known. Aleatico di Puglia is a wine dating back to the early 13th century, when it was first produced for the table of the Holy Roman Emperor Frederick II.

puina, puvina [pu-**ee**-na] another name for RICOTTA.

Punt e Mes [punt e **mes**] a bitter flavoured vermouth, dark auburn in colour. The name, in Piedmontese dialect, is supposed to signify one degree (*punt*) of sweetness and half a degree (*mes*) of bitterness.

puntarelle [pun-ta-**rel**-le] wild chicory spears, eaten raw dressed with olive oil and anchovies. Typical of Rome.

punte d'ago [**pun**-te **da**-go] 'needle points', a pasta shape.

punte di asparagi [**pun**-te di as-**pa**-ra-ji] asparagus spears.

pupi di zucchero [**poo**-pi di **tsook**-ke-ro] painted festival dolls made of sugar (Sicily and the south), sometimes known as *pupi di cena*.

purea [pu-**re**-a] purée.

purezza [pu-**ret**-sa] literally 'purity'. A wine is *in purezza* when it is a varietal, i.e. made from a single grape variety.

purpetti [pur-**pet**-ti] in Sicily, baby octopus, usually fried, stewed or eaten in salad.

purpo [**poor**-po] octopus (Sicily).

pussacaffè [**pus**-sa-caf-**fe**] see CAFFÈ.

puttanesca [put-ta-**nes**-ca] a sauce for pasta of capers, black olives, garlic, olive oil, pepper, anchovies and tomatoes. The name derives from *puttana*, a whore. Theories abound as to origin: because it is quick to produce, some say it may derive from the fact that wayward wives, who had misbehaved all day rather than slaved at the stove, found it a swift way of providing their homecoming husbands with a good dinner.

puzzone di Moena [put-**zo**-ne di mo-**e**-na] famously smelly cheese from Trentino-Alto Adige.

quadrefiore [**qua**-dre fi-**o**-re] 'four flowers' PASTA CORTA shape.

quadrucci [qua-**dru**-chi] pasta squares that are added to soups or broth.

quaglia [**qual**-ya] quail.

quagliata [qual-**ya**-ta] curds; newly-made cheese before the salting process has begun.

quaresimali [qua-re-zi-**ma**-li] Lenten biscuits, made with almonds, sometimes in the form of alphabet letters coated in chocolate.

quartirolo [quar-ti-**ro**-lo] a soft, crumbly, agreeably sour cheese from Lombardy.

quarume [qua-**roo**-me] a dish of well seasoned boiled veal offal (Palermo).

quasi crudo/a [**qua**-zi **cru**-do] almost raw, very rare.

quattro formaggi [**quat**-tro for-**mad**-ji] see PIZZA.

quattro stagioni [**quat**-tro stad-**jo**-ni] see PIZZA.

quecciuolo see MURICE.

quinquinelle [quin-qui-**nel**-le] fish dumplings, quenelles.

quinto quarto [**quin**-to **quar**-to] the 'fifth quarter' of the animal: its entrails. A slaughtered animal is always slaughtered animal is divided into cuts graded by quality. When the choice bits have been sold, what remains is the so-called 'fifth' quarter: the offal, which in Rome, Palermo and Catania in particular traditionally formed the staple food of the poor, who found (and still find) inventive ways of making it taste good. See PAJATA and PALERMO.

rabarbaro [ra-**bar**-ba-ro] rhubarb.

Raboso [ra-**bo**-zo] a red-wine grape from the Veneto, high in tannin and acid.

racina [ra-**chee**-na] grapes (Sicily).

radiatori [ra-di-a-**to**-ri] pasta pieces resembling old-fashioned tubular radiators.

radicchio [ra-**dik**-ki-o] not radish, which is *ravanello*, but endive or chicory. There are two main varieties the round-leafed *radicchio di Verona* and the long,

Radicchio di Treviso, the sought-after, bitter-tasting red endive from the Veneto region, with its slender, curling leaves.

curly-leafed *radicchio di Treviso*. The leaves are red, veined in white, and the taste is subtly bitter. It is a great delicacy of the Veneto region, often added to RISOTTO or cooked *alla* PIASTRA.

rafano [**ra**-fa-no] horseradish; also called *barbaforte* or *cren*.

raffermo [raf-**fer**-mo] *pane raffermo* is stale bread, used to thicken soups and stews or to make dumplings.

ragù [ra-**goo**] a thick, meat-based sauce, with onions, red wine and often tomatoes, slowly cooked and reduced. See also BOLOGNESE.

ramato [ra-**ma**-to] a style of wine made with PINOT GRIGIO, typically in Friuli in northeast Italy. The process of long skin contact during maceration gives the wine a distinctive amber or coppery hue.

ramerino [ra-mer-**i**-no] rosemary.

ramolaccio [ra-mo-**la**-cho] white radish.

rana, ranocchio [**ra**-na, ra-**nock**-yo] frog (pl. *rane*), the edible *Rana esculenta*. They abound in the wetlands of Lombardy and Piedmont and can be eaten whole, either deep fried or simmered with wine and herbs.

rana pescatrice [**ra**-na pes-ca-**tri**-che] the frogfish or monkfish.

rapa [**ra**-pa] turnip. *Rape armate* ('turnips in armour') is a medieval dish that resurfaces from time to time. The 'armour' consists of a topping of cheese, butter and spices. The dish is ironically named, the point being that instead of protecting the turnips, the 'armour', the delicious cheesy carapace, renders them more vulnerable to assault (i.e. more appetising) than they might normally be.

rapa tedesca [**ra**-pa te-**des**-ca] Jerusalem artichoke.

rapanello see RAVANELLO.

rape see RAPA.

raponzolo, raperonzolo [rap-**ont**-zo-lo, ra-per-**ont**-zo-lo] rampion, a vegetable with a parsnip-like root used in broth or served hot with cheese. The fairytale character Rapunzel is named after it.

Raschera [ras-**ke**-ra] tangy, semi-hard DOP cheese made mainly from cow's milk with a dash of sheep's or goat's milk added in. From Piedmont.

Ratafià [ra-ta-fi-**a**] a sweet cherry liqueur. Also known as *rattafia* [rat-ta-**fi**-a]. It is sometimes used to flavour confectionery.

ravanello [ra-va-**nel**-lo] radish.

ravaggiolo, raveggiolo, raviggiolo [ra-va-**jo**-lo] a fresh sheep or goat's cheese. See CACIO.

ravioli [ra-vi-**o**-li] PASTA RIPIENA, an ancient type and still one of the best known, both in Italy and beyond. Etymologists derive its name from *rape* ('turnips'), because early *ravioli* were typically filled with turnip greens. The earliest mention of *ravioli*, in the 13th-century *Cronica* of the Franciscan friar Salimbene da Parma, does not mention this. In fact he describes eating a '*raviolus*' without a pastry casing. *Ravioli* today have their own official website (*www.ravioli.it*), which lists almost 30 recipes with fillings of meat, fish, vegetables and cheese. It also shows how

Ravioli, one of the most popular and best-known forms of *pasta ripiena*.

square *ravioli* are made: not one by one, but from a single pasta sheet, dotted with blobs of filling, covered with a second sheet, and divided with a pastry cutter.

razza [**rat**-za] 1. a skate or ray; *razza bianca* (white skate); *razza quattrocchi* ('four-eyed' skate), so-called because of its markings; 2. a breed or 'race', especially of cattle, e.g. *razza Agerolese*, a brown-coloured milking cow from Campania, whose milk is used for PROVOLONE; or the *razza Valdostana*, whose milk is used for REBLEC.

Razza Rendena [**rat**-za ren-**de**-na] 1. a cheese made from the milk of Rendena cows, native to the Val Rendena in Trentino. Rendena milk is also used for SPRESSA; 2. the cows themselves, also used as beef cattle.

reblec [reb-**leck**] fresh cow's milk cheese from the Valle d'Aosta.

Recioto [re-**cho**-to] one of the four styles of VALPOLICELLA red wine, in fact the original and most ancient style, made following a time-honoured ancient method by partially drying the grapes before crushing them. The wine is then fermented, carefully not leaving enough time for the yeasts to convert all the sugar to alcohol, so that a residual sweetness remains in the finished product. Compare AMARONE.

Refosco [re-**fos**-co] red-wine grape grown in the Friuli-Venezia Giulia region, producing fully-flavoured, fruity wines.

regina [re-**jee**-na] carp.

regine [re-**jee**-ne] literally 'queens', pasta named in honour of the House of Savoy, the royal family that supplied kings of Italy from Unification until the foundation of the modern republic in 1946; *reginelle* [re-ji-**nel**-le], 'little queens', are another Savoy pasta; *reginette* [re-ji-**net**-te] are wavy-edged strips of pasta, the same as MAFALDE; but in Palermo (Sicily) they are small shortbread biscuits sprinkled with sesame seeds.

renga see ARINGA.

resentin [re-sen-**tin**] see CAFFÈ.

rete [**re**-te] literally a 'net'; caul, a fatty membrane. See OMENTO.

rhum [**rroom**] rum.

ribes [**ree**-bes] redcurrants.

Ribolla gialla [ri-**bol**-la **jal**-la] a white-wine grape cultivated in Friuli.

ribollita [ri-bol-**li**-ta] bean and vegetable stew of Tuscan origin. The soup is made a day in advance and is then reboiled (*ribollita*) to intensify and mature the flavour. Red cabbage, kale and stale bread are the main ingredients and there are variations on the theme throughout the region.

Ricasoli, Baron Bettino [ri-**ca**-zo-li] (1809–80) second Prime Minister of united Italy and a native Tuscan, credited with drawing up the first official 'recipe' for the CHIANTI blend.

ricci di donna [**ree**-chi di **don**-na] 'a woman's curls', a type of pasta.

ricciarelli [ri-cha-**rel**-li] delicate honey and almond biscuits from Siena, Tuscany.

riccio di mare [**ree**-cho di **ma**-re] sea urchin (pl. *ricci*).

ricciola [ri-**cho**-la] amberjack, a saltwater fish with firm white flesh.

riccioli amalfitani [**ree**-cho-li a-mal-fi-**ta**-ni] little curl-shaped pieces of pasta.

ricciolina [ri-cho-**lee**-na] *torta ricciolina* is a kind of marzipan tart.

ricotta [ri-**cot**-ta] a soft cheese made from whey, the name meaning literally 'recooked", alluding to the manufacturing process. Standard cheese is made from milk by extracting the curds. To make *ricotta*, the leftover whey is heated, resulting in a runny, protein-rich and highly versatile cheese, ideal for adding to sauces. There are many regional variants, using milk from cows, sheep, buffalo and goats, and including smoked *ricottas* and *ricotta salata*, a *ricotta* preserved with salt and then left to age and harden in just the same way as a conventional PECORINO.

rigaglie [ri-**gal**-ye] offal from poultry.

rigate, rigati [ri-**ga**-te, ri-**ga**-ti] of pasta, ridged.

rigatoni [ri-ga-**to**-ni] pasta in the form of short, ridged tubes.

rinforzo, insalata di [in-sa-**la**-ta di rin-**fort**-zo] a salad of cauliflower, anchovies, olives and pickled peppers served

in Naples over Christmas and
Epiphany.

rinfresco [rin-**fres**-co]
refreshment (pl. *rinfreschi*).

Ripasso [ri-**pas**-so] type of
VALPOLICELLA made by a second
fermentation of a non-SUPERIORE
wine on used RECIOTO skins.

ripieno/a [ri-pi-**e**-no] stuffed
or filled. *Olive ripiene* are stuffed
olives.

riserva [ri-**zer**-va] reserve: a
high-quality version of a wine,
often with a greater alcoholic
content, aged for longer.

risi e bisi [**ri**-zi e **bi**-zi] rice with
young peas, a speciality of the
Veneto.

riso [**ree**-zo] rice.

risotto [ri-**zot**-to] rice simmered
slowly in stock (*brodo*) until
the liquid has been absorbed.
ARBORIO rice is widely held to
be the best for *risotto*, capable of
absorbing the various attributes
of the other ingredients—stock,
wine, butter, olive oil—without
losing its own texture and
flavour. Its home is certainly
the north of Italy, where rice is
grown. Delicious truffle *risotti*
are also common, and in the
Veneto they make *risotto* with
RADICCHIO. *Risotto* is not the
same as *riso in brodo* ('rice in
broth'), in which rice is one of
several ingredients in a runny
soup.

ristretto see CAFFÈ.

robiola [ro-bi-**o**-la] a soft,
creamy cheese from Piedmont,
made from sheep's, cow's or
goat's milk, popular as a basis
for sauces.

rococò [ro-co-**cò**] a Neapolitan
ring-shaped Christmas biscuit.

rognoni, rognoncini [ron-
yo-ni, ron-yon-**chi**-ni] kidneys.
Rognoncini trifolati are sliced and
braised in wine.

Romagna see EMILIA-ROMAGNA.

romanesco [ro-ma-**nes**-co]
green or yellow-green broccoli
with tightly-packed, pointed
florets.

rombo [**rom**-bo] turbot. *Rombo*

Rigatoni, ridged, tubular pasta
used in Rome as a vehicle for
pajata.

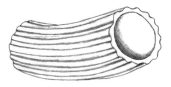

Rucola, a pungent and popular salad leaf.

liscio [**rom**-bo **lee**-sho] is brill.

Rondinella [ron-di-**nel**-la] red-wine grape known for its generous yields, grown in the Veneto and used in VALPOLICELLA and BARDOLINO blends.

Rosa Camuna [**ro**-za ca-**moo**-na] a mild cheese from Val Camonica, Lombardy.

rosato [ro-**za**-to] rosé.

roscani see AGRETTI.

rosetta [ro-**zet**-ta] see MICHETTA.

rosmarino [ros-ma-**ri**-no] rosemary.

rosolio [ro-**zo**-li-o] a distilled liqueur. The name comes from the Latin word *ros*, meaning dew. The idea was that early *rosoli* were made from herbs, flower petals and other botanicals gathered in the very early morning, with the dew still fresh upon them.

rospo [**ros**-po] frogfish, monkfish or angler fish.

Rossignola [ros-sin-**yo**-la] red-wine grape from the east shore of Lake Garda, sometimes used in VALPOLICELLA. It is the Veneto name for GROPPELLO.

rossi leggeri [**ros**-si-lej-**je**-ri] light red wines.

rosso [**ros**-so] 1. red. *In rosso* means cooked with tomatoes; 2. *rosso d'uovo*: egg yolk.

rosticciana [ros-ti-**cha**-na] grilled spare ribs.

rotini [ro-**tee**-ni] corkscrew-shaped pasta.

rotolo [**ro**-to-lo] 1. a swiss roll; a roly poly; 2. a wrap or roulade.

rrau see RAGÙ.

ruccolo, ruccul [**roo**-co-lo, ruc-**cool**] 1. a kind of flatbread; 2. bread filled with chunks of ham and sausage.

Ruchè [ru-**ke**] Piedmontese red-wine grape.

rucola, rughetta, ruchetta [**ru**-co-la, ru-**get**-ta, ru-**ket**-ta] rocket or arugula, a pleasantly peppery-tasting salad vegetable. It has been popular in Italy since Roman times, when it was thought to have aphrodisiac properties (it was often grown near statues of the fertility god,

Priapus). Today it is found not only in salads but in pasta sauces and rice dishes.

ruote [ru-**o**-te] wheel-shaped pasta.

ruspante [rus-**pan**-te] free-range (chicken).

russuliddu [rus-su-**lid**-du] in Sicily, fried red mullet.

rustica, alla [**ru**-sti-ca] 'country' style.

ruta [**roo**-ta] rue.

saba, sapa [**sa**-ba, **sa**-pa] grape must.

sa fregula [sa **fre**-gu-la] pasta balls, couscous.

sagne chine [**san**-ye **ki**-ne] a rich Calabrian lasagne where the pasta is interleaved with a stuffing of meatballs, artichokes, mushrooms, herbs, PECORINO and egg.

sagne a pezze [**san**-ye-a-pet-ze] a lozenge-shaped flat pasta from Molise, also known as *tacconelle*.

sagra [**sag**-ra] a festival, often celebrating the food or wine of a town, region or province.

Sagrantino [sag-ran-**ti**-no] red-wine grape from Umbria, much prized and often blended with SANGIOVESE to make ink-dark,

fruity wines that age very well, e.g. Sagrantino di Montefalco, a DOCG wine made from 100 percent Sagrantino.

salada [sal-**a**-da] salted, as in *carne salada*, salt beef. Also known as *carne salà*.

salama da sugo [sa-**la**-ma da **su**-go] a kind of Ferrarese haggis, consisting of pork neck, belly, throat, liver and tongue salted and seasoned, mixed with unpasteurised red wine and packed into a stout pig's bladder.

salame and **salume** [sa-**la**-me, sa-**lu**-me] cured meats (*see box opposite* and also see SPECK, PROSCIUTTO, BRESAOLA, etc).

salami *see box.*

salamino [sa-la-**mi**-no] a kind of spiced pork SALAMI.

salamoia [sa-la-**mo**-ya] brine.

salamora [sa-la-**mo**-ra] a marinade, made by steeping herbs and spices in oil. Many recipes exist, depending on what kind of meat or fish the marinade is intended for.

salatino [sa-la-**ti**-no] a savoury snack, an appetiser.

salato/a [sa-**la**-to] 1. savoury, the opposite of *dolce*; 2. salted, salty.

sale [**sa**-le] salt.

salicornia [sa-li-**cor**-ni-a] glasswort or marsh samphire, a succulent maritime plant, a popular accompaniment to fish dishes, sometimes pickled. It is also known as *asparagi di mare*, sea asparagus.

salignoun [sa-lin-**yoon**] a RICOTTA from the Valle d'Aosta, flavoured with herbs and PEPERONCINO.

salimora see SALAMORA.

salmì, in [sal-**mi**] a way of cooking game involving lengthy stewing in wine with herbs and seasoning. *Lepre in salmì* is jugged hare.

salmistrata [sal-mis-**tra**-ta] cured, as in *carne salmistrata*, cured meat. It is a speciality of the South Tyrol (Alto Adige), where beef and sometimes pork is salted and flavoured with pepper, juniper etc.

salmone [sal-**mo**-ne] salmon.

Salume, *salame* and salami

In Britain and the USA *salami* is the accepted term to denote the distinctive cured sausages, sold whole or in slices in delicatessens and supermarkets or served in sandwiches and as *hors d'oeuvres*. The usage is incorrect, albeit harmlessly so, since *salami* is the plural of *salame*.

Both *salame* and *salume* are derived from the Latin word *sal*, meaning salt, the main ingredient in the curing process. But while *salume* is the general term for all cured, cold meats, a *salame* is just one example. A *salame* tends to be made of cheaper, leftover bits of meat, which is salted, seasoned and cured uncooked. Some *salume* are called *insaccati* ('en-sacked', because they are stuffed into intestines to keep their shape). Important subgroups of these are *salsicce* (roughly the equivalent of the English 'sausages') and *soppressate* (from the verb 'to crush'). Many kinds of meat are used in *salume*, though by far the most common is pork. A *salumeria* is a shop specialising in cured meats and sausage.

Traditional *Salumeria* with its old shop sign, in Mantua.

salmorigano see SALMORIGLIO.

salmoriglio [sal-mor-**il**-yo] a sauce made of olive oil, lemon juice, garlic, salt, parsley and oregano. It can be eaten hot or cold or used as a fish marinade. It is also known as *salmorigano*.

salpa [**sal**-pa] a type of sea bream (*Sarpa salpa*), patterned with thin gold stripes.

salsa [**sal**-sa] sauce. See also VERDE.

salsiccia [sal-**si**-cha] a sausage, an INSACCATO made of raw seasoned meat stuffed into an intestine. They can be eaten hot or cold, but must be cooked first. *Salsicce* differ widely from region to region.

salsicciotto [sal-si-**chot**-to] a large banger or frankfurter.

saltato/a [sal-**ta**-to] sautéed.

saltimbocca [sal-tim-**boc**-ca] a Roman speciality, veal cutlets topped with PROSCIUTTO and simmered in white wine and butter with sage. The name means 'jump in the mouth', alluding to the irresistible taste of the dish.

salume see SALAME.

salumeria [sa-lu-me-**ri**-a] shop specialising in salted and cured meats.

salvia [**sal**-vi-a] sage.

sambuca [sam-**bu**-ca] an anise-flavoured DIGESTIVO often served with coffee beans set alight on its surface, which set off an incandescent blue glow.

sambuco [sam-**bu**-co] elderberry.

sambudello [sam-bu-**del**-lo] a coarse SALAME from Arezzo, Tuscany.

sammurigghiu [sam-mu-**rig**-yu] Sicilian for SALMORIGLIO.

Sampiero [sam-pi-**e**-ro] John Dory.

sanato [sa-**na**-to] young, milk-fed veal from Piedmont.

sangele see SANGUINACCIO.

Sangiovese [san-jo-**ve**-ze] red-wine grape used to produce the fine wines of Tuscany such as CHIANTI CLASSICO, and BRUNELLO di Montalcino (Brunello is a clone of Sangiovese Grosso). The principal grape in all Chianti wines, Sangiovese is intense in colour and high in acidity.

sangue [**san**-gwe] blood. *Al sangue* = rare.

sanguinaccio [san-gwi-**nat**-cho] 1. a blood sausage, in Catania (Sicily) also known as *sangele*; 2. a chocolate dessert.

sanguinello [san-gwi-**nel**-lo] blood orange.

santoreggia [san-to-**red**-ja] savory (herb).

Saonara [sa-o-**na**-ra] a town in the province of Padua in the Veneto known for its horsemeat. Some say the tradition of eating horsemeat in the Veneto dates back to the early trade routes from Genoa and other cities to Venice. Many horses were too broken down to make the return journey and were therefore slaughtered and eaten. The slaughter of horses is a contentious subject today. Enjoy *prosciutto di cavallo* while you can...

saor [sa-**or**] a marinade of onions, sage and white wine typical of the Veneto, where it is used with sardines.

sapa [**sa**-pa] grape must.

sapore [sa-**po**-re] flavour, taste.

saracinesca [sa-ra-chi-**nes**-ca] sauce made of almonds, raisins, ginger, cinnamon, cloves and black pepper. It imparts a distinct Middle-Eastern ('Saracen') flavour to certain Venetian dishes.

saraghina [sa-ra-**ghee**-na] a sprat.

sarago fasciato [**sa**-ra-go fa-**sha**-to] the two-banded sea bream.

sarda [**sar**-da] a pilchard, sardine; *sardina*: a young pilchard, i.e. a sardine.

Sardegna see SARDINIA.

sardenaira, sardenara, sardinara [sar-de-**na**-i-ra, sar-de-**a**-ra, sar-di-**na**-ra] a Ligurian FOCACCIA with a topping of tomato, capers and anchovies. It is also known as *pizza all'Andrea* or PISCIALANDREA.

Sardinia a land of long-standing tradition, breathtaking landscapes and intact coastline and beaches. Although the island is named after the sardine, Sardinia is not famed for its fish dishes. Pirate raids historically forced the population inland, so the most representative dishes focus instead on lamb, rabbit, game and sheep's cheese. Myrtle is commonly used as a flavouring, notably in the famous roast suckling pig. One maritime ingredient that is still prevalent is BOTTARGA, the 'Sardinian caviar'. The CANNONAU red wine is said to be unusually rich in antioxidants.

sardon [sar-**don**] in Venice, a sardine.

sartù [sar-**tu**] the *sartù di riso* or *sartù napoletano* is a Neapolitan baked rice pie, filled with meatballs, sausage, cheese, mushrooms and peas (though recipes vary) .

Sassella [sas-**sel**-la] DOCG wine from Valtellina, Lombardy, typically made from the NEBBIOLO grape.

Sassicaia [sas-si-**ca**-ya] an all-Cabernet SUPERTUSCAN from the Bolgheri region.

sasizza [sa-**sits**-za] in Sicily, a sausage.

sas alisanzas see ALISANZAS.

sa taccula see TACCULA.

savoiardi [sa-vo-**yar**-di] sponge fingers.

savor see SAOR.

sbagliato [sbal-**ya**-to] bungled, spoiled, messed up. See NEGRONI.

sbombata [sbom-**ba**-ta] a dish of baked pasta, cheese and chicken giblets.

sbriciolata, sbriciolona, sbrisolona [sbri-cho-**la**-ta, sbri-cho-**lo**-na, sbri-zo-**lo**-na] 1. a sweet crumbly cake from Lombardy and the north, originally Mantua; 2. *sbriciolata* (masc. *sbriciolato*) means 'crumbled'.

sbrofadej [sbro-fa-**de**-i] pasta from Lombardy resembling stout VERMICELLI, made with egg, flour and grated nutmeg, served in broth.

scabeggio [sca-**bed**-jo] fried fish marinated in garlic, lemon juice and sage (vinegar and white wine may also be added). The dish is typical of Moneglia in Liguria. The word shares a root with the Spanish *escabeche*, also a sour marinade.

scacciata [scat-**cha**-ta] Sicilian sacvoury pie, made with bread dough, especially during the Christmas season. It can have a variety of fillings, e.g. potato, cheese and anchovies, broccoli and sausage.

scaglie [**scal**-ye] shavings. As in *scaglie di Parmigiano*, Parmesan shavings.

scaldatelli [scal-da-**tel**-li] ring-shaped bread rolls flavoured with onion, oregano, olives, sesame or fennel seeds, cooked in boiling water and then baked in the oven until golden brown (Puglia).

scalille [sca-**lil**-le] pastry knots fried and then glazed in syrup of figs (Calabria).

scaloppino [sca-lop-**pi**-no] an escalope, a thin, pounded piece of meat, commonly veal (pl. *scaloppini*).

scalogna [sca-**lon**-ya] scallion, shallot.

scamone [sca-**mo**-ne] rump (of beef).

scamorza [sca-**mort**-za] small and pear-shaped, a pulled cow's milk cheese from southern Italy (in Naples it is sometimes made with buffalo milk) with a characteristic little 'neck' to hang it up by while maturing. The smoked version, *scamorza affumicata*, is delicious.

scampi [**scam**-pi] the Italian name for Norway lobsters, langoustines, Dublin Bay prawns.

scapece [sca-**pe**-che] a method of pickling fish or vegetables. See SCABEGGIO.

scarcedda [scar-**ched**-da] Easter cakes from Puglia and Basilicata. Both sweet and savoury versions exist; the sweet type are often iced.

scarola [sca-**ro**-la] escarole, broad-leaved endive.

scarpazza [scar-**pats**-za] a vegetable tart, also known as *stirpada* and *scherpada*.

scarpazzone [scar-pats-**zo**-ne] see ERBAZZONE.

scarpena [scar-**pe**-na] the red scorpion fish.

scarpinocc [scar-pi-**nock**] cheese-filled ravioli from Lombardy.

scarteddate [scar-ted-**da**-te] fried Christmas biscuits in southern Italy. A version of

CARTELLATE.

scelta [**shel**-ta] choice, e.g. *contorno a scelta*, a choice of vegetables.

scherpada see SCARPAZZA.

schiacciata [ski-at-**cha**-ta] a thin Tuscan flatbread, usually topped with olive oil and salt.

schiacciato/a [ski-at-**cha**-to] crushed, mashed.

schiaffoni [ski-af-**fo**-ni] see PACCHERI.

Schiava [**skya**-va] red-wine grape grown largely in the Trentino and South Tyrol (Alto Adige), where it is known in German as Vernatsch or Trollinger.

schie [**ski**-e] small grey shrimp of the Venetian lagoon, eaten whole in RISOTTO.

schienale [ski-e-**na**-le] bone marrow from the spine.

Schioppettino [ski-op-pet-**ti**-ni] dark red Friulan grape, used for eating and to make fruity red wines.

schiuma [ski-**u**-ma] froth, foam.

schlutzer tirolesi [**shloot**-zer ti-ro-**le**-zi] spinach and ricotta-filled RAVIOLI from Trentino-Alto Adige.

sciabola [**sha**-bo-la] see PESCE

SPATOLA.

scialatielli [sha-la-ti-**el**-li] square-section noodles from Campania, typical of the Amalfi Coast, somewhat resembling short TAGLIATELLE. They are often served with seafood sauces.

sciarrano [shar-**ra**-no] the saltwater perch.

sciatt [shatt] buckwheat pancake with cheese and GRAPPA (Lombardy, Valtellina).

sciroppo [shi-**rop**-po] syrup.

sciule piene [**shu**-le pi-**e**-ne] Piedmontese stuffed onions. Stuffing recipes vary: some use raisins, while others call for meat and cheese. The stuffing is thickened with bread soaked in milk.

sclupit, sclopit [sclu-**pit**, sclo-**pit**] the fresh young shoots of the bladder campion, picked wild in Friuli-Venezia Guilia and used in risottos, pasta dishes and FRITTATE.

scoglio, allo [**al**-lo scol-yo] literally 'rock style', used to describe a dish (usually pasta) served with *fruits de mer*, mixed seafood.

sconciglio see MURICE.

scorfano [**scor**-fa-no] scorpion

fish. There is more than one
type: *scorfano rosso* (red),
scorfano nero (black) and the
scorfanotto (a mottled variety).
They are a staple of fish stews
and can also be eaten roasted or
grilled.

scorzato/a [scort-**sa**-to] peeled.

scorza [**scort**-sa] the peel (of
a fruit or vegetable), or rind
(of a cheese). *Scorza candita* is
candied peel. *Scorze d'arance
candite* are candied orange peels.

scorzonera [scort-so-**ne**-ra] a
type of salsify, a plant prized for
its edible root, which is cooked
in the same way as a parsnip.

scottato/a [scot-**ta**-to] for
vegetables, blanched, parboiled.
When talking about meat or
fish, especially tuna, in means
seared.

scremato [scre-**ma**-to]skimmed
(milk).

scrippelle 'mbusse [scrip-**pel**-
le im-**bus**-se] crêpes in broth,
sprinkled with cheese, from
Abruzzo.

scrocchiarella [scroc-ki-a-**rel**-
la] as in *pizza scrochiarella*, pizza
with a very crunchy dough.

scuccuzzu [scuc-**coot**-zu] a type
of pasta from Liguria, rather like

Select, garnet-red mixer drink
marketed as the 'Aperitif born
in Venice', distilled in the
lagoon city since 1920. A 'Spritz
Select' is a popular *aperitivo*
made with Select and Prosecco.

couscous.

scungilli [scun-**jil**-li] whelks,
served sautéed in sauce, often
spicy. It was while eating a dish
of *scungilli* that the gangster Joe
Gallo was gunned down in Little
Italy, Manhattan, on his 43rd
birthday in 1972.

scuro/a [**scu**-ro] dark.

Above: *seppia*, a cuttlefish, fatter in the body than the *calamari*, or squid (pictured opposite).

seadas, seattas, sebadas [se-**a**-das, se-**at**-tas, se-**ba**-das] Sardinian RAVIOLI, large, round and sweet, filled with cheese and grated lemon, and served fried and drizzled with honey.

secale see SEGALE.

secco/a [**sec**-co] dry, dried (pl. *secchi, secche*).

sedanini rigati [se-da-**ni**-ni ri-**ga**-ti] pasta in the form of small celery stalks, i.e. ribbed and grooved in the same way as the plant.

sedano [**se**-da-no] celery.

segale [**se**-ga-le] rye, a kind of grass that has been cultivated since ancient times in northern Italy, where the climate and terrain is unfriendly to wheat. It is prized for its grain, which is suitable both for human consumption and for animal feed. Today, many regional breads and pastas are made from a mixture of wheat and rye flour. Recent Swiss research has shown that bread made from *segale bianca*, the kernel of the rye grain, acts as an excellent natural insulin regulator and can therefore help those at risk from diabetes. Many breads are made from a mixture of wheat flour and rye bran, which does not have the same beneficial effect.

Select [**se**-lect] a mixer drink for making the Venetian APERITIVO known as 'SPRITZ Select'. Made with juniper and rhubarb (and 28 other botanicals), it is very similar in colour to CAMPARI but a little less bitter, and not as sweet as APEROL. Popular in Venice (where it originates) .

sella [**sel**-la] saddle, e.g. *sella d'agnello*: saddle of lamb.

selvaggina [sel-vaj-**ji**-na] game.

semelle [se-**mel**-le] round bread rolls with a cleft in the middle (Florence). The name derives from the German *Semmel* and dates from the period of Austrian rule in Tuscany.

semi [**se**-mi] seeds.

semifreddo [**se**-mi **fred**-do] literally 'half cold', a dessert made of ice cream and sponge cake.

semola battuta [**se**-mo-la bat-**tu**-ta] irregular little lumps of pasta cooked in broth (Puglia).

semolino [se-mo-**li**-no] a flour ground from durum wheat, widely used to make pasta dough. See FARINA.

semplice [**sem**-pli-che] simple.

senape [**se**-na-pe] mustard.

senza [**sent**-sa] without.

seppia [**sep**-pi-a] cuttlefish. There are several types, of which *seppietta* and *seppiola* are two. Styles of cooking do not differ: the flesh is either grilled, fried or stewed, and is also eaten cold in salads. *Seppioline* are very small cuttlefish; *uova di seppia* is cuttlefish roe. *Nero di seppia* is the ink, used to colour and flavour GNOCCHI, pasta and RISOTTO. *Seppia* is similar to, but not the same as, squid (CALAMARI).

seras [**se**-ras] tangy cheese from the Valle d'Aosta.

serpentone [ser-pen-**to**-ne] coiled or spiral-shaped pastry from Umbria and Lazio, made of ground almonds. Also known as *torciglione*.

serra see PESCE SERRA.

serviti con contorno [ser-**vi**-ti con con-**tor**-no] served with vegetables (meaning you do not need to order these separately).

servizio compreso [ser-**vit**-si-o com-**pre**-zo] service charge included.

sesamo [**se**-za-mo] sesame.

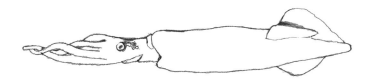

sevadas see SEADAS.

sfarricciato [sfar-ri-**cha**-to] blood pudding (Molise).

sfinciuni [sfin-**chu**-ni] soft pizza topped with tomato, onion, anchovies, oregano and CACIOCAVALLO cheese, served as street food in Palermo.

sfogio [**sfo**-jo] Venetian name for sole (fish), SOGLIOLA.

sfoglia matta [**sfol**-ya **mat**-ta] lit. 'crazy pastry', a term for puff pastry or *pasta sfoglia*.

sfogliatella [sfol-ya-**tel**-la] Neapolitan dessert: a ruffled pastry shaped like a scallop shell, filled with RICOTTA or custard (pl. *sfogliatelle*).

sfoglio, sfogghiu [**sfol**-yo, **sfog**-yu] a puff pastry pie (Sicily).

sformato [sfor-**ma**-to] a vegetable flan or soufflé.

Sfurzat [sfurt-**zat**] the AMARONE of the Valtellina, northeast of Lake Como.

sfuso [**sfu**-zo] *vino sfuso* is loose wine, wine from a cask or demijohn (*see picture overleaf*).

sgabei [sga-**be**-i] strips of fried bread dough, eaten either plain or with a ham or cheese filling.

sgombro [**sgom**-bro] mackerel.

sgroppino [sgrop-**pi**-no] the Italian equivalent of a coupe colonel: a DIGESTIVO or palate cleanser between courses consisting of lemon sorbet laced with vodka. Popular in the Veneto.

sguazzabarbuz see MALTAGLIATI.

sgusciato/a [sgu-**sha**-to] shelled, e.g. of nuts (pl. *sgusciati, sgusciate*).

siccioli see CICCIOLI.

Sicily the large island at the toe of Italy, with a very varied gastronomic tradition reflecting its geographical position and complex history. The soil is fertile and the climate good, meaning that bread, fruit, vegetables, fish, cheese and meat are all excellent. Sicilians eat a lot of fish, and their confectionery is second to none, thanks in part to the introduction of sugar cane by the Arabs and chocolate by the Spanish. Sicily and her offshore islands also produces abundant wine: according to legend, vines first grew here on the slopes of Etna, springing up under the feet of Dionysus.

sidro [**si**-dro] cider.

siliquastro [si-li-**quas**-tro] 1. the Judas tree. Its flowers (*fiori di siliquastro*) are sometimes seen on recherché menus; 2. siliquastrum was the medieval name for PEPERONCINO.

Silter [**sil**-ter] a mild cow's cheese made in the lower Val Camonica, Lombardy.

simenza e calia [si-**ment**-za e **cal**-ya] on feast days in Sicily street stalls sell roasted chickpeas (*calia*) and pumpkin seeds sprinkled with salt (*simenza*).

sindria [**sin**-dri-a] watermelon (Sardinia).

slattato [slat-**ta**-to] soft, fresh cow's milk cheese from the Marche.

Slow Food A movement inspired by an organisation called Arcigola, founded in 1986 as a protest against the proposed opening of a branch of McDonald's near the Spanish Steps in Rome. There is now an international network of towns and villages that subscribe to the Slow ethic: residents are encouraged to cook and eat in a leisurely way, using local produce and respecting local

Simple establishment dedicated to *vino sfuso*, in other words wine that has not been bottled (*imbottigliato*) but which is sold direct to the customer from the barrel, cask or demijohn.

traditions. Slow Food also publishes restaurant and wine guides.

smacafam [sma-ca-**fam**] the 'hunger-beater', potato polenta baked with cream and SALAME (Trentino-Alto Adige).

smetana [**sme**-ta-na] a sauce made of onion, cream or sour cream and wine. It goes well with game birds.

soaso [so-**a**-zo] brill, a flatfish in the turbot family.

Soave [so-**a**-ve] dry white wine from the Verona area of the Veneto, mainly made from the Garganega grape.

sodo [**so**-do] of an egg, hard-boiled: *uovo sodo* (pl. *uova sodi* or *sode*).

sofficini [sof-fi-**chee**-ni] fried crispy pancakes.

soffritto [sof-**frit**-to] a combination of celery, onion and carrot lightly fried in olive oil, the foundation of many Italian recipes. Garlic, parsley, fresh sage and other herbs may be added to taste.

sogliola [**sol**-yo-la] sole. *Alla mugnaia* = meunière.

soia [**so**-ya] soya.

Solaia [so-**la**-ya] like TIGNANELLO, a wine from the Chianti region that is made from Bordeaux grape varieties and does not label itself a Chianti. It is one of the so-called SUPERTUSCANS.

soppressata [sop-pres-**sa**-ta] lit. 'crushed' or 'squashed', a kind of SALUME, a sausage packed into an animal's intestine,

often (but not always) soft and suitable for spreading.

sorana [so-**ra**-na] in the Veneto, beef from a young heifer.

sorbetto [sor-**bet**-to] a sorbet. The word derives from sherbet, a cold drink introduced to Sicily by the Arabs and consisting of water and fruit pulp sweetened with sugar. An *aria di sorbetto,* the 'sorbet aria', was a convention in 19th-century Italian opera, a song performed by one of the minor singers during which ice cream vendors would circulate through the theatre. A *sorbetto* is finer-grained than a GRANITA.

sorcetti [sor-**chet**-ti] a type of GNOCCHI typical of the Abruzzo, often made with spinach.

s'oriattu [so-ri-**at**-tu] Sardinian barley bread.

sospiri [sos-**pi**-ri] 'sighs', little sweetmeats that can take a wide variety of forms, from biscuits to fairy cakes.

sottaceti [sot-ta-**che**-ti] pickles (lit. 'under vinegar').

sotto [**sot**-to] in, on or under, e.g. *tonno sott'olio*: tuna in oil.

spadellato [spa-del-**la**-to] sautéed.

spaghetti [spa-**get**-ti] literally, 'small strings', the most famous Italian pasta.

spaghettoni [spa-get-**to**-ni] extra thick, long spaghetti.

spagnolo [span-**yo**-lo] Spanish.

spalla [**spal**-la] shoulder, of veal, lamb or pork. *Spalla di San Secondo* is a cooked ham from Emilia-Romagna.

spalmare [spal-**ma**-re] to spread; *spalmabile* = spreadable.

sparacanaci [spa-ra-ca-**na**-chi] in Sicily, fried baby mullet.

sparaglione [spa-ral-**yo**-ne] the annular sea bream (*Diplodus annularis*).

sparo [**spa**-ro] Venetian dialect for SPARAGLIONE.

spatola see PESCE SPATOLA.

spätzli [**shpets**-li] *gnocchetti* from Trentino-Alto Adige.

specchio [**spek**-yo] literally, a mirror. On menus a *specchio* is an accompaniment designed to reflect or enhance the principal ingredient, e.g. *zucchini ripieni* (stuffed courgettes) *su specchio di* (on a 'mirror' of) *pomodoro fresco* (fresh tomato).

speck [shpek] juniper-flavoured ham, widely made in Trentino-Alto Adige and northern Italy.

spezie [**spet**-zi-e] spices.

On the origins of spaghetti

Patriotic Italians keen to refute claims that spaghetti was introduced to Italy from China by Marco Polo in the late 13th century seize with glee on the *Tabula Rogeriana*, a book of maps with accompanying commentary commissioned c. 1140 from the Arab cartographer Muhammad al-Idrisi by King Roger II of Sicily. In that book, al-Idrisi refers to the Sicilian town of Trabia, where 'an abundance of water turns numerous mills, where they grind flour used to make *itryah*, a particular type of pasta made up of exceedingly long strings...'. The word *itryah* survives today in Italianised form, as *tria*, a kind of long pasta still eaten in the south. Marco Polo may well have brought a similar food from China to the Veneto. But wheat-growing Sicily and Puglia were already enjoying spaghetti before he was even born.

spezzatino [spets-za-**ti**-no] meat stew.

spianata [spi-a-**na**-ta] a kind of FOCACCIA.

spicchio [**spik**-yo] (pl. *spicchi*) a piece, a segment. *Uno spicchio d'aglio* = a clove of garlic.

spiedini [spi-e-**di**-ni] anything grilled or roasted on skewers (*spiedi*); kebabs.

spiedo [spi-**e**-do] a spit for roasting.

spiga [**spi**-ga] an ear (of wheat, corn).

spighe [**spi**-ghe] pasta shaped like ears of wheat.

spigola [**spi**-go-la] a type of sea bass. *Persico spigola* is striped bass.

spina [**spi**-na] 1. a spine or thorn; 2. a tube, hence *birra alla spina*, draught beer.

spinaci [spi-**na**-chi] spinach (always plural), a popular vegetable served as a side dish, mixed with pasta dough to make green pasta, or used as a pasta stuffing.

spirali [spi-**ra**-li] spiral pasta.

spongata [spon-**ga**-ta] a Christmas pie with a shortcrust pastry exterior and a filling of nuts and dried fruit.

spratto [**sprat**-to] a sprat, pl. *spratti*, sprats.

spremuta [spre-**mu**-ta] freshly squeezed fruit juice.

spressa [**spres**-sa] a cow's milk cheese from Trentino-Alto Adige.

spritz [sprits] also *sprizz*; a popular aperitif in northeast Italy, made with wine and soda or PROSECCO plus the addition of a bitter such as APEROL or CAMPARI.

sproccolati [sproc-co-**la**-ti] dried figs filled with fennel seeds.

spruzzamusi [sprut-za-**mu**-zi] 'snout-sprayers', a regional name for pasta served in a sloppy sauce.

spugnole [spun-**yo**-le] morel mushrooms.

spumante [spu-**man**-te] sparkling, of wine.

spumone [spu-**mo**-ne] a general term for light, fluffy desserts, egg-meringues or mousses (pl. *spumoni*).

spuntini [spoon-**ti**-ni] snacks.

squacquero,
squacquerone [squack-we-ro, squack-we-**ro**-ne] very soft, almost runny cow's milk cheese

When there is an R in the month: fish in season in Venice and its lagoon

Fish, like vegetables, have their season (*stagione*). Many shellfish should not be eaten in the summer months because they are prone to go bad so quickly. Others are best in certain months.

Year round:	Eel, baby squid, clams, John Dory
Spring:	Cuttlefish, soft-shell crab
Spring to December:	Sea bass
Summer:	Mussels, soft-shell crab
Summer to autumn:	Gilt-head bream, grey mullet, baby cuttlefish, sardines, anchovies, sole
Autumn:	Red mullet, flounder, mantis shrimp, langoustines, soft-shell crab
Autumn and winter:	Shrimps, scallops, razor clams, baby octopus
Autumn to early spring:	Turbot

from Emilia-Romagna.

squaliato/a [squa-li-**a**-to] melted.

squalo [**squa**-lo] shark.

stagionato [sta-jo-**na**-to] lit. 'seasoned'; of cheese, aged or matured.

stagione [sta-**jo**-ne] season, e.g. *verdure di stagione*: seasonal vegetables; *fuori stagione*: out of season.

stambecco [stam-**bec**-co] the wild mountain goat of Valle d'Aosta and the alpine regions.

stecca di cioccolato [**stec**-ca di choc-co-**la**-to] chocolate bar.

stecchi alla genovese [**stec**-ki alla je-no-**ve**-ze] wooden skewers stuck with chicken, chicken liver and mushrooms dipped in béchamel sauce, breaded and fried.

stelline [stel-**li**-ne] tiny stars, a pasta shape, also known as *stellette, stellettine, stelle, astri, fiori di sambuco*.

STG *Specialità Tradizionale Garantita*, official appellation awarding 'traditional' status to certain products to protect them from imitations.

stigghiole [stig-**yo**-le] lamb or kid intestines, flavoured with salt, pepper and herbs, wound around a bamboo stick and cooked on a brazier. Traditional street food from Palermo, Sicily.

stile [**sti**-le] style.

stinco [**stin**-co] as in *stinco di maiale* [**stin**-co di ma-**ya**-le], pork hock or pork knuckle, typical winter food in Trentino-Alto Adige, oven-roast with potatoes.

stirpada see SCARPAZZA.

stoccafisso [stoc-ca-**fis**-so] cod or other white fish that has been dried and preserved without the use of salt (compare BACCALÀ, which is salt cod). Both *baccalà* and *stoccafisso* are thoroughly soaked in water before being used.

storione [sto-ri-**o**-ne] sturgeon.

straccetto [stra-**chet**-to] a strip. *Straccetti di manzo* are beef strips.

stracchino [stra-**ki**-no] Lombard cow's milk cheese

with a soft, creamy texture. See CRESCENZA.

stracciamus [stra-cha-**moos**] see SPRUZZAMUSI.

stracciatella [stra-cha-**tel**-la] 1. broth made by adding beaten eggs and PARMESAN cheese to stock; 2. *fior di latte* ice cream (see GELATO) with chocolate chips.

strachin [stra-**kin**] see STRACCHINO.

stracotto [stra-**cot**-to] 1. a stew, often of beef in red wine; 2. overcooked, the opposite of *al dente*.

strafatto [stra-**fat**-to] over-ripe, of fruit.

strangolapreti [stran-go-la-**pre**-ti] 'priest choker', an example of anti-clerical gastroterminology. 1. a potato GNOCCHI, sometimes made with spinach. The idea is that a greedy priest, while gorging himself, might get one stuck in his throat and choke; 2. In some parts of Italy the term is a synonym for STROZZAPRETI.

strangozzi [stran-**gots**-zi] thick Tuscan spaghetti.

strangujët [stran-gu-shet] GNOCCHI with tomato sauce and plenty of basil, an ARBËRESH dish.

straniero/a [stra-ni-**e**-ro] foreign. Wine lists are often divided into *vini Italiani* ('Italian wines') and *vini stranieri* ('foreign wines').

strapazzate [stra-pats-**za**-te] scrambled (eggs).

strascinati [stra-shi-**na**-i] pasta similar to FETTUCCINE or TAGLIATELLE. Sometimes called *penchi*.

strattu [**strat**-tu] in Sicily, tomato purée, lit. 'extract' (*estratto*) of tomato, made by cooking tomatoes and spreading the pulp on large dishes in the sun to evaporate.

stravecchio [stra-**veck**-yo] of a cheese, 'extra aged', in other words even older than a *vecchio*. *Stravecchio* cheeses are typically aged for three years. Cheeses aged for four years or more are sometimes described as *stravecchione*. Brandy can also be *stravecchio* (the equivalent of X.O. on the label).

Strega [**stre**-ga] a herbal DIGESTIVO coloured with saffron and flavoured with mint, consumed, in fiction, by Don Vito Corleone in Mario Puzo's *The Godfather*. The name means 'witch', an allusion to the ancient traditions of witchcraft supposed to have existed in its place of manufacture, Benevento (Campania).

streppe e caccialà [**strep**-pe e cat-cha-**la**] a simple shepherds' dish native to the Maritime Alps of Liguria. It consists of roughly-made piece of pasta boiled in water with cabbage leaves, turnips and potatoes.

striguli, strigoli [**stri**-gu-li, **stri**-go-li] the young shoots of the bladder campion (*Silene vulgaris*), used in parts of Umbria for springtime risotto. In Friuli-Venezia Giulia, where it is a popular ingredient of FRITTATA, it is known as *sclupit* and in Romagna as *strigoli*.

stringozzi [strin-**gots**-zi] thick spaghetti from Umbria, very similar to PICI.

stroncatelli [stron-ca-**tel**-li] spaghetti-like pasta made of flour and egg, popular in Italian Jewish cuisine and traditionally eaten at Rosh Hashanah (Jewish New Year).

strozzapreti [strots-za-**pre**-ti] pasta shape, the 'priest strangler', so called because it resembles a rope or rolled length of cloth.

strucolo [**stru**-co-lo] strudel.

struffoli [**struf**-fo-li] honey-glazed pyramids of fried dough (Campania).

strutto [**strut**-to] lard, reduced pork fat, used in baking and in stews. Not to be confused with the more sophisticated LARDO.

struzzo [**strut**-zo] ostrich, reared in ever increasing numbers throughout Italy.

stufato, stufatino [stu-**fa**-to, stu-fa-**ti**-no] a stew; as an adjective, *stufato* means stewed, braised (fem. *stufata*).

stuzzicadenti [stoots-zi-ca-**den**-ti] toothpicks.

stuzzichini [stoots-zi-**ki**-ni] titbits, finger food that can be served on STUZZICADENTI.

su ordinazione [su or-di-nat-si-**o**-ne] made to order.

succo [**sook**-ko] juice (pl. *succhi*).

sgarello [su-ga-**rel**-lo] the common scad, a type of Altantic mackerel.

sugeli [su-**je**-li] pasta characteristic of the Ligurian alps, small *gnocchetti*

traditionally served with BRUZZO cheese.

sughitti [su-**git**-ti] sweetmeats made from cooked must and cornflour (Marche).

sugna [**soon**-ya] suet.

sugo [**su**-go] sauce or gravy.

suino [su-**i**-no] pig.

superiore see VINO.

Supertuscan term coined by the America wine critic Robert Parker to describe wines from the BOLGHERI region, and also TIGNANELLO from CHIANTI, which revolutionised Italian winemaking in the 1970s by their pioneering use of Bordeaux grape varieties (Cabernet Sauvignon, Cabernet Franc and Merlot). Italian wine classification rules originally prevented these wines from obtaining DOC status. This situation has now been rectified.

suppa cuata [**sup**-pa cu-**a**-ta] a thick soup from Sardinia made by pouring meat stock over alternate layers of bread, PECORINO, parsley and nutmeg and slowly baking until the bread has absorbed the stock and a crust has formed.

supplemento [sup-ple-**men**-to]

extra charge or supplement.

supplì [sup-**pli**] Roman rice balls, stuffed with cheese.

sursuminata [sur-su-mi-**na**-ta] scrambled eggs with tomatoes (Calabria).

susamelli [su-za-**mel**-li] honey-sweetened sesame-seed biscuits.

susianella [su-zi-a-**nel**-la] a well seasoned sausage of pork meat and offal, from the province of Viterbo, Lazio.

susina [su-**zi**-na] plum (pl. *susine*).

tacchino [tac-**ki**-no] turkey.

tacconelle = SAGNE A PEZZE.

tacconi [tac-**co**-ni] 1. large squares (pasta shapes). 2. runner beans.

taggiasche, olive [o-**li**-ve tad-**jas**-ke] the *taggiasca* is a highly prized variety of black olive from Liguria, used for eating and to make oil.

tagliata [tal-**ya**-ta] lit. 'cut'; *tagliata di manzo* is grilled beef entrecôte seasoned with herbs and served in slices. The inside of the meat must be left rare.

tagliatelle [tal-ya-**tel**-le] broad ribbons of egg pasta.

tagliato/a a cubetti [tal-**ya**-to a cu-**bet**-ti] diced.

taglierini [tal-ye-**ree**-ni] thin noodles.

tagliolini [tal-yo-**lee**-ni] egg-pasta noodles.

Tai [tie] white grape used to produce the peachy wine of Friuli. Its full name is Tocai Friulano, but EU regulations forbid the Italian wine to use the name Tocai, because of possible confusion with the Tokaj wine of Hungary. Hence the invented name Tai.

tajarelle [ta-ya-**rel**-le] ribbon pasta from Abruzzo.

tajarin [ta-ya-**reen**] egg noodles (Piedmont).

taleggio [ta-**ledg**-jo] a mild cow's milk cheese from Lombardy, similar in texture to STRACCHINO. Taleggio now enjoys DOP status.

tanaceto [ta-na-**che**-to] tansy, a bitter plant used to make the DIGESTIVO called *arquebuse*. Tansy is held to be good at soothing headaches and joint pain, and effective in preventing infestations of worms.

tangelo [tan-**je**-lo] sometimes called 'honeybell', a large, sweet, seedless citrus fruit, a hybrid of the tangerine or mandarin orange with pomelo or grapefruit. It is grown in Calabria and in eastern Sicily.

tannura [tan-**nu**-ra] a small clay portable oven (Sicily).

taragna [ta-**ran**-ya] see POLENTA.

tarallo [ta-**ral**-lo] a ring-shaped bread roll or biscuit, typical of southern Italy. The diminutive form is *taralluccio*; pl. *taralli*.

tarantella [ta-ran-**tel**-la] tuna SALAME from Taranto, Puglia.

tarocco [ta-**roc**-co] blood orange.

taroz [ta-**rodz**] a kind of north Italian version of bubble and squeak: mashed potatoes and green beans blended with cheese and butter. A hearty dish made from leftovers. Typical of the Valtellina region of Lombardy.

tartina [tar-**ti**-na] a canapé or open sandwich

tartufato/a [tar-tu-**fa**-to] flavoured with truffles.

tartufo [tar-**tu**-fo] truffle, a rare, expensive and highly prized arboreal fungus, a significant component of Italian cuisine (*see box*).

tartufo di mare [tar-**tu**-fo di **ma**-re] a Venus clam, the 'Warty Venus' as opposed to the smooth variety, which is known as *cappa liscia*.

Taurasi [ta-u-**ra**-zi] perhaps the finest red wine from southern Italy. Made mainly from the AGLIANICO grape, grown in Campania.

tavola calda [**ta**-vo-la **cal**-da] literally 'hot table', a snack bar offering pre-cooked food.

tavolozza [ta-vo-**lots**-za] literally, a painter's palette; by association an assortment, e.g. *tavolozza di formaggi morbidi*: an assortment of soft cheeses.

tazza [**tat**-sa] cup

té [tay] tea.

tegamaccio [te-ga-**ma**-cho] a thick fish stew from Umbria, made mainly from eels and perch, served on slices of toasted stale bread.

tegame [te-**ga**-me] a pan, hence *al tegame* or *al tegamino*, braised.

tellina [tel-**li**-na] wedge clam, a shellfish related to the COZZA and the VONGOLA (pl. *telline*).

temolo [**te**-mo-lo] grayling (freshwater fish).

tendaio [ten-**da**-yo] a medium-flavoured cow's milk cheese made in Castiglione di Garfagnana, Tuscany.

Truffles

The truffle is a fungus that grows on or around the roots of trees. The relationship is mutually beneficial, the truffle gaining access to the tree's reserves of carbohydrate and sucrose, the tree benefiting from the water and minerals that the truffle absorbs from the soil. There are several types of truffle to be found in Italy, all of them either white or black.

The best known **white truffle** is the *Alba madonna*, the 'diamond of Piedmont', which grows in the Langhe area and in the countryside around Alba. Also found in Croatia, it flourishes around the roots of oak, hazel, poplar and beech trees and is harvested in autumn, coinciding with the town's annual truffle fair. Another kind of white truffle, the *Tuber magnatum pico*, grows in the Marche and other parts of central Italy.

There are two main kinds of **black truffle**: *Tuber aestivum*, the summer truffle, which grows throughout Italy; and *Tuber melanosporum*, which grows well with oak, hazel and hornbeam. The finest examples come from Norcia and Spoleto in Umbria. Acqualagna, a town in the Marche, is famous for its international festivals for white, black and summer truffles.

Fittingly, given their elusive nature, truffles are 'hunted' by farmers who use sniffer dogs specially trained for the purpose. In former times pigs were used, but they had a dangerous tendency to eat the truffles once they had found them, possibly as a result of becoming over-excited by the truffle's scent, which bears a resemblance to that of the porcine sex hormone. Dogs are more tractable. The preferred breed in Italy is the *Lagotto romagnolo*, a gundog native to Romagna with an obedient nature and a gentle mouth. Such dogs are known as *cani da tartufo* [**ca**-ni da tar-**tu**-fo]: 'truffle hounds'. For a long time the best-known truffle hound in Italy was Diana, who belonged to the Italian-Croatian farmer Giancarlo Zigante. In 1999 she found, near Buje in Croatia, what was recorded in the *Guinness Book of Records* as the largest truffle in the world, weighing 1.31 kg (2lb 14oz). Though this truffle was found in Croatia it did much to stimulate the industry around Alba in Italy, largely as a result of Zigante's imaginative PR initiatives which included refusing to sell the truffle, getting it cast in bronze, giving a lavish banquet to celebrate its discovery, and having Diana hunt truffles on stage in Carnegie Hall. Diana's Croatian record remained unbroken for several years until the autumn of 2007, when a truffle hound named Rocco and his owner Luciano Savini discovered a gigantic example near Pisa, Tuscany. This weighed 1.5kg (3.3lb) and Savini determined to offer it to the highest bidder. At the end of a high-profile auction held simultaneously in Macau, Hong Kong and Florence, the flamboyant Macau casino owner Stanley Ho hazarded USD 330,000 for the truffle, making it at the time not only the largest but also the most expensive ever recorded.

tenerine [te-ne-**ri**-ne] sweet cherries.

tenero/a [te-ne-ro] tender.

tenerumi [te-ne-**ru**-mi] in Sicily, the tender green leaves of the snake-squash, which are cooked and eaten like spinach, or mixed with tomato and morsels of sharp cheese and used to dress spaghetti.

Teroldego [te-**rol**-de-go] grape from Trentino-Alto Adige producing fresh and fruity reds.

testa di maiale [**tes**-ta di ma-**ya**-le] pig's head.

testa in cassetta [**tes**-ta in cas-**set**-ta] brawn or head cheese, a SALUME made from leftover pork cuts, especially meat taken from the head.

testaroli [tes-ta-**ro**-li] typical of the Lunigiana, the area between Liguria and Tuscany, this is an old version of pasta, known to the ancient Romans, consisting of flour-and-water batter cooked on a hot iron, the *testa*. The fat little pancakes are then cut into diamonds, boiled in water and served with PESTO.

teteun [te-te-**oon**] a SALUME made from cooked cows' udders, salted and heavily seasoned with herbs, considered a delicacy in the Valle d'Aosta.

tiella [ti-**el**-la] a layered dish named after the utensil it is cooked in and thus occurring in many manifestations. In general it is a kind of hotpot, containing whatever is at hand: rice, potatoes, shellfish, vegetables and so on.

tigelle [ti-**jel**-le] small circular pastries like Scotch pancakes, waffles or drop scones (Emilia-Romagna), eaten with a variety of sweet and savoury toppings or fillings.

tiglio, fiori di [fi-o-ri di **til**-yo] lime blossom.

Tignanello [tin-ya-**nel**-lo] premier wine from CHIANTI, which blends native SANGIOVESE with Cabernet Sauvignon and Cabernet Franc. Because of the inclusion of non-native grape varieties, it was not permitted to call itself a Chianti according to the classification

rules of the time (the early '70s), and the producer left the Chianti consortium amid much publicity. Tignanello became famous as one of the SUPERTUSCANS. Today the rules have changed, and should it wish, it may now label itself a Chianti.

timballo [tim-**bal**-lo] a baked dish of one staple ingredient (potatoes, pasta or rice) with accompaniments such as cheese, mushrooms, tomatoes.

timo [**ti**-mo] thyme.

timpano SEE TIMBALLO.

tinca [**tin**-ca] tench.

Tintilia [tin-**ti**-li-a] a red grape native to Molise, producing a strong regional wine of the same name.

tiramisù [ti-ra-mi-**su**] a rich dessert of sponge cake sharpened with brandy or other spirit together with ESPRESSO, layered with MASCARPONE fluffed with beaten egg white, and sprinkled with chocolate powder. The name means 'pick-me-up', an allusion to its supposed restorative properties.

tiropatina [ti-ro-pa-**ti**-na] the ancestor of modern creme

Fishmonger cutting up a large *tonno*, with a slightly anxious customer proffering a coin. Scene from a painted vase of the 4th century BC from Lipari in the Aeolian Islands, off northern Sicily.

caramel. A recipe for it is linked to the 1st-century Roman gourmet Marcus Gavius Apicius (*see box opposite*).

tisana [ti-**za**-na] herb tea.

toast not a toasted slice of bread, but a ham and cheese sandwich, a *croque monsieur*.

Tocai Friulano [toc-**ai** fri-u-**la**-no] see TAI.

tocco di funghi [**toc**-co di **foon**-ghi] a 'touch of mushrooms', a Ligurian sauce comprising PORCINI cooked in wine with parsley, garlic, pine nuts and butter. Some versions also use tomatoes.

toma [**to**-ma] a type of alpine cow's milk cheese made from skimmed milk, similar to the French *tomme de Savoie*. A good example is *Toma di Gressoney*, made in the Valle d'Aosta. *Tomini* are small cheeses from Piedmont preserved in oil and spices.

tombarello [tom-ba-**rel**-lo] a kind of tuna, found in tropical waters as well as the Mediterranean (mainly the Adriatic).

tonnarelli [ton-na-**rel**-li] egg pasta cut in fine strands, similar to spaghetti. They are very typical of Roman cuisine, often served with the sauce known as CACIO *e pepe*.

tonnato [ton-**na**-to] served with a tuna mayonnaise or *salsa tonnata*. *Vitello tonnato*, cold poached veal served in a tuna mayonnaise, is an effective collision of tastes and still a widely popular dish (though perhaps now a little *démodé*).

tonno [**ton**-no] tuna. *Tonno alla*

siciliana is tuna cooked with garlic, wine and mint or basil, served in a tomato sauce, to which olives and capers are sometimes added.

tonno del Chianti [ton-no del ki-an-ti] not tuna at all, but pork, cooked long and slowly in white wine until it is meltingly tender. Cut up while still warm, it is mixed with olive oil and herbs and can even be packed into glass jars for future use. For best results, use meat from CINTA SENESE pigs, and serve with *cannellini al* FIASCO.

topinambur [to-pi-nam-boor] Jerusalem artichoke.

topini [to-pi-ni] Tuscan pasta, a little like gnocchi, made with spinach, potato, RICOTTA and egg, formed into little 'mice' and boiled for a few minutes.

torcetti [tor-chet-ti] malted biscuit loops from Piedmont.

torchi [tor-ki] PASTA CORTA shaped like hand torches or flashlights.

torciglione see SERPENTONE.

torcinello [tor-chi-nel-lo] a

Tiropatina, the ancestor of creme caramel

Marcus Gavius Apicius (AD 14–37) was a famous epicure whose name is pseudo-epigraphically linked to a book of ancient Roman recipes, *De Re Coquinaria*, 'The Art of Cooking'. It is unlikely that Apicius wrote these recipes down, though he would certainly have eaten many of them: he has gained a reputation for lavishness and extravagance that is not entirely fair. It is true that gourmet recipes do form a chapter in the book, but the main accent is on the method of preparation and the importance of condiments. The version of *agrodolce* (sweet and sour) sauce mentioned in Apicius, for example, recommends the use of 'pepper, mint, pine nuts, sultanas, carrots, honey, vinegar, oil, wine and musk'. His recipe for 'Tyropatinam', a kind of early creme caramel, calls for a mixture of milk, honey and beaten eggs, heated over a slow flame and then sprinkled with pepper before serving.

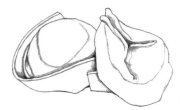

Tortellini, a type of *pasta ripiena* said to resemble the navel of Venus.

lamb's intestine filled with sweetbreads, well seasoned and grilled (pl. *torcinelli*).

torcolo [tor-co-lo] a large, thick CIAMBELLA.

tordi [tor-dee] thrushes. See UCCELLINI.

törggelen [törg-ge-len] an autumn tradition in the wine-making parts of Alto Adige, a sort of cellar crawl involving a walk in the vineyards followed by some glasses of wine and platters of ham, SPECK and cheese. A *Törggl* is the Tyrolean word for a wine press.

tornagusto [tor-na-**goos**-to] literally a 'taste reviver', a sauce devised by Vincenzo Corrado, chef at the court of Naples in the 18th century, to reawaken the jaded palates of his employers.

His *tornagusto* for PROSCIUTTO *di Parma* was made of a mixture of sugar and lard: Corrado died at the age of 103; he may not have eaten too much of his own cooking.

torresano [tor-re-**za**-no] farmed pigeon or squab (pl. *torresani*).

Torrette [tor-**ret**-te] DOC red wine from Valle d'Aosta.

torrone [tor-**ro**-ne] nougat, either hard or soft.

torta [tor-ta] 1. a cake, tart, flan or pie; 2. chickpea flatbread from Livorno, Tuscany.

torta al testo see CRESCIA.

torta salata [tor-ta sa-**la**-ta] the 'savoury pie' of Liguria, filled with whatever ingredients are to hand; a quiche.

tortelli [tor-**tel**-li] PASTA RIPIENA similar to RAVIOLI. *Tortelli di zucca*, stuffed with pumpkin, are popular in northern Italy; *tortelli di patata* are Tuscan potato-filled ravioli.

tortellini [tor-tel-**li**-ni] small egg pasta pockets originally from Emilia-Romagna, made with a variety of fillings including ham, cheese, spinach and potato. In Modena the filling must be based on PROSCIUTTO *crudo* while in Bologna they prefer MORTADELLA. A *tortellino* resemble a navel and there are a number of appealing stories about their origin. One relates that when Venus, Mars and Bacchus stopped one night at an inn near Bologna, the innkeeper could not resist peeping through the keyhole. Upon beholding Venus's exquisite navel, he rushed straight to the kitchen and recreated it in pasta form.

tortelloni [tor-tel-**lo**-ni] large TORTELLINI.

tortiglioni [tor-til-**yo**-ni] short, fat pasta tubes with grooves.

tortino [tor-**ti**-no] a patty, e.g. *tortino di pesce*: fishcake.

tortlòt [tort-lot] in Piedmont, large ravioli filled with a mixture of previously cooked and minced leeks, spinach and chickpeas, bound with parmesan and egg and baked in the oven.

tortora [**tor**-to-ra] turtle dove.

Toscana [tos-**ca**-na] see TUSCANY.

toscanelli [tos-ca-**nel**-li] 1. white Tuscan beans; 2. the small cheroots still much appreciated by Italian smokers, especially in the south.

tosèla [to-**ze**-la] fresh curd cheese, a little like RICOTTA,

The art of folding table linen

If you have ever sat in a restaurant and marvelled at the work of art that is your serviette, you would appreciate the *magnum opus* of Matthias Geiger (d. 1630), a Bavarian professor at the University of Padua, whose *Tre Trattati* are three treatises on tablecraft. The first deals with the art of decorative table linen sculpture and is a step-by-step manual beginning with simple three-way geometric designs and progressing to more intricate confections including bishop's mitres, hunting dogs, lettuces, ships in full sail, wood grouse, the double-headed Habsburg eagle and lion of St Mark. The other two treatises deal with how to lay a table, the proper season for all viands, and how to trim, dress, carve and serve them.

typical of the Primiero valley in Trentino. It is made of cow's milk.

totano [**to**-ta-no] tattler, a type of squid, the end of its body shaped like an arrow (*see picture on p. 169*; pl. *totani*). Abundant around the Aeolian islands, it is delicious cooked in ragout.

tovagliolo [to-val-**yo**-lo] table napkin.

tozzo [**tots**-zo] a crumb or fragment.

tramezzini [tra-mets-**zi**-ni] sandwiches; a filling placed between two slices of square white bread, which is then cut into to triangles. Although very similar to the English prototype, they claim to have been in invented in Turin, and there is even a precise date: 1925. The name was dreamed up by the patriotic poet, aviator and First World War hero Gabriele d'Annunzio: in Mussolini's day there was a Fascist drive to rid the Italian language of what were seen as foreign barbarisms, thus 'sandwich' was deemed unacceptable. See also MARINETTI.

trancio [**tran**-cho] a slice (pl. *tranci*), e.g. *due tranci di pizza*.

tranquillo [tran-**quil**-lo] still (not sparkling).

trattoria [trat-to-**ri**-a] a restaurant, often family-run, and with an informal atmosphere.

Trebbiano [treb-**ya**-no] white-wine grape grown throughout Italy and used to produce pale, dry wines such as FRASCATI. For Trebbiano di Lugana, see TURBIANA.

treccia [**tre**-cha] a plait or braid, used of cheese such as MOZZARELLA or bread.

trenne [**tren**-ne] hollow pasta tubes characteristic of Liguria, flattened on one side; *trennette* are a smaller equivalent.

trentingrana [tren-tin-**gra**-na] hard cheese from the mountains of Trentino. A little like a GRANA in texture. It is made in round truckles and is cellar-aged.

Trentino-Alto Adige [tren-**ti**-no al-to **a**-di-je] northeastern region of Italy bordering Austria and Switzerland, the South Tyrol. It has a dual gastronomic heritage, Trentino being distinctly Italian and Alto Adige being Tyrolean. Game stews and alpine cheeses are the hallmark of the latter, while

POLENTA, freshwater fish from the lakes and pasta characterise the former. Many of the grape varieties have German names: Rosenmuscateller, Gewürztraminer—an appropriately *gemütlich* reminder of Austria.

tretarielle see MENUZZE.

tria 1. (in Puglia) see CICERI; 2. (in Venice) the striped red mullet; see TRIGLIA.

tricolore [tri-co-**lo**-re] lit. 'three colours', a style of many republican flags. The Italian tricolor dates back to the Repubblica Cispadana, a northern Italian state set up by Napoleon in 1796 (the stripes on its flag were horizontal; the vertically-striped flag seen today, with the same colours turned clockwise through 90º, was first used by patriots in the Risorgimento, the movement for Italian unity, and was adopted as the flag of the new Kingdom of Italy in 1861. In 1946 it was again officially adopted as the flag of the republic). In gastronomic terms the colours are also symbolic: green for forests and alpine pastures,

or any number of indigenous strains of spinach, cabbage, wild herbs or artichokes; white for cheese and pasta; red for wine, CHIANINA beef, marbled sections of PROSCIUTTO, and glossy sun-ripe tomatoes.

tridarini [tri-da-**ri**-ni] a type of PASTA GRATTATA.

triddi [**trid**-di] Puglian PASTA GRATTATA.

triglia [**tril**-ya] red mullet. There are two kinds of mullet: *triglia di fango*, the 'mullet of the mud', red mullet, thrives in shallow, sandy or muddy water; *triglia di scoglio* [**scol**-yo], the 'mullet of the rocks' or striped red mullet, which lives in clearer, deeper water and has a better diet, is more highly prized. It is known is Venetian dialect as *tria*.

tripoline [tri-po-**li**-ne] a wavy noodle named in honour of Italy's conquest of Tripoli.

trippa [**trip**-pa] tripe, once street food in most Italian cities, but now building up a gourmet following as CUCINA POVERA becomes more fashionable. As it is one of the cheapest cuts, it was often used as cat food. To say that times are hard, people

Trofie al pesto, a typical dish of Liguria.

often use the expression *Non c'è trippa per gatti*! (There's no tripe for cats!).

triscule [**tris**-cu-le] wild strawberries (Friuli dialect).

trito/a [**tri**-to] minced.

troccoli [**troc**-co-li] a coarse kind of TAGLIOLINI.

trofie, trofiette [tro-fi-e, tro-fi-**et**-te] PASTA CORTA in the form of flattened corkscrews. It is commonly eaten in Liguria, with a PESTO sauce.

Trollinger [**trol**-ling-er] see SCHIAVA.

trota [**tro**-ta] trout; there are many types, both freshwater and saltwater. *Trota salmonata* [sal-mo-**na**-ta] is not a subspecies, it refers to a trout whose flesh is pink due to plenty of carotein in its diet; these fish are farm-raised and purposely fed with carotein-rich mixtures.

trucioli [tru-cho-li] 'wood shavings' a form of PASTA GRATTATA.

truffles see TARTUFO.

tuma [**tu**-ma] in Sicily, fresh sheep's milk cheese, not yet salted. *Tuma all'argentiera* is a popular dish consisting of slices of fried *tuma* dressed with a little balsamic or white wine vinegar, sea salt, pepper and oregano.

tuma persa [**tu**-ma **per**-sa] strong-tasting cow's milk cheese from Sicily, made only in the village of Castronovo di Sicilia. During the maturing process the rind is hand-rubbed daily with olive oil and black pepper.

tuorlo d'uovo [**twor**-lo **dwo**-vo] egg yolk (pl. *tuorli*).

tuppo [**tup**-po] brioche

Turbiana [toor-bi-**a**-na] white-wine grape formerly known as Trebbiano di Lugana. It is used to make LUGANA wines.

turciniuna [tur-chi-ni-**oo**-na] lamb or goat intestines and offal stewed with onions and lemon, popular at Easter in Ragusa,

Sicily.

turtiddi [tur-**tid**-di] sweet fried GNOCCHI (Calabria).

Tuscany region of central Italy known as much for its food and wine as for the cultural treasures of Florence and Siena. Tuscan land is good for agriculture, for vines and olives, and the woods are full of game. The cuisine is firmly tied to the land, and preparation is simple, the main ingredients, such as bread (rigorously unsalted), meat and oil, being allowed to speak for themselves without the augmentation of elaborate sauces. The strong fish soups of Livorno are unique. Wild boar and steak are popular dishes, and the peppery beef stew known as PEPOSO is a classic. Tuscany produces some of the most famous of all Italian wines, including CHIANTI, BRUNELLO di Montalcino, Vino Nobile di Montepulciano, and the sweet dessert wine VINSANTO. There are fine Tuscan SALUMI, and truffles also abound.

tutto mare [**tut**-to **ma**-re] lit. 'all sea'; a seafood sauce.

uccelli scappati [oo-**chel**-li scap-**pa**-ti] 'escaped' birds, morsels of liver, meat or sausage cooked in ways more usually associated with small birds and game, especially with POLENTA, now the traditional song birds or migratory birds are not available.

uccelletto [oo-chel-**let**-to] general term for a small game bird, although there is a Tuscan bean dish, *fagioli all'uccelletto*, in which the beans are slow-cooked in a tomato and sage sauce of a type traditionally served with game birds.

Umbria [**um**-bri-a] the 'Green Sea' of central Italy, beautiful region known for the Apennine mountains and their foothills, for the enchantments of Lake Trasimene, and for the great monastery of St Francis at Assisi, with its frescoes by Giotto. The hillside city of Perugia is the capital and there are numerous picturesque smaller towns. The cuisine of Umbria is varied and reflects a quietly prosperous pastoral heritage dating back to Etruscan times. Wild pigeon, roast suckling pig, black truffle omelette and chilli-infused sauces are characteristic of the region. Norcia sausages are famous. Sagrantino di Montefalco is a well-regarded wine.

umbricelli [um-bi-**chel**-li] pasta noodles typical of Orvieto in Umbria.

umido, in [**u**-mi-do] stewed, in other words cooked slowly in liquid, in a covered pan.

uova di bufala [**wo**-va di **bu**-fa-la] 'buffalo's eggs', small mozzarella cheeses.

uovo [**wo**-vo] egg (pl. *uova*); *uova fritte* = fried eggs; *uova strapazzate* = scrambled eggs.

uova e curcuci see ova.

uva [**u**-va] grapes; *uva bianca/ nera* = white /red grapes; *uva passa* [**pas**-sa], *uva secca* [**sec**-ca] and *uvetta* [u-**vet**-ta] are raisins.

uva spina [**u**-va spi-na] gooseberry.

uvetta [u **vet**-ta] a raisin, pl. *uvette*.

uvetta sultanina [u **vet**-ta sul-ta-**ni**-na] a sultana.

Valle d'Aosta [**val**-le da-**os**-ta] small, northwestern region renowned for dramatic alpine views, feudal castles and abundant wildlife. The Parco del Gran Paradiso was Italy's first national park. The regional cuisine shows notable examples of French and Swiss influence, and because of the cold climate, the emphasis is on preserved food: cheese and cured meats. Polenta is the local staple. Lardo d'Arnad, made from the fat of chestnut-fed pigs, is famous. *Caffè Valdostano*, served in a communal cup with many spouts, is flavoured with orange and laced with grappa. See grolla dell'amicizia.

Val di Chiana see Chianina.

Valdobbiadene [val-dob-**ya**-de-ne] wine-growing area of Treviso province in the Veneto, known for its prosecco.

valeriana [va-le-ri-**a**-na] valerian; *valernianella* is lamb's lettuce.

Valpolicella [val-po-li-**chel**-la] popular red wine made in the province of Verona from a blend of three main grape varieties: Corvina (or sometimes Corvinone), Rondinella and Molinara. Essentially it takes four distinct forms: **1. Valpolicella Classico:** This is basic Valpolicella, made from grapes straight from the vine.

Lighter ones are often served chilled, somewhat in the manner of young Côtes du Rhône; **2. AMARONE**. Made from semi-dried grapes, fermented to complete dryness; **3. RECIOTO**. This most ancient form of Valpolicella, also made from semi-raisined grapes but with residual sweetness; **4. RIPASSO**, made from a second fermentation of Valpolicella Classico on used Recioto or Amarone skins.

vaniglia [va-**nil**-ya] vanilla.

vapore [va-**po**-re] steam; *al vapore* = steamed.

varolo, variolo [va-**ro**-lo, va-ri-**o**-lo] Venetian for sea bass.

Varzi [**vart**-si] a village in the Oltrepò Pavese area of Lombardy, famous for its SALAME.

Vastedda del Belice [vas-**ted**-da del-**be**-li-che] a delicatey-flavoured pulled cheese, DOP, of whole raw sheep's milk, made only along the banks of the Belice in southwest Sicily.

vastunaca [vas-tu-**na**-ca] in Sicily and Calabria, the wild carrot.

VdT *vino da tavola*, table wine.

vecchio/a [**veck**-yo] old; of a cheese, aged.

vegano/a [ve-**ga**-no] vegan.

vegetariano/a [ve-je-ta-ri-**a**-no] vegetarian.

velenoso/a [ve-le-**no**-zo] poisonous.

vellutata [vel-lu-**ta**-ta] a velouté, a dish of creamed vegetables or a sauce made from vegetable stock and roux.

venature [ve-na-**tu**-re] veining; in a ham, streaks.

vendemmia [ven-**dem**-ya] grape harvest; *vendemmia tardiva* [tar-**di**-va] is late harvest.

Venerdì gnocolar [ve-ner-**di** ni-o-co-**lar**] 'Gnocchi Friday' in Verona, the first Friday after Shrove Tuesday, a festival devoted to GNOCCHI. The master of ceremonies is the Papà del Gnoco, whose sceptre is a giant fork impaling a *gnoco*.

Veneziana [ve-net-zi-**a**-na] 1. pertaining to Venice; 2. *veneziane* are almond-glazed brioches.

ventresca [ven-**tres**-ca] the tender underbelly of tuna (though the word can be applied to other fish) often served as grilled steaks.

ventricina [ven-tri-**chi**-na] a pork SALUME from the Abruzzo with its own website (*www.ventricina.com*), complete with appetising photos.

verde all'italiana, salsa [ver-de al-it-tal-i-**a**-na] Italian green sauce of olive oil, garlic, parsley, anchovies, capers, cucumbers and vinegar.

Verdicchio [ver-**dik**-ki-o] grape from the Marche producing white wines, generally crisp and pleasant. The DOC Verdicchio dei Castelli di Jesi is highly respected.

verdure [ver-**du**-re] vegetables; *verdure di stagione* [stad-**jo**-ne] are seasonal vegetables.

Verduzzo [ver-**doots**-zo] grape from the Friuli region, yielding fruity, perfumed white wines.

Vermentino [ver-men-**ti**-no] white-wine grape cultivated in Sardinia and in coastal regions of Tuscany and Liguria. Produces dry wines that go well with fish.

vermicelli [ver-mi-**chel**-li] literally, 'little worms', very thin pasta used in soups.

vermouth (in Italian, *vermut*) a dry fortified wine, flavoured with herbs, said to have been invented in Turin in the late 18th century. Italian vermouth comes in two varieties, dry white and sweet red (made sweet with the addition of caramel). White vermouth is often used in cooking as a substitute for white wine. The best known brands of Italian vermouth are MARTINI and CINZANO.

Vernaccia [ver-**nat**-cha] 1. a white-wine grape grown in central Italy, used in Tuscany, for the DOC Vernaccia di San Gimignano; 2. Vernaccia di Serrapetrona is a ruby-red, sparkling DOCG dessert wine from the Marche.

Vernatsch [fer-**natsh**] see SCHIAVA.

verza [**vert**-sa] Savoy cabbage. *Verze ripiene* are stuffed cabbage leaves. *Verza nera* is red cabbage.

verzelata [vert-se-**la**-ta] in Venice, a type of mullet.

vialone [vi-a-**lo**-ne] a type of rice used for RISOTTO.

vicentina, alla [vi-chen-**ti**-na] 'Vicenza style'. BACCALÀ *alla vicentina* is stockfish cooked with onions and milk.

vincisgrassi [vin-chis-**gras**-si] LASAGNE from the Marche made with the addition of béchamel sauce. Vincisgrassi is a corruption of the name of Alfred Candidus Ferdinand, Prince of Windisch-Grätz, commander of the Austrian forces against Napoleon at the siege of Ancona (1799). The dish was allegedly created for him by a local chef and constitutes an interesting fusion, encountered elsewhere in northern Italian cooking, of lean local produce and middle-European creaminess.

vinicolo [vi-**ni**-co-lo] wine-producing; *produzione vinicola* = wine production.

vino [**vi**-no] wine. Italy is one of Europe's most important producers and the range is vast. Major grape varieties and types of wine are indexed by name (e.g. Barolo, Sangiovese) .

Basic wine terms
Colour: *rosso* (red); *bianco* (white); *rosato* (rosé).

Taste: *secco* (dry; *abboccato* (semi-dry); *amabile* (semi-sweet); *dolce* (sweet); *frizzante* (sparkling).

Quality: *vino del paese* (country wine); *vino da tavola* (table wine); *vino della casa* (house wine); *vino sfuso* (loose wine, which you can order by the carafe, *caraffa*). *Vino superiore* indicates a grade above the standard wine; more prestigious still is the *Riserva*. *Vino d'annata* is vintage wine.

Wine classification
In Italy, as in other wine-producing nations, the quality of a wine depends on measurable factors such as grape type, climate, soil and age. Immeasurables, such as the resourcefulness, integrity and vision of individual wine producers, are the subject of as much debate in Italy as they are elsewhere. Italy also has stringent wine laws that dictate what grapes may be used for what wines, and for blended wines, in what proportions those grape varieties may be mixed.

Wine (and also some foods) are carefully classified in Italy. Wine is bottled and sold under four classifications which commonly appear on wine bottle labels, either written out in full or in abbreviated form: VdT, IGT, DOC and DOCG.

VdT: *vino da tavola*, for the most part good, honest table wine that varies from area to area and vintage to vintage.

IGT (*Indicazione geografica tipica*): used to classify wines that are produced to a high standard in a defined geographical area but which do not meet the stricter requirements necessary for a DOC or DOCG classification.

DOC (*Denominazione di origine controllata*): used to classify wine that is produced to strict standards in specified regions. In its zeal to implement the new system in the wake of new legislation in 1992, the awarding bodies handed out what many felt to be an excessive number of DOCs, with the result that it was soon necessary to implement a new. 'super' classification:

DOCG (*Denominazione di Origine Controllata e Garantita*). Here the product's quality and authenticity is 'guaranteed' by official, government-licensed tasters.

---

vino arancione [vi-no a-ran-**cho**-ne] orange wine, a speciality of Friuli-Venezia Giulia, indicating a very tart, astringent wine, orange in colour, obtained by a process of very long contact with the skin, stems and pips. Grape varieties used include RIBOLLA GIALLA and PINOT GRIGIO.

vino biodinamico [vi-no bi-o-di-**nam**-i-co] biodynamic wine, made using organic methods but also taking into account the rhythms of the planets, moon etc.

vino biologico [vi-no bi-o-**loj**-i-co] organic wine.

vino novello [vi-no no-**vel**-lo] the new vintage, drunk in October or November of the year it is produced; often delightfully FRIZZANTE.

vino sfuso [vi-no **sfoo**-zo] *see*

Reading a wine label

Logo or symbol

Name of the
estate or producer

**TENUTA
LA MORRA**

VIGNACCIO

Name of the wine

Grape variety, *vitigno*

Gaglioppo

INDICAZIONE GEOGRAFICA TIPICA
IMBOTTIGLIATO ALL'ORIGINE CIRÒ (KR) ITALIA

Classification

2014

Vintage

750ML℮13.5%VOL

ALC13.5% BY VOL

Alcoholic strength

Imbottigliato da means 'bottled by'; *imbottigliato all'origine* means
'estate-bottled'; *imbottigliato dal viticoltore* means that the wine
was bottled by the grower.

sfuso.

vino speziato [**vi**-no spet-si-**a**-
to] spiced, mulled wine, served
in winter.

vino da tavola [**vi**-no da ta-**vo**-
la] table wine.

vino visciolato [**vi**-no vi-sho-
la-to] red wine infused with wild

cherries.

Vinsanto [vin-**san**-to] or Vin
Santo; amber-coloured dessert
wine from Tuscany, typically
made from TREBBIANO or
MALVASIA grapes, which are
traditionally dried on straw to
concentrate the sugars. The

name means 'holy wine' because it is always made in Holy Week. It requires a lot of care and attention and must age in the barrel for at least three or four years before bottling. Families would put down a bottle of Vinsanto on the arrival of a baby girl, to be drunk at her wedding. The wines vary in sweetness; some are almost dry.

violino di capra [vi-o-**li**-no di **ca**-pra] 'The goat's fiddle', a goat leg marinated in wine with juniper berries, bay leaves and other seasoning. Originally from the Valtellina and Valchiavenna in Lombardy it is carved in a striking manner, the joint held like a violin, the carving knife its bow. Tradition says that once started, the whole thing must be eaten before the guests may leave the table.

virtù [vir-**too**] spring vegetable soup.

visciole [**vi**-sho-le] wild cherries.

viscotta [vis-**cot**-ta] in Sicilian dialect, biscuits.

vite [**vi**-te] vine (pl. *viti*).

vitello [vi-**tel**-lo] calf, veal.

vitigno [vi-**tin**-yo] grape variety.

Vitovska [vi-**tov**-ska] white-wine grape producing dry, complex, medium-bodied wines. It is grown in Friuli-Venezia Giulia.

vongole [**von**-go-le] clams (sing. *vongola*). *Spaghetti alle vongole*, a popular dish in the Veneto, is served with a sauce of garlic, parsley, pepper and olive oil with a hint of dried chilli. *Vongole veraci* [**von**-go-le ve-**ra**-chi] are carpet shell clams, distinguishable from *vongole* by the bands on their shells (*see illustration*).

vredocchie [vre-**doc**-ki-e] indented GNOCCHI from Molise, traditionally served with cauliflower in the dish *vruocchele con vredocchie*.

vuliata [vu-li-**a**-ta] in Puglia, a bread roll baked with olives (*puccia e uliate*).

weinsuppe [**vein**-zup-pe] *zuppa di vino* in Italian, a light soup made with white wine, beef broth, egg yolks and cream seasoned with cinnamon, characteristic of Trentino-Alto Adige. *Terlanerweinsuppe*, made in the town of Terlano, is the best known version.

wine see VINO.

xeres [**tse**-rez] sherry.

zabaglione [tsa-bal-**yo**-ne] a creamy dessert made with beaten eggs, sugar and MARSALA.

zaeti [tsa-**e**-ti] see ZALETTI.

zafferano [tsaf-fe-**ra**-no] saffron, the stamen of a particular kind of crocus (*Crocus sativus*), cultivated mainly in the Marche, Abruzzo and Sardinia. It is a highly prized (and highly priced) flavouring and colouring ingredient for risotto, soups, cakes and pasta. It was introduced into Italy from Spain in the 13th century, by a Dominican monk from Navelli in the Abruzzo, who first came across the plant in Toledo, while attending a meeting on the extirpation of heresy. The saffron crocus throve in Italian soil and made fortunes for the residents

Two types of *vongole*. The simple *vongola* (above) has a pale brown or greyish shell patterned with a distinctive zigzag. *Vongole veraci* (shown below) have darker shells marked with radiating vertical bands.

of Navelli and also the town of L'Aquila, which celebrated its wealth by building and endowing churches, libraries and colleges.

zaletti [tsa-**let**-ti] little butter biscuits from the Venice region, made with added sultanas and a dash of grappa. Known in dialect as *zaeti*.

zammù [tsam-**mu**] a Sicilian thirst-quencher, of Arab origin, consisting of cold water and a drop of anise essence, which clouds the water.

zampa, zampetta [tsam-pa,

tsam-**pet**-ta] foot or claw.

zampone [tsam-**po**-ne] a SALUME from Modena. Seasoned pork stuffed into the skin of a pig's front leg. It is typically served in slices, often accompanied by lentils, beans, pickles, etc.

zanchetta [tsan-**ket**-ta] small fish, particularly the scaldfish; small fry.

zappatora, alla [tsap-pa-**to**-ra] 'navvy style'; see CARRETIERA.

zelten [**tsel**-ten] a rich cake of dried fruit and nuts, from Trentino-Alto Adige.

zenzero [**tsen**-tse-ro] ginger.

zeppola [**tsep**-po-la] a fritter, in southern Italy; *zeppole di San Giuseppe* are fritters for Saint Joseph's Day, made in Naples, noted for their rich, creamy fillings.

zeraria [tse-**ra**-ri-a] a pork and beef galantine from Liguria, traditionally made by the whole family for Christmas festivities.

zibba [**tsib**-ba] also known as *merca*, a Sardinian name for glasswort or SALICORNIA. In *muggine sulla zibba*, grey mullet is served on a bed of it.

Zibibbo [tsi-**bib**-bo] a white grape from Pantelleria, from which the DOC *Moscato di Pantelleria* and *Moscato Passito di Pantelleria* are made. The vines are grown in shallow pits surrounded by dry-stone lava walls to protect them from the winds and provide them with moisture (humidity condenses onto the stone at night). The cultivation technique is now UNESCO World Heritage.

zighe [**tsi**-ghe] see ARSELLE.

zighera [tsi-**ghe**-ra] round curd cheese, seasoned or smoked, from Trentino.

zigoinr [tsi-**go**-i-ner] a species of wild oregano unique to the area surrounding Cortina d'Ampezzo in the Veneto Dolomites, used to flavour PUCCIA DI CORTINA.

zigrinate [tsi-gri-**na**-te] small snails.

zimino, in [tsi-**mi**-no] used mainly of fish, meaning cooked in a sauce of finely minced onion and celery with spinach or chard. Some versions also include tomatoes.

zippuli [**tsip**-pu-li] a Sardinian term for fritters. See ZEPPOLA.

zite, ziti [**tsi**-te, **tsi**-ti] large, tubular MACCHERONI originally from Southern Italy, also known as *boccolotti*, *zitoni*, *zituane* or *candele*.

zolfini [tsol-**fi**-ni] a Tuscan variety of FAGIOLI, known also as *fagioli burrini* ('butter beans'), suitable for cooking *al* FIASCO. Tradition relates that before retiring to bed, Tuscan labourers would fill their empty terracotta wine flasks with beans and leave them nestling overnight in the dying embers of the hearth. The following day the slowly-cooked beans would form the basis of a sustaining snack.

zolletta [tsol-**let**-ta] a cube, e.g. *zollette di zucchero*, sugarlumps.

zucca [**tsuk**-ca] pumpkin, squash, marrow (pl. *zucche*).

zucchero [**tsuk**-ke-ro] sugar. *Zucchero greggio* [**gredg**-jo] = brown sugar.

zucchine, zucchini [tsuk-**ki**-ne tsuk-**ki**-ni] courgettes, zucchini; baby marrows.

zuccotto [tsuk-**cot**-to] a dome-shaped SEMIFREDDO with a sponge exterior and an ice cream and candied fruit filling.

zuf [tsuf] in Friuli, a gruel or porridge made of corn POLENTA and milk. It can also refer to a dish of creamed pumpkin.

zufi [**tsu**-fi] a fermented RICOTTA from northern Piedmont.

zuncà see GIUNCATA.

zuppa [**tsup**-pa] soup.

zuppa inglese [**tsup**-pa in-**gle**-ze] literally 'English soup,' the Italian version of trifle: layers of custard and chocolate cream, laced with ALCHERMES and containing crumbled sponge cake for texture. A plausible theory as to its origin is that the Dukes of Este instructed their chefs to recreate the dramatically rich English puddings they had been served at the court of Elizabeth I.

zuppa alla Pavese see PAVESE.

zuppetta [tsup-**pet**-ta] 1; a little soup; 2: a cream and sponge slice from Naples.

USEFUL PHRASES

Cordiality, courtesy, a polite use of the conditional tense, a clearly expressed readiness to part with money and sincerely expressed gratitude all go a long way in Italy. The following twelve basic phrases are well worth rehearsing until you have them by heart. They can be attached with minimal adaptation to virtually any word, phrase or concept contained in this book.

I. THE TWELVE BASICS

Good morning *Buon giorno* [buon **jor**-no]
Good afternoon *Buon pomeriggio* [buon po-me-**ridg**-jo]
Good evening *Buona sera* [buo-na-**se**-ra]
Please *Per favore* [per fa-**vo**-re]
Thank you *Grazie* [**grat**-si-e]
I would like *(Io) vorrei* [yo vor-**re**-i]
We would like *Vorremmo* [vor-**rem**-mo]
He would like *(Lui) vorrebbe* [**lu**-i vor-**reb**-be]
She would like *(Lei) vorrebbe* [**le**-i vor-**reb**-be]
The bill please *Il conto per favore* [il **con**-to per fa-**vo**-re]
This is for you *Ecco a lei!* [**ec**-co a **le**-i] (when giving a tip)
Goodbye and thank you *Arrivederci, grazie!* [ar-ri-ve-**der**-chi **grat**-si-e!].

II. FINDING A RESTAURANT

The next step is to find a good restaurant. Research on the internet sometimes works, and guide books can be a great help. But nothing can beat asking real people for their opinion. Concierges, chambermaids, policemen, the couple at the next table at breakfast—all these are fair game and may well be able to impart useful local knowledge.

Where is the nearest restaurant?
Dove si trova il ristorante più vicino? [**Do**-ve si **tro**-va il ri-sto-**ran**-te pi-**u** vi-**chi**-no]

Is there a restaurant near here?
C'è un ristorante qui vicino? [Che un ri-sto-**ran**-te kwi vi-**chi**-no]

Can you recommend...
   ...a good restaurant?
   ...an exclusive restaurant?
   ...a reasonably priced restaurant?
   ...a restaurant where they serve authentic Italian cooking?
Mi può consigliare... [Mi **pwo** con-sil-**ya**-re]
   ...un buon ristorante? [un **bwon** ri-sto-**ran**-te]
   ...un ristorante esclusivo? [un ri-sto-**ran**-te es-clu-**zi**-vo]
   ...un ristorante a prezzi ragionevoli? [un ri-sto-**ran**-te a **prets**-zi ra-jo-**ne**-vo-li]
...un ristorante dove si offre autentica cucina italiana? [un ri-sto-**ran**-te **do**-ve si **of**-fre a-u-**ten**-ti-ca cu-**chi**-na i-ta-li-**a**-na]

Where is the best pizzeria?
Dov'è la migliore pizzeria? [do-**ve** la mil-**yo**-re pits-ze-**ri**-a]

Can you recommend a bar where they sell good snacks?
Mi può consigliare un bar dove vendono spuntini buoni? [Mi **pwo** con-sil-**ya**-re un bar do-ve **ven**-do-no spun-**ti**-ni **bwo**-ni]
We would like a quiet candlelit dinner.
Vorremmo una tranquilla cena a lume di candela. [vor-**rem**-mo un-a tran-**quil**-la **che**-na a **lu**-me di can-**de**-la]

We would like to go to a place with dancing and live music.
Vorremmo andare in un luogo con dansing e un gruppo live. [vor-**rem**-mo an-**dar**-e in un **luo**-go con **dan**-sing e un **grup**-po **la**-iv].

III. BOOKING

The likelihood is that you will either ask a concierge to make a booking for you or, failing that, take your chances and explore the city, town or village. If you feel sufficiently confident to make a booking yourself, the following phrases will be useful.

I'd like to make a reservation.
Vorrei fare una prenotazione. [Vor-**re**-i **fa**-re u-na pre-no-tats-**yo**-ne]

What time do you open this evening?
A che ora apre stasera? [a ke **o**-ra **a**-pre sta-**se**-ra]

I would like to book a table for seven o'clock / 7.30.
Vorrei prenotare un tavolo per le sette / le sette e mezzo. [vor-**re**-i pre-no-**ta**-re un **ta**-vo-lo per le **set**-te / **set**-te e **mets**-zo]
There are four of us.
Siamo quattro. [si-**a**-mo **kwat**-tro]
1, 2, 3, 4, 5, 6, 7, 8, 9, 10, 11, 12
uno, due, tre, quattro, cinque, sei, sette, otto, nove, dieci, undici, dodici [**u**-no, **du**-e, tre, **kwat**-tro, **chin**-kwe, **se**-i, **set**-te, **ot**-to, **no**-ve, di-**e**-chi, **un**-di-chi, **do**-di-chi]

IV. BASIC QUESTIONS

Is there a fixed price menu?
C'è un menù a prezzo fisso? [che un me-**nu** a **prets**-zo **fis**-so]

Can we bring the children?
Possiamo portare i bambini? [pos-si-**a**-mo por-**ta**-re i bam-**bi**-ni]

Is there a high chair?
C'è un seggiolone? [che un sedg-jo-**lo**-ne]

Do you have vegetarian dishes?
Avete piatti vegetariani? [a-**ve**-te pi-**at**-ti ve-je-ta-ri-**a**-ni]

I am allergic to...
  ...nuts.
  ...dairy products.
  ...gluten.
Sono allergico / allergica... [**so**-no al-**ler**-ji-co / al-**ler**-ji ca]
  ...alle noci [**al**-le **no**-chi]
  ...ai latticini [**a**-i lat-ti-**chi**-ni]
  ...al glutine [al **glu**-ti-ne]

Can you prepare dishes without...?
Potete preparare piatti senza...? [po-**te**-te pre-pa-**ra**-re pi-**at**-ti **sent**-sa...]

Do you take credit cards?
Accettate carte di credito? [a-chet-**ta**-te car-te di **cre**-di-to]

V. ARRIVING AT THE RESTAURANT

If you have not booked and the restaurant seems busy, ask if you can wait. The manager will tell you if a table will be available soon or apologise is he is unable to accommodate you (*mi dispiace, ma siamo al completo stasera*: I'm sorry but we're fully booked this evening). Once a table is available, or if you have already booked, you will need to choose where to sit.

I have a reservation in the name of ------------.
Ho una prenotazione a nome di --------. [**o** u-na pre-no-tats-**yo**-ne a **no**-me di]

Can we wait for a table?
Possiamo aspettare un tavolo? [pos-si-**a**-mo as-pet-**ta**-re un **ta**-vo-lo]

Can we come back in half an hour?
Possiamo tornare tra mezz'ora? [pos-si-**a**-mo tor-**na**-re tra mets-**so**-ra]

May we sit here?
Possiamo sederci qui? [pos-si-**a**-mo se-**der**-chi kwi]
Can we sit...
   ...inside / outside?
   ...by the window?
   ...in the corner?
Possiamo sederci... [Pos-si-**a**-mo se-**der**-chi]
   ...all'interno / all'esterno? [al in-**ter**-no / al es-**ter**-no]
   ...vicino alla finestra? [vi-**chi**-no al-la fi-**ne**-stra]
   ...all'angolo? [al **an**-go-lo]

We are in a hurry.
Abbiamo premura. [ab-bi-**a**-mo pre **mu**-ra]

VI. ORDERING YOUR MEAL

You are seated and ready to order drinks and inspect the menu. Try to gauge the relative seniority of the staff and to judge if it would be better to use the more respectful *Signora* or *Signore* when attempting to attract their attention. Get a fix on where the bathrooms are, especially if you are with children. Remember that children are welcomed even if they make a lot of noise.

Decoding an Italian menu

A typical menu will list courses as follows: *antipasti* (appetisers); *primi piatti* (usually pasta and risotto); *secondi piatti* (meat and fish dishes); *contorni* (accompanying vegetables); *formaggi* (cheese); *dolci* (desserts). You do not have to order all courses. It is perfectly acceptable just to have a starter and a pasta dish, or a starter, meat and dessert. Fixed-prize menus are also sometimes available, for example a *menu del giorno* at lunchtime or a *menu degustazione* (taster menu).

Waiter! Waitress!
Cameriere! Cameriera! [ca-me-ri-**e**-re! ca-ma-ri-**e**-ra!]

Madam! Sir! Miss!
Signora! Signore! Signorina! [sin-**yo**-ra! sin-**yo**-re! sin-yo-**ri**-na!]

We would like something to drink.
Vorremmo qualcosa da bere. [vor-**rem**-mo kwal-**co**-za da **be**-re]
Could we have the menu please?
Potremmo avere il menu? [po-**trem**-mo a-**ve**-re il me-**nu**]

Do you have a menu in English?
Avete un menu in inglese? [a-**ve**-te un me-**nu** in in-**gle**-ze]

May I see the wine list?
Potrei vedere la carta dei vini? [po-**tre**-i ve-**de**-re la **car**-ta de-i **vi**-ni]
We would like a bottle of...
   ...still water.
   ...sparkling water.
   ...this wine.
Vorremmo una bottiglia di... [vor-**rem**-mo u-na bot-**til**-ya di]

...*acqua liscia* [**ac**-kwa-**li**-sha]
...*acqua frizzante.* [**ac**-kwa frits-**zan**-te]
...*questo vino.* [**kwe**-sto **vi**-no]

I would like...
The little girl would like...
The little boy would like...
Vorrei... [vor-**re**-i]
La bambina vorrebbe... [la bam-**bi**-na vor-**reb**-be]
Il bambino vorrebbe... [il bam-**bi**-no vor-**reb**-be]

For me / her / him/ us / them.
Per me / lei / lui / noi / loro [per me / **le**-i / **lu**-i / **no**-i / **lo**-ro]

What are the dishes of the day?
Quali sono i piatti del giorno? [**kwa**-li **so**-no i pi-**at**-ti del **jor**-no]

What do you recommend?
Che cosa mi consiglia? [ke **co**-za mi con-**sil**-ya]

We are not ready to order.
Non siamo pronti per ordinare. [non si-**a**-mo **pron**-ti per or-di-**na**-re]

We would like what they're having.
Vorremmo un piatto uguale al loro. [vor-**rem**-mo un pi-**at**-to u-**gwa**-le al **lo**-ro]

We'd like to order now.
Vorremmo ordinare ora. [vor-**rem**-mo or-di-**na**-re **o**-ra]

I'd like something light.
Vorrei qualcosa di leggero. [vor-**re**-i kwal-**co**-za di ledg-**je**-ro].
Which wine do you recommend for the fish / meat / dessert?

Quale vino mi consiglia per il pesce / la carne / il dolce? [kwa-le **vi**-no mi con-**sil**-ya per il **pe**-she / **car**-ne / **dol**-che]

We would like to share a selection of antipasti.
Vorremmo condividere una selezione di antipasti. [vor-**rem**-mo con-di-**vi**-de-re u-na se-lets-i-**o**-ne di an-ti-**pas**-ti]

Which vegetables are in season?
Quali sono le verdure di stagione? [**kwa**-li **so**-no le ver-**du**-re di stadg-**jo**-ne]

May I have...
  ...spinach with the steak?
  ...**more bread, oil and vinegar?**
  ...some ice?
Posso avere... [**pos**-so a-**ve**-re]
  ...spinaci con la bistecca? [spi-**na**-chi con la bi-**stec**-ca]
  ...più pane, olio e aceto balsamico? [pi-**u pa**-ne, **o**-li-o e a-**che**-to bal-**sa**-mi-co]
  ...un po' di ghiaccio [un **po** di ghi-**a**-cho]

I'd like to try...
  ...a local cheese.
  ...a traditional dish.
Vorrei provare... [vor-**re**-i pro-**va**-re]
  ...un formaggio locale. [un for-**mad**-jo lo-**ca**-le]
  ...un piatto tradizionale. [un pi-**at**-to tra-dit-si-o-**na**-le]

Please bring...
  ...another bottle of wine / water.
  ...another orange juice.
  ...a knife / spoon / napkin.
  ...a fork.
  ...the salt and pepper.

Si prega di portare... [si **pre**-ga di por-**ta**-re]

   ...un'altra bottiglia di vino / d'acqua. [un **al**-tra bot-**til**-ya di **vi**-no / **d'ac**-kwa]

   ...un altro succo d'arancia [un **al**-tro **suc**-co da-**ran**-cha]

   ...un coltello / cucchiaio / tovagliolo [col-**tel**-lo / cu-ki-**aï**-o / to-val-**yo**-lo]

   ...una forchetta [**u**-na for-**ket**-ta]

   ...il sale e il pepe. [il **sa**-le e il **pe**-pe]

What grape variety is this wine?
Che vitigno è questo vino? [ke vi-**tin**-yo e **kwe**-sto **vi**-no]
Just a drop [when the waiter offers to pour you more wine]
Solo un goccio. [**so**-lo un **got**-cho]

VII. SPECIAL NEEDS & REQUESTS

NB: For dietary requirements, see IV. Basic Questions.

Could you heat this [baby] bottle for me?
Potrebbe fare scaldare questo biberon? [po-**treb**-be **fa**-re scal-**da**-re **kwe**-sto bi-be-**ron**]

Where is the bathroom?
Dov'è il bagno? [do-**ve** il **ban**-yo]

Please could you close the window/door.
Potrebbe chiudere la finestra / porta. [po-**treb**-be ki-**u**-de-re la fi-**nes**-tra / **por**-ta]

Please could you open the window/door.
Potrebbe aprire la finestra / porta. [po-**treb**-be ap-**ri**-re la fi-**nes**-tra / **por**-ta]

Is this spicy?
È questo piccante? [e **kwe**-sto pi-**can**-te]

Does this contain.....?
Questo contiene.....? [**kwe**-sto con-ti-**e**-ne]

Is this sweet?
È questo dolce? [e **kwe**-sto **dol**-che]

VIII. WHEN THINGS GO WRONG

I did not order...
   ...this dish.
   ...this drink.
   ...this wine.
Non ho ordinato... [non o or-di-**na**-to]
   ...questo piatto. [**kwe**-sto pi-**at**-to]
   ...questa bevanda. [**kwe**-sta-be-**van**-da]
   ...questo vino. [**kwe**-sto **vi**-no]

I ordered...
   ...the vongole / the lamb / the tiramisu.
   ...orange juice / sparkling water.
Ho chiesto... [o ki-**e**-sto]
   ...le vongole / l'agnello / il tiramisù. [le **von**-go-le / lan-**yel**-lo / il ti-ra-mi-**su**]
   ...succo d'arancia / acqua frizzante [**suc**-co da-**ran**-cha / ac-kwa frits-**zan**-te]

We have been waiting a long time.
È molto tempo que aspettiamo. [e **mol**-to **tem**-po ke as-pet-ti **a**-mo]

This food / coffee is cold.
Questo cibo / caffè è freddo. [**kwe**-sto **chi**-bo / caf-**fe** e **fred**-do]

This is underdone.
Questo è poco cotto/a. [**kwe**-sto e **po**-co **cot**-to/ta]

This is overcooked.
Questo è troppo cotto/a. [**kwe**-sto e trop-po **cot**-to/ta]

Excuse me, but the wine is corked.
Scusi, ma il vino sa di tappo. [**scu**-zi ma il **vi**-no sa di **tap**-po]

IX. PAYING THE BILL

Could I have the bill please?
Il conto per favore. [il **con**-to per fa-**vo**-re]

May I pay with a credit card?
Posso pagare con una carta di credito? [**pos**-so pa-**ga**-re con u-na **car**-ta di **cre**-di-to]

Is service included?
Il servizio è incluso? [il ser-**vit**-si-o e in-**clu**-zo]

The bill isn't right.
Il conto non torna. [il **con**-to non **tor**-na]

Keep the change.
Tenga il resto. [**ten**-ga il **res**-to]

We will pay all together

Pagheremo tutti insieme [pa-ghe-**re**-mo **tut**-ti in-si-**e**-me]

We will all pay separately
Facciamo alla romana (in the 'Roman' way, the equivalent of going
Dutch) [fatch-**ya**-mo al-la ro-**ma**-na]
We've eaten really well here
Abbiamo mangiato molto bene. [ab-bi-**a**-mo man-**ja**-to **mol**-to **be**-ne]

The food was great.
Il cibo era ottimo. [il **chi**-bo e-ra **ot**-ti-mo]

Could you call me a taxi?
Potrebbe chiamarmi un taxi. [po-**treb**-be ki-a-**mar**-mi un **tak**-si]

X. IN THE BAR, CAFÉ OR GELATERIA

It is important to remember, when ordering in cafés or bars, that you
should pay at the till (*cassa*) and then take your receipt (*scontrino*) to the
bar or to collect your order. The essential thing to be aware of in bars is
the difference between bar service and table service. Do not order at the
bar and then surreptitiously attempt to sit at a table.

I'd like a small / medium / large ice cream please.
Vorrei un gelato piccolo / medio / grande per favore. [vor-**re**-i un je-**la**-to **pic**-
co-lo / **me**-di-o / **gran**-de per fa-**vo**-re]

I'd like one scoop / two scoops....
  ...in a cone / in a cup...
  ...with a little whipped cream.
Vorrei una pallina / due palline... [vor-**re**-i u-na pal-**li**-na / **du**-e pal-**li**-ne]
  ...in un cono / in una coppetta... [in un **co**-no / in **u**-na
  cop-**pet**-ta]

...con un po' di panna. [con un **po** di **pan**-na]

I would like…
   ...a glass of————.
   ...two croissants.
   ...two jam tarts.
   ...one of those.
   ...a slice of that cake.
   ...two slices of pizza.
Vorrei… [vor-**re**-i]
   ...un bicchiere di————. [un bic-ki-**e**-re di]
   ...due cornetti. [**du**-e cor-**net**-ti]
   ...due crostate di marmellata. [**du**-e cros-**ta**-te di mar-mel-**la**-ta]
   ...uno di questi / una di queste. [**u**-no di **kwe**-sti / **u**-na di **kwe**-ste]
   ...una fetta di questa torta. [**u**-na **fet**-ta di **kwe**-sta **tor**-ta]
   ...due fette di pizza. [**du**-e **fet**-te di **pits**-za]